LIBRARY
MURRAY STATE UNIVERSITY

GANDHI
in South Africa

GANDHI

in South Africa

British Imperialism and the
Indian Question, 1860–1914

by Robert A. Huttenback

Cornell University Press

ITHACA & LONDON

DT
764
E3
H84

Copyright © 1971 by Cornell University

All rights reserved. Except for brief quotations in a review, this
book, or parts thereof, must not be reproduced in any form without
permission in writing from the publisher. For information address
Cornell University Press, 124 Roberts Place, Ithaca, New York 14850.

First published 1971

International Standard Book Number 0-8014-0586-6
Library of Congress Catalog Card Number 73-124723

Printed in the United States of America by Vail-Ballou Press, Inc.

For John S. Galbraith

265542

LIBRARY
MURRAY STATE UNIVERSITY

Preface

To MOST modern readers, the name Mahatma Gandhi brings to mind an emaciated *dhoti*-clad figure who, through the imaginative use of nonviolence, drove the British raj from India. It is rarely remembered that Gandhi spent the first twenty-one years of his adult life in South Africa and that he forged there, through unceasing "experiments with truth," a startling new philosophy of revolution.

Gandhi had originally intended to remain in South Africa for no more than a year, but the situation of the Indian community there so outraged his moral sensibilities that his conscience would not allow him to depart. The Indians were victims of a dilemma rooted in a historic change in the evolution of the British Empire. In the early days of the so-called dependent empire in Africa and Asia, Englishmen had merely lingered in the imperial domain. A whole sea of problems was encountered, however, when white men started settling in areas inhabited by colored peoples, or when Indians, who were second only to the British themselves as colonists within the empire, moved to East, Central, and South Africa, to Fiji, Mauritius, the West Indies, British Guiana, Burma, Ceylon, Hong Kong, and Malaya, and, for that matter, to Britain itself. The nineteenth century was a great era of liberal reform and growing humanitarianism in Britain, and it became increasingly difficult for the British Government to justify what was in practice a double imperial standard—one for white men and the colonies of settlement and another for non-Europeans and the dependent empire. The only escape from this dilemma was to imply the equality of all subjects of the crown, regardless of their color or place of residence.

Indians, particularly, had been assured that inclusion in the empire implied the sharing of equal rights with all other British subjects. Queen Victoria's postmutiny proclamation had guaranteed that the monarch felt herself bound "to the Natives of our Indian territories by the same obligation of duty which binds us to all our other subjects . . . that so far as may be, our subjects, of whatever race or creed, be freely and impartially admitted to offices in our service, the duties of which they may be qualified by their education, ability, and integrity, duly to discharge." To be sure, the proclamation applied only to India; yet if an Indian moved to Britain, he assumed the same rights as any Englishman. Thus, at the turn of the century, two Indians, Dadabhai Naoroji and Sir Mancherjee Bhownaggree, were able, on different occasions, to win seats in Parliament at a time when they could have shared but little in the government of their own country. And Indians anticipated similar treatment in the other British possessions to which they began to immigrate in the mid-nineteenth century.

The actual conditions immigrant Indians encountered, however, fell far short of their expectations, and this book is the story of their struggle for survival in South Africa under the leadership of Gandhi and of how, in the process, he imprinted himself on the country and it on him. The book is also a study in the dynamics of British imperial administration, of the interrelationship and interaction of the British, the Indian, and the several South African governments catalyzed and focused by an Indian community which was inspired and guided by Gandhi.

As is so often the case, the author has made extensive use of earlier research by other scholars. He wishes therefore to express his debt particularly to Professor Leonard M.

Thompson, whose monograph, *Indian Immigration into Natal (1860–1872)*, published in the *Archives Year Book for South African History* (1952), so ably describes the early years of the Indian presence in South Africa. Without the cooperation of many individuals and archives this book could never have been written. Especial thanks are due to the Indian community of Durban, to the officials of the South African National Archives in Pretoria and the Natal and Cape archives in Pietermaritzburg and Cape Town respectively. Mr. S. Roy of the National Archives of India in New Delhi, as he has for so many scholars on so many different occasions, put himself to endless trouble to be helpful. The staffs of the Public Record Office, the India Office Library, and the British Museum in London, as well as the librarians of Birmingham and Cambridge Universities and the Bodleian and Rhodes House in Oxford went out of their way to make a difficult task more easy.

Finally, without an improved research technique suggested by Professor Norman Davidson, the assistance of the author's wife, the encouragement and advice of Professors Robert Conhaim and John Benton, the support of the Division of Humanities and Social Sciences of the California Institute of Technology and of the Carnegie Corporation, the deciphering and typing skills of Mrs. Lucille Lozoya, and the imagination of Professor E. S. Munger, who first suggested the subject, the author could have neither commenced nor completed his task.

ROBERT A. HUTTENBACK

Pasadena, California
September 1970

Contents

Illustrations

Map

Footnote Abbreviations

CO   Colonial Office series in the Public Record Office, London
IOL   India Office Library, London
NA   Natal Archives, Pietermaritzburg, Natal, Republic of South Africa
NAI   National Archives of India, New Delhi
PRO   Public Record Office, London
RA   Rhodesian Archives, Salisbury, Rhodesia
SANA   South African National Archives, Pretoria
TA   Transvaal Archives in the South African National Archives, Pretoria

GANDHI
in South Africa

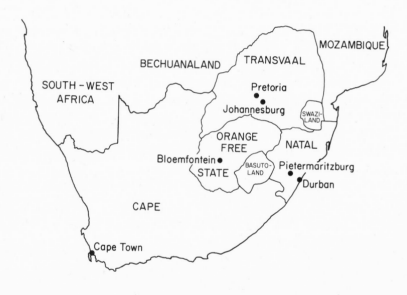

SOUTH AFRICA

I / The Birth of a Problem

NATAL, the verdant land on the southeast coast of Africa, first greeted European eyes on Christmas Day, 1497, when Vasco da Gama sailed along its coastline. It did not, however, come under the British flag until 1843, and its early days as a colony were far from prosperous. No precious metals or gems were ever discovered in significant quantities, and attempts to raise cotton and coffee were disappointing. It was only when sugar was initially rendered from cane in 1851 that the key to the future was discovered. Within seven years the sugar industry was firmly rooted in the colony, and only a lack of labor—for the local Africans were in general disinclined to work for any length of time on the coastal plantations—blocked the path to the establishment of a thriving plantation economy.

It so happened that Natal was not alone in its predicament. Other British colonies had faced a similar labor shortage after the emancipation of the slaves in the British Empire in 1834. Wed to a plantation economy, without adequate labor they faced extinction. In desperation they turned for rescue to that great reservoir of manpower, India, and a vast program for the importation of indentured labor was commenced. Inadequate controls and the resulting abuses prompted denunciations in Parliament and a suspension of the system pending Parliamentary investigation. Although a majority of the committee that in due course undertook the task opposed the utilization of indentured labor,

Parliament, in 1842, voted to accept the minority report which favored the renewed emigration of indentured labor under a system of safeguards to be provided through subsequent legislation. The prosperity of Mauritius and the sugar islands of the West Indies was consequently restored; for the Government of India permitted the emigration of indentured labor to Mauritius (1842), Jamaica, British Guiana, and Trinidad (1844), St. Lucia (1856), and Granada (1858) once laws adequate to protect the Indian immigrants had been passed by the various legislatures.

Natal confidently determined to adopt the same solution, and in 1856 placed on the statute books what was at best a general ordinance, "empowering the Lieutenant-Governor to make rules and regulations for Coolies introduced into this District from the East Indies." Things were, however, not as simple as the colonial government had rather naïvely supposed. The Government of India imposed strict regulations on colonies wishing to import indentured labor. Recruiting in India was conducted by Indians working under the supervision of approved emigration agents appointed by the colonial governments. Contracts were for five years, and had to be concluded in the presence of the protector of emigrants, an official of the local presidency government, whose duty it was to supervise emigration, which was permitted from only three ports—Calcutta, Bombay, and Madras. The protector was to prevent the recruitment of Indians by fraudulent means, to provide for a pre-embarkation medical inspection, to arrange for the safeguarding of the laborers' savings, and to prescribe conditions for their return voyage. In all these matters, he was to work closely with the various colonial emigration agents. The proportion of women to men was from time to time stipulated, and the minimum specifications for emigrant ships were rigidly prescribed. Colonies more distant from India than Mauritius had to provide a free return passage to India to all immigrants at the conclusion of ten years' overseas residence, and the governor-general in council could suspend emigration to any or all colonies.

The Natal ordinance was in a sense comparable to existing enactments in colonies already utilizing imported Indian labor. Consequently, the land and emigration commissioners and the court of directors of the East India Company approved Natal's proposal in principle.[1] The Government of India was, not surprisingly, less sympathetic. After consulting the Bengal Presidency, the governor-general concluded that as the recruiting agencies for Mauritius and the West Indian colonies, areas offering greater opportunities to Indian laborers than Natal, had difficulty filling their quotas, "no useful purpose would be gained by authorizing the emigration of labourers from any of the ports of India to . . . Natal." [2] The Natal ordinance of 1856 was thus destined to remain largely a dead letter—doomed by the failure of the Natal administration to realize that Calcutta required not vague generalities but specific and carefully thought out details.

Natal was, of course, still in desperate need of labor and consequently, in spite of the Government of India's rebuff, the colonial authorities determined to persevere. Further negotiations ensued, and the Government of India finally conceded that, "if the Colony of Natal agrees to the rules, it would be unjust to it, and the Indian labourers, to refuse to allow such labourers to go to the Colony, if they can be prevailed on by legitimate offers to do so." So saying, Calcutta announced itself ready to promulgate an enabling act as soon as Natal passed legislation containing the same minimum guarantees for Indian laborers that prevailed in other colonies importing indentured Indians.[3]

The year 1859 ushered in a labor crisis in Natal severe enough to alarm even the greatest optimists. Once more petitions inundated the colonial administration demanding "the

[1] NAI, Aug. 7, 1860, procs. (Note: see bibliography for relevant department into which emigration proceedings fall during any particular year.)

[2] L. M. Thompson, *Indian Immigration into Natal (1860–1872)* (Cape Town, 1952), 11.

[3] *Ibid.,* 12.

introduction *by the Government* of Coolie labourers." [4] The
Natal Mercury claimed, in April 1859, that, *"the fate of the
Colony hangs on a thread* and that thread is Labour." [5] A select committee was promptly appointed by the legislative
council to consider the petitions, and as a result of its recommendations, three bills were introduced into the legislature
designed to end Natal's labor shortage once and for all. The
first granted validity to contracts made outside Natal but not
in British India.[6] Its purpose was to allow the acquisition of
contract labor from sources other than India. The second en-
abled the Government of Natal to introduce workers from
British India into Natal "at the public expense" under conditions similar to those in operation in colonies already importing Indian labor.[7] The third empowered private persons
to introduce Indian laborers into Natal at their own expense.[8]

Of the three measures only the second, Law 14, aroused
much debate as its provisions required considerable government expenditure for the benefit, its opponents claimed, of
only part of the colony's population. The *Natal Mercury,*
the planter organ, on July 28, 1859, rendered its version of
the discussion:

The jealous feeling with which our up-country friends view the
enterprise of our coast settlers was amusingly exhibited . . .
when they [said], should we pay to make the planters rich? In
answer to these pathetic protestations, the coast members assume
the aspect of injured innocence, declaim energetically as to the
colonies having only one common object in view, the general
good of all, relate the harrowing tale of their own struggles,
losses and difficulties, and then meekly pocket, not only the
smothered wrath of their colleagues, but the successful issue of
their legislation.[9]

[4] *Ibid.*   [5] *Ibid.,* 8.   [6] Natal Law 13, 1859.
[7] Natal Law 14, 1859.   [8] Natal Law 15, 1859.
[9] Quoted in Thompson, *op. cit.,* 13.

The opposition to Law 14 was in fact slight, but the arguments associated with its passage inaugurated a controversy between coast planters and up-country settlers that was to be a running sore until indentured immigration came to an end in 1911. Law 14 did indeed provide for the defrayment of all initial expenditures by the government, but the planters were to pay three-fifths of the passage of all Indian immigrants introduced into the colony and "other expenses chargeable upon him [the immigrant]." [10] Indentured Indians were to be assigned to a plantation for three years in the first instance, and a planter would have to pay the further two-fifths of a laborer's passage costs should the worker be reassigned to him for an additional two years.[11]

Despite these provisions, the government heavily subsidized Indian indentured immigration to Natal. It paid the expenses of the special agent sent to India to inaugurate the immigration scheme. It had to absorb the passage costs of Indians who died in transit, and it had to provide for the return to India of those Indians who wished to take advantage of the free passage guaranteed them at the end of ten years' residence in Natal, and of those who were invalided home.

To facilitate the immediate implementation of Indian immigration, the legislative council voted a subsidy of £5,000.[12] And to balance the resulting deficit in the colonial revenue, customs duties were increased on such items as beads and blankets—used almost exclusively by the African population —and on machinery used by the planters.[13] The yields from these new exactions on the two classes of merchandise were £4,135 and £3,480 per year, respectively.[14]

The chief object of Law 14 was, of course, to satisfy the In-

[10] Natal Law 14, 1859. Chargeable expenses included the cost of importing the required proportion of women and accompanying children.

[11] One-fifth for each year; Natal Law 14, 1859, section 6.

[12] Natal Law 20, 1859.   [13] Natal Law 19, 1859.

[14] Thompson, op. cit., 14.

dian Government that Natal intended to provide adequate protection for the welfare of indentured Indian immigrants. To this effect a "Coolie Immigration Department" was created which was to be the responsibility of the "Coolie Immigration Agent." This department was to receive the monies due from the employers of Indian labor, and the agent was to maintain a register of Indian immigrants and to assign them to individual planters. The Indian immigrants were to complete five years of indentured service at wages of no less than ten shillings a month, and for a time they could purchase back the last two years of this obligation by a payment of five pounds.[15] At the end of five years, the immigrants became free. And ten years after their arrival in Natal, they became eligible for the free return passage to India, although the governor could, at his discretion, commute the cost of the fare (approximately ten pounds) into a grant of crown land, if an immigrant so desired. Nothing in the legislation, however, forced the immigrants to return to India at the end of ten years, and section 9 of the law stated: "On the expiration of the first five years after his introduction into this colony every Coolie immigrant . . . shall be at liberty to hire or dispose of his services, or to change his residence, in the same manner as any other labourer, not being a Coolie immigrant."

While he was in indentured service, the Indian laborer was not subject to the ordinary master and servants ordinance of the colony, but to special conditions. He was guaranteed medical care, food, lodging, clothes, and wages, and any employer violating the stipulations of the law in these regards could have his labor contracts canceled by the governor. On the other hand, should a laborer miss a day's work without proper cause or leave his employer's estate without a signed pass, he was liable to fine or imprisonment. When a

[15] The privilege of buying back the last two years of indenture was established under the terms of Law 14 of 1859. This provision was rescinded by Law 17 of 1864.

laborer had completed five years indentured labor, he became subject to the normal legislative code of the colony. Once the laws governing Indian immigration to Natal had received the royal assent, the India Office, in London, authorized the Government of India to pass the necessary enabling legislation, and India Act XXIII of 1860 consequently extended the system of indentured Indian emigration to include Natal. The act established standards for the feeding, clothing, and general care of the laborers in any consignment,[16] as well as the method of recruitment. Natal, for its part, dispatched the colony's postmaster-general, W. M. Collins, to India to conclude final arrangements with the authorities in Calcutta, and between October 12, 1860, and February 5, 1861, five vessels left the Indian ports of Madras and Calcutta carrying 1,029 men, 359 women, and some children. The first Indians were thus introduced into southern Africa. They carried with them Natal's hopes for a prosperous future and, unsuspected by the colonists, the seeds of discord and traumatic confrontation.

The first years of Indian immigration to Natal provided only a halting stream of laborers. Competition from other, more experienced colonies was stiff, and the passage of Natal Law 17 of 1864, which extended the term of compulsory indentured service from three to five years, combined with India Act XIII of 1864, with its provisions for more rigid control of recruiting procedures, to frustrate Natal in its efforts. It became progressively more difficult to charter vessels to carry Indian emigrants to Natal, and, as a result, the Natal requisitions for 1863 and 1864 were not filled until 1866. Between August 14, 1863, and May 21, 1864, however, fourteen ships landed 2,814 adult male Indians at Durban.[17]

[16] NA, sec. of state to Natal, March 29, 1875. The Indian Government had established the minimum required percentage of women at 25% of the number of men in any consignment. In 1866 this figure was raised to 50%, and in 1875 it was stabilized at 40%.

[17] Thompson, op. cit., 18.

No sooner had Natal apparently overcome the obstacles associated with the establishment of a system of indentured Indian immigration than a severe depression struck the colony, bringing the importation of laborers to a halt in 1866. When the planters wished to recommence the immigration scheme some four years later, they found the legislative council unenthusiastic about providing the necessary financial support and, more significantly, the Government of India actively hostile.

It so happened that between November 1870 and March 1871, the first group of immigrants who had entered Natal ten years previously became eligible for the free return passage to India. Of the 1,431.5 statute adults [18] who had arrived in the colony in the year 1860–1861, 131 had died in Natal, while 43 had previously been repatriated due to sickness; 96 had left Natal for the diamond fields, and 739 had decided to postpone their return passage. Most of this last group, under the blandishments of the planters, continued to labor in the sugar fields, although a large number worked independently as domestic servants, fishermen, and market gardeners.[19] However, 413 chose to return to India on the *Red Riding Hood* and *Umvoti,* which sailed from Natal in February and May 1871, respectively.

Upon landing at Madras, many of these returning Indians carried tales of mistreatment and indifference to the officials of the Government of India. They claimed an almost total lack of funds as a result of illegal fines and withheld wages. During the depression, for instance, Indians on estates that went bankrupt were left unpaid and without food or adequate clothing. As it was often cheaper for an employer to hire free labor on which no sum was due to the government to offset the cost of importation, some Indians who were introduced into the colony before Law 17 of 1864 took effect in July 1865 were simply refused reassignment at

[18] Children under ten were considered half a "statute adult."
[19] Thompson, *op. cit.,* 55.

the end of three years, for it was not legal to reassign indentured labor on whom the requisite sum had not been restored to the government. Where there was employment for
free labor, indentured Indians were precluded by law from
assuming it. Consequently, in May 1868, there were two
hundred and sixty Indian laborers, with unexpired indentures, living at a subsistence level in Durban, with not a
penny among them. They survived on the most meager of
government rations. Natal was clearly not assuming its obligations to these unfortunates and when, with the waning of
the depression, they were finally reassigned, they were not
compensated for the time they had been out of work, even
though their plight had been the result of the colony's violation of an agreement which the Indians had entered into
in good faith. The returned Indians also told of floggings,
inadequate medical attention, and an inability to get their
grievances fairly heard or redressed by magistrates, most of
whose interpreters were, they asserted, biased against them.[20]

The complaints of the repatriated immigrants in the first
instance turned the attention of the Indian authorities toward the cleansing of their own house. In India, before the
passage of the ameliorative Act XIII of 1864, the method of
recruiting laborers for overseas service had been filled with
abuse, especially in Bengal. The duties of the protector of
Indian emigrants and of the colonial emigration agents had
not been sufficiently clearly defined. Individual recruiters
operating in Bengal had not been licensed and did not have
to submit to any effective control by the presidency government. The immigrants who returned in 1871 indicated that
the Natal recruiters had not made them sufficiently aware of
the conditions they would face in Natal, and convinced the
Government of India that despite the passage of the Act of
1864 much yet remained to be done. For one thing, the emigrants were not asked to sign a formal agreement detailing
the terms of engagement. They were merely informed ver-

20 *Ibid.*, 57.

bally of the terms and conditions they were expected to meet.[21] The closest approximation to a contract to which the emigrant fixed his signature or mark was a general statement at the head of the emigrant ship list, which in the case of the *Scindian* read as follows:

We the undersigned Male Adult Emigrants do hereby agree to serve the Employers to whom We may respectively be allotted by the Natal Government under the Natal Act No. 14 of 1859, and we all understand the Terms under which We are Engaged; Wages, for the first Year to be 10 shillings, for the 2nd Year 11 shillings and for the 3rd Year 12 shillings.[22]

It seemed to be but slightly appreciated that the emigrants came from widely diversified social and caste backgrounds—a complicating factor both for the journey to Natal and for the Indians' life there. As the salaries of the emigration agents depended on the fulfillment of their assigned quota of Indian Laborers, it is not surprising that many Indians were recruited under false pretenses, even after 1864, when such practices were made more difficult; and that many emigrants were so aged or infirm that they were unable to work when they reached Natal and had to be returned to India at the colony's expense.

Due in no small part to reports such as those filed by the repatriated Indians, the Government of India passed Act VII of 1871,[23] which once more tightened the regulations concerned with the recruitment of Indian labor for the various British colonies. More significantly, the governor-general wrote the secretary of state, "We cannot permit emigration thither [Natal] to be resumed until we are satisfied that the colonial authorities are aware of their duties towards Indian emigrants and that effectual measures have been

[21] *Ibid.,* 20.   [22] *Ibid.*

[23] "An Act to Consolidate the Laws Relating to the Emigration of Native Labourers."

taken to ensure that class of Her Majesty's subjects full protection in Natal." [24]

Not only the Government of India, but the British Government, in the shape of the secretary of state for the colonies and the land and emigration commissioners, manifested
an interest in the information imparted by the returned immigrants from Natal. As a consequence, Kimberley wrote to
Governor Keate:

I transmit to you a copy of a Report from the Emigration Commissioners upon the explanations furnished by the Immigration
Agent of Natal and several magistrates in answer to complaints
made to the Protector of Emigrants at Calcutta by certain coolies
who had returned from Natal to India.

In accordance with the suggestion of Sir Clinton Murdoch I
have to request you to furnish me with a Report showing the
number of Indian Immigrants now in Natal, their condition, the
mode in which as a general rule they are employed.

If at any time in future there should be a question of renewing
the immigration of coolies to be employed as indentured labourers in Natal these statements will require serious consideration.[25]

Murdoch, himself a member of the land and emigration
board, discussed the complaints of the returned Indians and
concluded by saying:

It seems clear . . . that the system of supervision over Cooly [sic]
Immigrants in Natal has been very lax. It does not appear
whether the semi-annual inspection of Estates on which coolies
are employed has been carried out as required by the Ordinance
of 1859 and it is alleged that the medical care of the people has
been neglected.[26]

[24] NAI, dept. of rev., ag. and comm. (em.), viceroy in council to sec.
of state, 11, May 10, 1872. Quoted in Natal leg. coun. sess. paps., 1872.

[25] NA, no. 155, sec. of state to gov., March 14, 1872.

[26] *Ibid.*, encl., Sir Clinton Murdoch, emigration board, to Colonial
Office, Feb. 24, 1872.

On March 29, 1872, Kimberley restated his position:

> If it is contemplated to apply for a renewal of indentured labour in Natal, full and accurate information must be furnished as to the condition and treatment of Immigrants now in the Colony, and as to the truth, or otherwise, of the charges made by the Returned Emigrants to the Protector at Calcutta.[27]

There is no doubt that very few of the up-country settlers and, in general, many of Natal's non-sugar-growing citizens shared the planters' enthusiasm for indentured Indian labor. But the latter group were sufficiently influential to force the appointment of a commission to investigate the Indian question, consisting of Michael Gallway, the attorney general of Natal, and Colonel B. P. Lloyd, an Indian civil servant on sick leave in the colony. The commissioners devoted only three months to their task and were unable to obtain valuable information from the laborers who had been emancipated in 1871. But given these limitations, they carried out their inquiries honestly and dispassionately. The "Coolie Commission Report," as the commissioners' findings were termed, recommended the abolition of flogging as a punishment, improved medical services, and, most important of all, the appointment of a protector of Indian immigrants—the existing coolie immigration agent shorn of his offensive title and given vastly increased powers. The protector, the commissioners stipulated, should be "an active and efficient officer . . . [with] some experience in India, or among Coolies, and . . . some knowledge of Indian languages.[28] He was to be charged with the general supervision of all Indians in Natal.

The recommendations of the "Coolie Commission Report" were implemented by Natal Law 12 of 1872, and when adjustments in the financial arrangements for Indian immigration were subsequently also enacted, both Whitehall and

[27] *Ibid.,* no. 164, sec. of state to gov., March 20, 1872.
[28] Thompson, *op. cit.,* 62.

the Government of India were prepared to countenance a resumption of indentured Indian immigration to Natal.

Between June 26, 1874, and May 1, 1875, eleven ships from Calcutta, bearing 5,974 Indian immigrants, arrived in Durban.[29] The renovated financial system appeared to provide needed stability, as well as being a triumph for the employers, to whom it guaranteed ten thousand pounds annually from the colonial exchequer. A constant supply of much-needed labor seemed assured. Colonel Lloyd, who assumed the position of protector soon after its creation, brought to the office not only his Indian experience and a knowledge of Hindustani, but administrative ability and energy. The importance of the new post was recognized when Colonel Lloyd was appointed to the governor's executive council. In 1874, General Cunynghame, commanding officer in South Africa, visited five of the major sugar estates and was able to report that "it was a credit to the Natal Planters, the contentment which he universally found amongst the Indian Immigrants recently arrived." [30] Lloyd himself, in his report for 1875, contended that Indian immigrants were receiving the best of treatment, that they were obtaining immediate redress for injuries and injustices incurred, and that many of them were purchasing land.[31]

The optimism engendered by the new order of things was to be of but short duration. The revised fiscal arrangements were found still to be inadequate to the task of supplying Natal with indentured laborers in sufficient numbers, and the colony's recruiting establishment in India was bedeviled with difficulties. Of the 1,710 laborers for which Natal applied in 1877, only 519 ever arrived in the colony.

Nevertheless, the number of Indians in Natal steadily increased. Over the months and years, vessel after vessel depos-

[29] Of this number, 3,511 were adult males and 1,397 adult females. Natal leg. counc. sess. paps. protector of Indian immigrants' report for 1875.

[30] Thompson, *op. cit.,* 66.   [31] Protector's report for 1875.

ited its human cargo on the quays of Durban. And, of course, time-expired "coolies" did not return to India as had been anticipated by Natal at the time of the inauguration of the indentured immigration scheme. They took advantage of the rights procured for them by the Government of India, commuted their guaranteed return passage into grants of land, during the years that the colony continued to countenance the practice, and remained firmly planted in Natal. By 1891, there were 41,142 Indians in Natal, 46,788 Europeans and 455,983 Africans.[32]

The presence of a significant body of Indians permanently resident in Natal became progressively more odious to the majority of white settlers as the number of immigrants grew. And that these undesirables should, upon becoming free, have the same rights as all other British subjects in the colony was particularly galling. But if many of the colonists felt that Indians in Natal had too many rights, the Government of India thought they did not have enough. It concluded that Indian laborers were paid too little and that excessive deductions were made in time of sickness.[33] The viceroy was also concerned about the pollution of streams used by Indians and the employment of Indians as domestic servants, which required them to work on Sundays in violation of their contracts.[34] To exacerbate the situation, the protector,

[32] Natal Census of 1891.

[33] CO 179/144, June 30, 1882. Encl., Govt. of India, dept. of rev., ag. and comm. (em.), no. 16, viceroy to sec. of state, April 18, 1882.

[34] NA sec. of state to gov., Feb. 20, 1883. Governor H. Bulwer replied that Sunday work was indeed a violation of their terms of indenture, but that Indians considered employment as domestic servants a privilege and that it would be difficult to reverse the existing situation. He hoped that the Indian Government would sanction the continuing use of Indians as domestic servants. *Ibid.,* gov. to sec. of state, Aug. 5, 1882, Jan. 3, 1883. Bulwer also reported efforts to pass legislation limiting the pollution of rivers and streams. *Ibid.,* Jan. 16, 1883. And he agreed that the sixpence a day sickness deduction from the pay of Indians who were infirm was a heavy burden on Indians during the first two years of indenture. The governor indicated that he would attempt to gain a change in this last condition. *Ibid.,* May 19, 1883.

of all people, was, in 1876 arrested in Verulam for shooting and killing an indentured Indian.[35] When his successor attempted to gain grants of land for over two hundred time-expired Indians entitled to them, his plea fell on deaf ears.[36]

If Calcutta worried, so did the planters, and the Government of India's concern in 1885 combined with a second depression in the sugar industry to prompt the appointment of another commission—this time under the chairmanship of Mr. Justice Wragg—with instructions to restudy the whole Indian problem.[37] The commission's report, which appeared in 1887, was a document of little consequence. The complaints of both the Indians and the white colonists were discussed cursorily and in no particular order; nor did the commission make many recommendations, although such matters as marriage and divorce, the pollution of streams, the magisterial powers of the protector, prison regulations, the disposition of the estates of deceased Indian immigrants, Sunday labor and irregularities on certain estates, the use of alcoholic beverages, and rations for female laborers fell under its scrutiny. The commission came under heavy up-country pressure to recommend the abolition of indentured Indian labor in Natal. As a consequence, the commissioners urged weakly that "a bonus system for Kaffir labourers be introduced without delay." [38] Of greater significance, however, was the suggestion "that the revenue contribution in aid of further immigration from India shall cease and that the grant from the general revenue shall not be used save as may be necessary to meet liabilities already incurred." [39]

On one significant issue—the rights of Indians already in Natal—the commission placed itself firmly on record. When it was proposed to the commission that Indians whose inden-

[35] NA, gov. to sec. of state, Jan. 11, 1877.

[36] Protector's report for 1880.

[37] The other members of the Wragg Commission were Dr. R. Lewer, brigade surgeon, H. F. Richardson and J. R. Saunders, a justice of the peace and well-known sugar planter.

[38] Wragg Commission report, chap. XLIV.   [39] *Ibid.*

tures had expired would immediately have to return to India, Commissioner J. R. Saunders replied:

I wish to express my strong condemnation of any such idea. What is it but taking the best of our servants and then refusing them the enjoyment of their reward, forcing them back (if we could but we cannot) when their best days have been spent for our benefit. Where to? Why? back to the prospect of starvation from which they sought to escape when they were young. Shylock-like taking a pound of flesh and Shylock-like, we may rely on it, meeting Shylock's reward.[40]

Whatever its weaknesses and strengths, the Wragg Commission Report opened a major debate on the Indian question in Natal. One pole of popular opinion was characterized by the words of the chairman of the Victoria County Planters' Association, who wrote: "I am glad to say that the increasing number of free coolies now renting land will keep many of them here as useful and enterprising colonists. . . . They . . . are most industrious, working morning, noon, and night." [41] On the other hand, the up-country farmers continued to object to the importation of Indian laborers. The *Natal Witness,* the newspaper that represented their views, stated:

The primary object of offering free or assisted passage is to obtain colonists of the same blood as our own, men and women of the same religion, of the same social customs, with whom we can have friendly relations, whose children may intermarry with our children, whose practices do not violate the first codes of morality. The ordinary Coolie fulfills none of these conditions. He and his family cannot be admitted into close fellowship and union with us and our families. He is introduced for the same reason as mules might be introduced from Monte Video, oxen from Madagascar or sugar machinery from Glasgow. The object for which he is brought is to supply labour and that alone. He is not one

[40] *Ibid.,* 100.

[41] Protector's report for 1875, chairman Victoria Planters' Association to protector, Dec. 12, 1874.

of us, he is in every respect an alien; he only comes to perform a certain amount of work, and return to India. The editor of the Colonist and Mr. King may think the Coolie is a desirable member of society, such as the people of Natal ought to introduce as colonists, but almost every other person entertains a different opinion and would greatly prefer that not a Coolie should come amongst us to contaminate society and hinder moral progress, were it not that his labour is needed. Coolies are not regularly introduced into any country except those devoted to the growth of sugar and coffee, where obtaining money is of greater importance that the moral health of the people, where the white population are the mere representatives of British capitalists, and who remain in the country only so long as it enables them to accumulate a few thousand pounds with which to return to Europe.[42]

A letter addressed to the editor of the *Witness* was indicative of the continuing hostility of up-country opinion. "There are no greater thieves than Coolies," the writer opined, "imported for the sole use of the coast planters and for whose importation the up-country districts have to pay a large sum of money annually." [43] The Indians were not in need of protection, the paper editorialized: "It is rather the European community that requires protection against the heathen coolie." [44] Despite the efforts of the British and Indian governments, Natal was able slowly to erode the protective corpus of Indian rights in the colony. Local ordinances in Durban and Pietermaritzburg subjected Indians to borough vagrancy laws, "by which all persons of Colour, if found in the streets after 9 o'clock *without a pass* are liable to arrest as vagrants." [45] Law 21 of 1888, the Registration of Servants Law, classified Indians as members of "an uncivilised race," and Law 20 of 1890 limited the right of indentured Indians and their descendants to drink intoxicating liquor.

[42] *Natal Witness,* Jan. 8, 1875.   [43] *Ibid.,* July 20, 1877.

[44] *Ibid.,* July 10, 1876.

[45] NA, gov. to sec. of state, Sept. 7, 1878. Natal Law 15 of 1869 dealt with vagrancy.

But the anti-Indian feeling in Natal was to find expression in threats and actions that went well beyond the curtailment of some Indians' rights to consume alcoholic beverages. Although very few Indians were eligible for the franchise (181 in 1882, according to the protector's report of that year), their legal access to the voters' rolls nevertheless caused the greatest fear. On February 3, 1880, one representative (Miller) spoke with deep emotion in the legislative council:

The only feeling I have in this matter is one of disgust that these men [the Indians] should be on the electoral roll. (Mr. Cato (interposing): Hear, hear; turn them out) . . . Who are these people? The scum of Madras and Calcutta. The idea of them coming here to have the electoral franchise conferred on them is monstrous. It was amongst these men at the last election that bribery took place; they got their half-crown and they voted. It is a most disreputable thing in my opinion to have such men put on the roll. Because they came here under an indenture for five years and know little more than they did, and because they lease one or two acres of land, and grow mealies and pumpkins they are to be put on the electoral roll. When this charter was published it was never intended to confer this right on them.

Eight days later (February 11) another member (Garland) took a similar view. Indians, he claimed, "think no more of taking a white man's life than a dog's." Besides, "their indifference to the claims of a Christian Sabbath is a matter which strikes every Englishman."

During 1880–1881, several attempts to deprive the Indians of the right to vote in parliamentary elections were thwarted only through the combined efforts of the governor, the Colonial Office, and the planters, who feared that the passage of an act to this effect might induce the Government of India to halt indentured immigration to Natal. The course of future events was, however, presaged by some Colonial Office minuting. The writer (probably Sir Robert Herbert, the permanent undersecretary) said he did not think that

the welfare of either Coolie or Native would be directly or indirectly promoted by giving . . . [them] votes within the ordinary electorates, their votes could be obtained by treating and bribery, by candidates who had their own ends to serve and who might promise to obtain for them injurious concessions (such as the removal of restrictions on purchasing spirits) and would be obliged in order to obtain their votes to oppose measures disliked by Natives or Coolies but necessary for health and good order.[46]

The first shots in the campaign to deprive the Indians of the franchise coincided with continuing debate on the whole subject of Indian immigration. The *Natal Witness* set the tone by delivering a passionate broadside against Indians in general, both indentured and free:

There is probably not a single person in Natal who does not, if spoken to on the subject deplore the Asiatic invasion, but personal and selfish considerations raise a barrier to any movement here to stem the tide. We want labour, is the cry; the Government will not force the native to work; and so we must take what offers and what is cheap. Of the social evil and evils to the body politic which such indifference is fostering, they take no account. Posterity must look after themselves. That is not the fashion in which nations have been built. . . . The ridiculous notion [is] that all nations have been made of the same idea that because a man happens to be born under a certain flag he may roam as he pleases where that flag flies and domicile himself wherever inclination or other considerations may dictate.[47]

In the legislative council, the discussion was heated, and the opinions of the planter and up-country interests sharply divided. L. Hulett, the influential sugar planter, asserted that "Indian labour is the only reliable labour for any dis-

[46] CO 179/144, Natal minute paper 1405, Jan. 23, 1882, minuting of Feb. 3, 1882.
[47] *Natal Witness,* July 17, 1890.

trict enterprise in the Colony." [48] Its introduction, he felt, had not only helped the sugar estates to prosper, but had also relieved the labor shortage in the up-country districts.[49] On the other hand, the representative from Durban (King) considered every white man in the colony an element of strength and each Indian a source of weakness.[50] Obviously incensed, he spoke with rising passion:

Never let me hear a planter talk of Responsible Government; it is a contradiction. It is impossible: you cannot have both. You cannot have a sound political life in the Colony and have a black population as well. Well, then, we will now go a little further and say—(laughter from several hon. members) Yes, you may laugh, Mr. Binns, but we will make you a laugh on the other side of your mouth, as we country people say it.[51]

It soon became evident, however, that neither the franchise question nor the achievement of a consensus on the future of indentured immigration was to be achieved quickly. The eyes of the colonists consequently turned to two other objectives, seemingly more attainable—the compulsory return to India of all indentured laborers at the termination of their contracts and the curtailment of the opportunities available to Indians already domiciled in Natal to interfere with the aspirations of the white population in any way.

To this effect, Natal hoped to convince the British and Indian governments to permit the termination of all indentures not in Natal but in India itself, and to accede to the colony's request that Indians be forced to remain in service for the entire ten-year period of their required residence in Natal.[52] As a *quid pro quo,* the legislative council proposed to abolish the £10,000 subsidy,[53] which had always been so

[48] Natal *Hansard,* Aug. 21, 1888.   [49] *Ibid.*   [50] *Ibid.*

[51] *Ibid.*   [52] NA, gov. to sec. of state, July 17, 1891.

[53] L. Hulett, one of the foremost planter representatives, argued that all those who used formerly indentured laborers should help pay the cost of importing indentured Indians. Hulett continued to point out that if there were no need for free Indian laborers, then they would

odious to the Colonial Office.[54] But the coating on the pill was evidently not sufficiently sweet, for the secretary of state's reply was, to say the least, cool:

> I have now the honour to inform you that the proposal that immigrants should be compelled to return to India after completion of their indentured service would be such an interference with the ordinary rights of British subjects that legislation in that sense could not be sanctioned.[55]

In regard to the proposed ten-year indentured service requirement, the secretary of state advised the Government of Natal to contact the Indian authorities directly.[56] This the governor of the colony did in early 1892,[57] but Calcutta was to be no more cooperative than Whitehall. The Bengal Presidency Government, in words similar to Saunders', argued that Natal merely wanted to prevent Indians from making an independent position for themselves; that the colony wished to use the best years of the immigrants' lives and then to return them to India when they were worn out and useless.[58] The viceroy stated the same position in greater de-

---

not be able to get jobs, which, of course, they could. Natal *Hansard,* May 13, 1892.

[54] Natal *Hansard,* July 14, 1891.

[55] NA, sec. of state to gov., Sept. 24, 1891.   [56] *Ibid.*

[57] *Ibid.,* letter book–general despatches, gov. to sec. of state, Jan. 4, 1892.

[58] NAI, Oct. 1892, procs. 14–17, W. Maude, offg. sec. to the Govt. of Bengal, to sec. to the Govt. of India, dept. of rev., ag. and comm., Aug. 25, 1892. The Bengali weekly *Pratikar* commented on May 3, 1889, that "one cannot but feel surprised at the spectacle of Englishmen who were so opposed to Negro slavery countenancing the system of coolie emigration within their dominions.

"The only difference between Negro slavery and coolie emigration is that the former was open slavery and the latter is slavery in disguise. . . . Coolie work is something very horrid with a cloak of philanthropy thrown over it. There is no sin in the world which is not committed in the course of coolie recruiting, and there are no words to express the abhorrence which coolie recruiting excites." Reports of the Native Press, Bengal, May, 1889.

tail. In view of the objections of the governments of Madras and Bengal, he could not countenance the proposal. In no other colony importing Indian labor did the term of indenture exceed five years, nor was reindenture compulsory.

The proposal would operate harshly on the Indian immigrant, by depriving him of the option of returning home at the end of five years, while at the same time preventing him from making the best use of the second five years of residence which under the law as it stands, he has to complete in the colony in order to secure the privilege of a free return passage to this country.[59]

Frustrated in all directions, Natal did what it could. No more land grants were made to Indians after 1891,[60] and Law 25 of 1891, "To amend and consolidate the Laws relating to the introduction of Indian Immigrants into the Colony of Natal, and to the regulation and government of such Indian Immigrants," attempted, with some small success, to satisfy the wishes of the white colonists. Previous legislation, notably Law 2 of 1870, had provided a method by which Indians could leave the colony after five years and become eligible for a free return passage to India at the end of ten years' residence in Natal, including at least five years' indentured service. The immigrant had three years after he first became eligible to apply for the free return passage.[61] Law 25 of 1891 now stipulated that no license to leave Natal would be issued to any Indian before the conclusion of ten years' residence in the colony, except under extraordinary circumstances.[62] Should an immigrant still be issued a license to depart the colony before the completion of ten years' resi-

[59] NA, Govt. House—high comm. and gen. dispatches, G. 366/92, minute paper, Oct. 18, 1892, encl., India no. 2498/58, dept. of rev., ag. and comm. (em.), viceroy to gov., Oct. 18, 1892.

[60] Thompson, *op. cit.,* 70.   [61] Law 2, 1870, Sec. 46.

[62] Law 25, 1891, section 91. Under very special conditions, the protector of Indian immigrants, with the approval of the Indian Immigration Trust Board, could return an Indian immigrant "to the place whence he may have come before the expiration of the said ten years."

dence, he would have to abandon his claim to the free return passage.[63] Section 110 of the law limited the period during which an Indian could apply for the free return passage to India to twelve months from the time he first became eligible.

Both the Colonial Office and the India Office insisted that Indian laborers recruited before the passage of the proposed new legislation be preserved in their prior rights. And Law 25 did not receive the royal assent until Governor Mitchell had informed the secretary of state that section 110 did not apply to those Indians who had vested interests as defined by law.[64] To further allay the doubts of the British and Indian authorities, the governor emphasized that section 1 of the new law clearly stipulated that "all matters and things done heretofore . . . shall be and continue in force in the same manner as if this Law had not been passed." [65] All in all, the 119 sections of Law 25 contained little that was new. The measure was more a document of consolidation than of amendment, and further developments would have to await Natal's increased independence from the control of the Colonial Office as a consequence of the granting of responsible government to the colony.

Meanwhile the nonelected officials of Natal tried to persuade the white colonists of the virtues not only of indentured Indians but also of those no longer under contract who, choosing not to return to India, engaged in occupations that complemented rather than competed with European enterprises. Governor Mitchell, for instance, defended the permanent settlement of Indian laborers in Natal. "Their general usefulness cannot be denied," he wrote,

and owing to the dislike of the Native labourers to a continuous engagement, the Indians are simply invaluable to those cultiva-

[63] *Ibid.,* section 92.   [64] NA, gov. to sec. of state, April 16, 1892.

[65] It should be noted that section 1 of Law 25 went on to state that the stipulations of previous laws would remain in effect "except where the same may be inconsistent with the provisions of this law."

265542

LIBRARY
MURRAY STATE UNIVERSITY

tors and stock farmers whose success depends on steady labour.

The cry to Natal's being a "White man's country" is untrue, so far as regards the White man's capacity for field labour in a semi-tropical climate, and there can, I think, be no doubt that if the Colony is to prosper, a supply of coloured labor will always be necessary.[66]

The protector saw it as his duty to urge those people who condemned the Indians as a race just to look around them, for they would see

hundreds of these Indians honestly and peaceably pursuing their several useful and desirable occupations.

If it were possible, even for a short time, to withdraw the whole of the Indian population from this Colony, I am convinced that with but very few exceptions every industry in existence at the present time would collapse, solely for the want of reliable labour. . . . Agriculture would collapse and almost every household be without domestic servants.[67]

But honeyed words were never very persuasive, and that colonial hostility was frequently translated into action was made clear in an article which appeared in the *Natal Advertiser* describing the evidence in a suit brought by an Indian:

Deponent got into a second-class carriage in the train leaving Charlestown at 1:30 p.m. Three other Indians were in the same compartment but they got out in Newcastle. A White man opened the door of the compartment and beckoned to witness saying: "Come out Sammy." Plaintiff asked: "Why," and the White man replied : "Never mind, come out, I want to place someone here." Witness said: "Why should I come out from here

[66] NA, gov. to sec. of state, July 17, 1891. The governor, in a colony without responsible government, was in a position to inform the Colonial Office of his own views. Once a colony gained responsible government, the governor was, in most cases, honor bound to reflect the policies of his ministers. He could, however, in informal and demi-official correspondence, still express his own opinions.

[67] Protector's report for the year ending June 30, 1894.

when I have paid my fare? . . . The White man then left and brought an Indian who, witness believed was in the employ of the railway. The Indian was told to tell the plaintiff to get out of the carriage. Thereupon the Indian said, "The White man orders you to come out and you must come out." The Indian then left. Witness said to the White man: "What do you want to shift me about for? I have paid my fare and have a right to remain here." The White man became angry at this and said: "Well, if you don't come out, I will knock hell out of you." The White man got into the Carriage and laid hold of the Witness by the arm and tried to pull him out. Plaintiff said: "Let me alone and I will come out." The witness left the carriage and the White man pointed out another second-class compartment and told him to go there. Plaintiff did as he was directed. The compartment he was shown was empty. He believed some people who were playing [in] a band were put into the carriage from which he was expelled. This White man was the District Superintendent of Railways at Newcastle. To proceed, witness travelled undisturbed to Maritzburg. He fell asleep, and when he awoke at Maritzburg, he found a White man, a White woman and a child in the compartment with him. A White man came to the carriage and said: "Is that your boy, speaking to the White man in the compartment?" Witness's fellow-traveller replied: "Yes," pointing to his little boy. The other White man then said, "No, I don't mean him. I mean the damned coolie in the corner!" This gentleman with the choice language was a railway official, being a shunter. The White man in the compartment replied: "Oh never mind him, leave him alone." Then the White man outside (the official) said: "I am not going to allow a coolie to be in the same compartment with White people." This man addressed plaintiff, saying: "Sammy, come out." Plaintiff said: "Why, I was removed at Newcastle to this compartment." The White man said: "Well, you must come out," and was about to enter the carriage. Witness, thinking he would be handled as at Newcastle, said he would go out and left the compartment. The White man pointed out another second-class compartment which witness entered. This was empty for a time, but, before leaving, a White man entered. Another White man (the official) afterwards came up and said: "If you don't like to travel with a stinking coolie I will find you another carriage." [68]

Whatever the governor and protector might publicly espouse, it was evident that those in the seats of power, the elected ministers of the colony, were more in tune with public opinion. They were determined to bring the terms of Indian immigration and the conditions under which Indians in Natal lived into conformity with the wishes of the majority in the colonial legislature.[69] For the Indians of Natal, consequently, the sky, already far from bright, was visibly darkening.

[68] M. K. Gandhi, *The Collected Works of Mahatma Gandhi* (hereafter referred to as *Works*) (Delhi, 1958–   ); II, 36–37; *Natal Advertiser*, Nov. 22, 1893.

[69] With the advent of responsible government, a legislative assembly was created and became the significant legislative body, although the council still remained as a second chamber.

II / The Setting

WHAT WAS the character of the Indian community that was slowly sinking its roots into the soil of Natal? The colony recruited laborers from both north and south of the subcontinent, and at first more immigrants were shipped from Calcutta than from Madras. The Madras agency was soon in the ascendancy, however, and in 1906 there arrived in Natal 6,019 laborers from Madras and only 476 from Calcutta.[1]

From available statistics of the time, it would appear that caste affiliation of the new arrivals approximated 60 per cent Sudra and untouchable, 25 to 35 per cent Vaishya, 10 to 15 per cent Kshatriya, and a sprinkling of Brahmins. Less than 20 per cent were non-Hindu.[2] In a random sample of Indians who arrived on eight different immigrant ships, the distribution was as follows: 2 per cent Brahmin, 9 per cent Kshatriya, 21 per cent Vaishya, 31 per cent Sudra, 27 per cent untouchable, 3 per cent Christian, and 4 per cent Muslim.[3] There was, of course, some fluctuation from year to year and from vessel to vessel—in the first group of immigrants from Madras, for instance, 12 per cent were Muslim[4] —but the constitution of the Indian population in Natal, as measured by caste, remained fairly constant from the first.

That such a large proportion of the Indian immigrants

[1] Protector's report for 1907.
[2] Hilda Kuper, *Indian People in Natal* (Pietermaritzburg, 1960), 7.
[3] *Ibid.*   [4] *Ibid.*

were of low caste or untouchable origin is no cause for wonder; for to them the doors of opportunity in India were firmly closed. Nor is it surprising that this majority element of the Indian population in Natal attempted to assume a new identity (albeit an Indian one) in its adopted South African home and manifested a marked disinclination to return to a land where the future held very little promise.

No matter how bad conditions were for Indians in South Africa, nothing altered the basic conviction of the entire Indian population, and especially those Indians of Sudra and untouchable background, that life in South Africa at its worst was better than life in India at its best. Strong as they may have been initially, at least among the "twice-born," over the years most caste distinctions among the Indians of South Africa became obscured, if not totally erased. Only endogamy tended to survive. Again, this happened first among those segments of the population lowest on the social scale which lacked the cohesiveness and group consciousness of the upper castes.

Whatever their background, the Indians found little common ground for communication with their new masters, and it was many years before some sort of *modus vivendi* could be established. Edmund Tatham, an early coolie immigration agent, wrote of his experience, "I was overwhelmed by the influx of a large number of strangers, the habits and manners of whom were entirely unknown here." [5]

From the first, the relation between the planters and the Indian laborers was not a happy one. The two groups understood each other but very little—temperamentally, linguistically, or socially. It was easy for Indians to avoid work by feigning sickness and very difficult for employers to punish them under existing legislation, except by imprisonment, which was hardly to the employer's benefit. Fines were permissible, but could by proper timing be avoided. Desertion

[5] L. M. Thompson, *Indian Immigration into Natal (1860–1872)* (Cape Town, 1952), 28.

was rife, and the planters, not without justice, sought to control this threat to their welfare. But the penalties imposed by Law 14 of 1865 were harsh—forfeiture of two days' wages for every day missed; and Law 2 of 1870 only slightly tempered the weight of the exaction. Despite new legislation, the planters continued to be provoked by desertions and apparently trivial complaints to magistrates, into illegally withholding rations, flogging, and fining in excess of the provisions of the law.[6]

If the planters had some grievances, the Indians had more. Justice appeared to be weighted in favor of the employers. Indians had the greatest difficulties in gaining the ear of judges or juries when they claimed mistreatment. Those who had the temerity to bring cases to trial almost invariably lost in courts not staffed with interpreters and were returned to the tender mercies of their oppressors. Although the governor had the power to transfer the Indian laborers from a planter guilty of mistreatment, he in fact never did so. In November, 1865, the coolie immigration agent, H. C. Shepstone, wrote the colonial secretary of Natal:

There is . . . [a] subject connected with Coolie management upon which I should be glad of advice, and that is the System now generally adopted of fining Coolies for any alleged misconduct, absence from work without leave, and sickness; and in many cases I believe that the Coolies, owing to these fines, have little or no wages to receive at the end of the month, and on

[6] *Ibid.,* 46. Wages for indentured Indians ranged from two shillings per month, for boys of eight during the first year of employment, to ten shillings a month, for males over eighteen also in their first year of employment. In the fifth year, a boy of twelve received eight shillings a month and a male adult fifteen shillings (CO 179/109, Natal Government notice 34, March 16, 1866). Rations provided for males beyond their ninth year included one and a half pounds of rice or two pounds of pounded maize (corn) daily, two pounds of dhall (lentils, split peas, etc.) per month, one pound of ghee (clarified butter) or oil per month, and a pound of salt per month. Women and children under ten received half the above ration (*ibid.*).

some estates I hear that this is carried to such an extent that when fines for sickness etc., as imposed by the Master exceed the wages of the Coolie for the month, they are carried to his debit in the next month's wages, so that, unless some measures are adopted for stopping this practice, Coolie employers may manage in such a way that they have little or nothing to pay to their Coolies for wages.

There is also I hear a system of flogging Coolies being now generally adopted, of which in most cases, I think the Coolies are afraid to go to the Magistrates to complain for fear of the consequences to them on their return from making such complaints.[7]

The attorney-general responded by recommending that the governor should punish offending employers by terminating their contracts.[8] Nothing, however, was done; rather section 44 of Law 2 of 1870 stated:

When all, or a large number of, the Coolies employed upon the same estate, shall absent themselves from their employment without leave, for the purpose or on pretence of making any complaint against their employer, such Coolies, or some one or more of them may, in the discretion of any competent Court, be liable to punishment by fine not exceeding two pounds sterling, or for imprisonment for any period not exceeding two months, whether such complaint shall or shall not be adjudged to be groundless or frivolous, and notwithstanding that such complaint may be successful.

Adequate supervision of the employers of Indian labor presented a continuing problem. Magistrates rarely visited the plantations; although they were required by law to do so; and any interference by reform-minded government agents could usually be counteracted by the politically powerful planters who treated their Indian employees at best unfairly and at worst cruelly. A typical case concerned the appointment of an unpopular Indian *sirdar* (foreman) on the estate of Henry Shire at Umhlanga. The other Indians protested vehemently, and Shire responded by increasing the

[7] Thompson, *op. cit.*, 48.   [8] *Ibid.*, 49.

hours of work and by reducing the pay and rations arbitrarily. He even had Indians flogged by Africans, for the Indians
a great humiliation. The laborers in retaliation refused to
work, and after some months deserted en bloc to Durban,
where they were apprehended, imprisoned for three successive terms, and finally returned to Shire. In February 1862,
the Indians hired an attorney to petition the government on
their behalf, and a commission consisting of two magistrates
and the agent was consequently appointed. After an exhaus-
tive inquiry, the commission concluded that Shire had indeed broken the law, but that the Indians for their part had
been "insubordinate and vexatious," and had deprived Shire
of a season's sugar crop. They urged that Shire not be deprived of his Indian laborers, a recommendation that the
governor accepted.[9]

In time, however, under pressure from the British and Indian governments, Natal slowly created a body of laws that
at least adequately protected Indian indentured laborers.
And despite all the handicaps of their situation, the Indians
in Natal, even while still under contract, were in many ways
much better off than their confreres in India. The climate
was healthier, and they, in general, ate more nutritious foods
in greater quantity and lived more comfortably. Once they
were free, many new opportunities were open to Indians.
The white population did not greatly resent the free Indians
during the years when their numbers were still small and as
long as they were illiterate and willing to work in positions
not threatening to the economic security of the Europeans.

In 1873, free Indians, in addition to the usual rations and
plots of land for private use, were earning from sixteen to
eighteen shillings a month as field laborers, one pound ten
shillings as mill hands, and from two to four pounds as fore-
men.[10] About half the Indians, upon the termination of
their five-year term of indenture, remained as workers on the
sugar estates. The rest spread throughout the colony as much

[9] *Ibid.,* 49.   [10] *Ibid.,* 52.

needed skilled and semiskilled laborers, although a small number, usually the second generation, became teachers and members of other professions. They were employed as cooks, artisans, domestic servants, tailors, and washermen. Bakers received from sixty to eighty shillings a month, railway porters twenty to thirty shillings, first-class cooks about one hundred and twenty shillings, blacksmiths forty to sixty shillings, domestic servants twenty to forty shillings, schoolteachers from one hundred to one hundred and twenty shillings, interpreters one hundred shillings, and "native doctors" twelve hundred to two thousand shillings.[11] A few Indians opened shops or became market gardeners, and they soon established a virtual monopoly of the fishing industry and of the cultivation of tobacco and of corn and other vegetables.[12] The protector's report for 1875 stated that there were 5,393 time-expired Indians in Natal, and that skilled workers in this class received an average monthly wage of sixty to one hundred shillings, while laborers received an average of eighteen to twenty-five shillings.[13] By 1885, about 2,000 Indians were in occupation of land within two miles of Durban.[14]

It seemed the best of all possible worlds, the Indians appeared to be prospering and the colonists were obtaining goods and services not heretofore available. "The Coolie Commission" report proclaimed: "The advantages of retaining in this country a race of men of industrial habits can scarcely be doubted." [15] Major-General Sir Garnet Wolseley,

[11] NAI, June 1873, A. proc. 22. A note on emigration by J. Geoghegan.

[12] Protector's report for 1883.

[13] NA, Natal leg. counc. sess. paps., protector's report for 1875. Working hours, the report pointed out, were from sunrise to sunset, and free Indians were not allowed to leave the colony without a license.

[14] Leo Kuper *et al., Durban—A Racial Ecology* (London, 1958), 20.

[15] NAI, Feb. 1875, procs.; Thompson, *op. cit.*, 63. In consonance with the commission's remarks, B. P. Lloyd, the protector, in July 1873

Gilbert's "very model of a modern major-general," who was Natal's administrator in 1875, reiterated the value of a permanent Indian population to Natal. He was convinced that Indian labor was vital,

not only to the maritime districts but to the whole Colony and to all the Provinces of Southern Africa. Without those industries [employing Indians] the commerce of Natal would languish, and its revenue would be seriously reduced; for although a large proportion of the sugar and coffee produced is consumed in these African provinces without bringing in any direct revenue, still their production and their transport by sea and land, foster commercial enterprises and give employment to numerous consumers of articles liable to duty.

Wolseley emphasized that the taxes paid by Indians and the profit realized from the sale of goods to the Indians in Natal, who now numbered in excess of 10,000, more than compensated for any expenditure from the colonial revenues for the importation of indentured labor. Indians, he thought, might also be most useful as soldiers should there be a major native uprising. "In my opinion," Wolseley concluded, "the Coolies are such an element of wealth and strength to the whole Colony that I recommend in the strongest terms Her Majesty's consent being accorded to the law under consideration [Law 28], as the loan sought for is urgently required at present." [16] The protector, in his report for 1881, contended

---

urged that 1,400 Indians due for the free return passage be induced to remain in Natal by a £10 bonus in lieu of the £8 passage. Children between two and twelve were to receive £5. Immigrants accepting the bonus would, according to Lloyd's plan, bind themselves to remain in Natal for an additional five years as free men and would forfeit the free return passage to India. Law 19 of 1874 provided for a £10 bonus to Indians who reindentured for five years, but this section of the law was repealed upon the insistence of the secretary of state for the colonies, who pointed out that in all other colonies only a one-year reindenture was permitted. Natal leg. counc. no. 7 of 1874, quoted in M. Palmer, *The History of Indians in Natal* (Cape Town, 1957), 38.

[16] NA, administrator to sec. of state, June 1, 1875.

that Indians in the colony were continuing to improve their position and that many of the free men were "extremely well off." One small cloud on the horizon, from the white colonists' point of view, was the reluctance of discharged Indians to reindenture. The protector, in his report for 1883, indicated that 4,548 Indians had received their discharge and that none had reindentured!

Despite the advantages gained from the Indian presence, white Natal was prepared to do very little for its new Indian fellow subjects. Education of the young should have been a vital social concern, for already in 1885 almost one-fourth of the Indians in Natal were children (7,430 out of 29,581).[17] By 1892 children numbered 11,988 out of a total Indian population of 40,510.[18] Had there been any inclination to integrate Indians more fully into the citizenry of Natal, education would have provided the means. At the insistence of Sir Michael Hicks-Beach, the secretary of state for the colonies from 1878 to 1880, Natal Law 20 of 1878, "To Provide for the Promotion of Education Among the Children of the Indian Immigrant Population," was passed. But its effects were never far-reaching. The protector in his report for 1880 pointed out that of the £1,000 provided by the legislature that year for Indian education, only £118-6-8 was spent, owing to the failure of an inspector, supposedly sent from India, to arrive.

From the very earliest days of the Indian presence in Natal, some sporadic attempts were made to educate both the adults and the young. In 1868, a certain Ralph Stoft opened a small evening school for adults which he supported and ran himself. The following year he received £25 from the local authorities to open a school for children. In 1871, Stoft was granted £36 to support a day and evening school for adults, and a George Robinson was allowed £16 for the opening of a school on his estate in Umkomanzi. A planter identified merely as Mr. Kennedy was given a similar

[17] Protector's report for 1887.   [18] *Ibid.*, 1892–1893.

amount in 1872 for the education of the "coolies" on his estate.[19] The goal of most of these early schools was the basic education of adults on the plantations, and by 1872 attendance was over one thousand.[20]

The main job of educating Indian children, however, insofar as it was even attempted, was left to the churches. In June 1872, there were in the colony only four schools, attended by 73 boys and 16 girls, and two months later the total enrollment had dropped by 29. The government contributed the princely sum of £68 per year to each school.[21] By 1880, the number of schools for Indians had no more than doubled, and even for the Natal of that day the level of government support was remarkably niggardly. Aid per month was set at two pounds for schools with 20 to 30 pupils,[22] two pounds ten shillings for schools with 30 to 40 students, three pounds for schools with 40 to 50 students, and four pounds for schools with 50 to 60 students. The Indians themselves contributed threepence per month per child if they were indentured and sixpence if they were free.[23] In 1885, there were 25 schools for Indians in Natal, 22 of which received government grants-in-aid totaling £1,461-4-3.[24] Support for individual students, always low, dropped from £1-1-6 per year in 1884 to 17/8 in 1886 [25] and 14/4 in 1888.[26] The trouble was that the total amount voted for Indian education by the legislative council remained relatively constant through the years, while the number of Indian students rose from 323 (10 schools) in 1882 to 1,591 (27 schools) in 1887.[27] In 1892 there were still just 27 schools for Indians but the enrollment had increased to 2,326 students, 713 of whom

[19] CO 179/107, J. Warwick Brooks, act. supt. of ed., to col. sec., Sept. 18, 1872.

[20] Ibid.   [21] Thompson, op. cit., 53.   [22] Ibid.

[23] Protector's report for 1881.   [24] Ibid., 1884.

[25] Annual report of the Indian immigrant school board, 1887. In Natal Blue Book, 1887.

[26] Ibid., 1888.   [27] Ibid., 1887.

were girls. The legislature nevertheless voted a subsidy of only £1,700 (compared to £31,989 spent on European schools and £3,396 on native schools) [28] for Indian education as the average expenditure per student dipped to 12/9¾.[29] Teachers for Indian schools, never easy to find, were usually from South India or Mauritius, although a few student teachers from Natal were also employed.[30]

The education available to Indians was inadequate in every way. The school buildings themselves were usually wretched and poorly equipped. Almost no provision was made for the education of girls. The inspector of Indian schools, F. Colepepper, forcefully described the situation in 1885. "Under present conditions," he wrote,

. . . we are only twisting a rope of sand, or worse, doing positive harm in half educating a number of boys and letting them loose upon the community at an age when they are ripe for any mischief, with minds in a state of unrest by means of what they have been taught, and with no apparent object for self-improvement —their future being the same as their uneducated fellows.

One hundred-and-seven boys who can read and write and do a little arithmetic are returned as having left school during the past year. The percentage who obtain employment, for which they would not be equally eligible without any education at all, is practically nil.[31]

At best, Indian education was elementary. The highest level Indian students could achieve until 1887 was Standard III, which meant that they could read from a Standard III reading book, recite "with intelligence and expression" sixty lines of poetry, identify nouns, adjectives, adverbs, and personal pronouns, and form simple sentences incorporating them. Students who passed the Standard III examination knew the major countries of the world and the physical fea-

[28] Ibid., 1892–1893.

[29] Annual report of the Indian immigrant school board, 1892–1893. Actually, £1,734-13-0 was expended on Indian education in 1892–1893.

[30] Ibid., 1887.   [31] Ibid., 1885.

tures of the continents. They could write six lines dictated from the standard reader, and they were able to inscribe in their copybooks capitals and figures in both the large and small hand. In arithmetic, they could demonstrate the four simple rules through the long division, addition, subtraction, and multiplication of money.[32] The addition of Standard IV to the curriculum of Indian schools in 1887 slightly raised the level of education available; reading was from the Standard IV rather than the Standard III reading book. A student had to recite eighty lines instead of sixty lines of poetry, and be able to explain words and allusions. He knew more geography and was introduced to weights and measures.[33] Most students, of course, never reached either Standard III or Standard IV level.[34]

The Natal statistical blue book for 1897, in its educational summary for government schools under inspection, showed that in 1885 there had been 51 European schools with 3,922 pupils as opposed to 25 Indian schools with 1,480 students. By 1896–1897 there were 297 schools for Europeans with an enrollment of 8,180 children and still only 28 schools for Indians with 1,842 boys and girls attending classes.[35] During these years the Indian population of Natal had more than doubled while the European population had increased but slightly. To keep the matter in context it is worth pointing out the figures for native African schools. In 1885, there had been 64 "native" schools with 3,783 students,[36] while in 1896–1897 there were 145 offering some form of education to 7,062 children [37] out of a population that was then listed as 377,581,[38] and by 1891 as 455,983.[39] The Natal census of 1904 classified 12.99 per cent of the Indian population

[32] *Ibid.*   [33] *Ibid.*, 1887.

[34] Of the 1,907 students (43 girls) enrolled in Indian schools in 1890, only nine passed Standard IV mathematics and thirty-seven Standard III. *Ibid.*, 1890.

[35] *Natal Blue Book*, 1897.   [36] *Ibid.*, 1885.

[37] *Ibid.*, 1897.   [38] *Ibid.*, 1885.   [39] Natal census, 1891.

as being "able to read and write" compared with 83.02 per cent of the Europeans.

As indicated above, the ex-indentured laborers were in many ways a convenience and hardly constituted an economic threat to the white population. Although very few chose to reindenture, some continued to perform as free men work very similar to that which they had undertaken while still covered by contract. Fishing, market gardening, hawking, the raising of tobacco, corn, and mealies, along with general unskilled labor, continued to be their metier. By 1886, Indians owned property worth but £18,983 adjacent to the two chief metropolitan centers of Durban and Pietermaritzburg,[40] and in 1898 they still cultivated only 35,000 acres compared with the 390,209 acres Europeans had under the plow.[41] Yet the population figures indicate a heavy concentration of Indians in just a few rural and urban districts. In 1872, there had been 123 Indians in the county and borough of Pietermaritzburg; 1,939 in the county and borough of Durban; 781 in the sugar-growing division of Inanda and 111 in Lower Tugela, where the major enterprise was also the raising of cane.[42] The comparable figures for 1908 were 5,-800, 15,027, 25,200, and 12,800.[43]

The Natal census of 1904 indicated that the Indian population was still heavily concentrated in the sugar-growing areas. Inanda was 70.58 per cent Indian and only 5.12 per cent European. Lower Tugela was 26.90 per cent Indian and 2.33 per cent European, and the figures for Umlazi were 34.44 per cent Indian to 9.35 per cent European. But there had also been a significant shift to the city with its greater economic opportunities. Indians constituted 23.04 per cent (46.13 per cent European) of the population of Durban; 19.62 per cent (48.58 per cent European) of Pietermaritzburg; 20.40 per cent (40.75 per cent European) of Ladysmith; 17.45 per cent (39.25 per cent European) of Newcastle,

[40] *Natal Blue Book*, 1886.   [41] *Ibid.*, 1898.
[42] *Ibid.*, 1880.   [43] *Ibid.*, 1898.

and 14.51 per cent (46.67 per cent European) of Dundee. The increasing urban concentration of Indians particularly frightened and offended many European settlers to whom it connoted both domestic propinquity and increased commercial competition. And it was a trend that was destined to continue. According to the Union census of 1951, Durban was 30.51 per cent European, 31.68 per cent African, and 33.98 per cent Indian. Indians, however, controlled only 13.70 per cent of the land wealth of the city.

The Indian population of Natal was increasing also in absolute terms, a circumstance which could not be laid entirely at the doorstep of continuing immigration. Natal's Indians, much like their cousins in India and other overseas places, were singularly fecund. In contrast to the Chinese in Australia, they clearly intended to remain in the land to which they had immigrated. Although many of the men left wives behind them in India and rarely sent for them at the expiration of their indentures, they usually remarried within the Natal Indian community. Taking two of the protector's reports more or less at random, the Indian birth rate is seen to have been close to 6 per cent in 1887 [44] and approximately 5 per cent in 1899.[45] Of the 133,031 Indians listed as residents of the Union in the census of 1911, 63,766 were born in South Africa.

If the specter of being swamped by a permanently resident Indian population—there were already 43,000 Indians to 40,000 Europeans in 1894 [46] —caused considerable concern among the white population of Natal, it was nothing compared to the alarm spread by the advent of the "Arab." First in a trickle and never in a flood, these new arrivals began entering Natal in the third decade of Indian immigration into the colony. They were in the main Muslims from Gujerat on the west coast of India, and they came not to labor in the fields of the white man but to engage in the retail trade.

By 1895, the *Mercury,* which thirty years earlier had

[44] Protector's report for 1887.　　[45] *Ibid.,* 1899.　　[46] *Ibid.,* 1894.

praised the contribution of the Indian to Natal as "a benefit to European mechanics and workmen" and a source of "enlarged production and increased prosperity," [47] contended that "the evils attendant upon the immigration of coolies, their low standard of living and morals, the introduction by them of disease and the ever-threatening outbreak of epidemics, not to mention other serious drawbacks—are too generally appreciated to leave room for contradiction." [48]

What had occurred to cause such a radical change in the attitude of the paper and of the white colonists was the advent of the "Arab." As has already been mentioned, the government and people of Natal had expected that the Indian immigrants would either return home at the end of ten years' labor, when they became eligible for a free return passage, or, at worst, remain in the colony solely in the capacity of laborers or domestic servants. The planters, in fact, feared rather that not enough Indians would remain in Natal at the expiration of their indentures,[49] and Sir Garnet Wolseley wrote the Colonial Office: "It may be confidently expected that . . . they [will] not only supply the planters with labour but to a large extent furnish the colonists generally with indoor servants for whom there is a pressing want in the province." [50] It has been noted that, by and large, these expectations were fulfilled by the Indians as their period under contract came to an end. It was their number and the rights, such as the franchise, that they acquired when they were free, not their occupations, which affronted the white colonists of Natal.

The "Arab" changed the entire picture. He came with his own finances and usually set himself up as the proprietor of a general retail store. He did business not only with Indians but with the white colonists and with Africans. He did not supplement or complement white enterprise, but competed

---

[47] *Natal Mercury,* Jan. 10, 1865.   [48] *Ibid.,* Jan. 24, 1895.

[49] H. Binns, Natal *Hansard,* July 29, 1883.

[50] NA, admin. to sec. of state, June 1, 1875.

with it directly. He tended to operate efficiently and on a small margin of profit, as many of his employees were relatives. The result was inevitable. The "Arab" began driving white shopkeepers into liquidation; for the colonial housewife, regardless of her general attitudes toward men of color, made her purchases where the prices were best; more often than not this was at her local "Arab's."

In 1880 there were seven "Arab" shopkeepers in Durban; [51] by 1885 there were already forty.[52] The census of 1891 listed 598 Indian storekeepers centered in Durban (132), Pietermaritzburg (74), Umlazi (67), Inanda (63), and Ladysmith (60). Another group was designated traders. They numbered 172, with 53 in Newcastle, 51 in Pietermaritzburg, and 29 in Durban. Still, the "Arabs" constituted only a small percentage of the total Indian population of some 41,-000, the vast majority of which continued to perform unskilled labor of some form or another but whose numbers also included sixty-six cigar makers, six engine drivers, three constables, and one hangman!

The Natal census of 1904 still showed the balance heavily in favor of the Europeans. At a time when the two elements of the population were about equal in number (97,109 Europeans to 100,918 Indians), there were 425 European grocers and assistants as compared to 75 Indian, 283 European "merchants and assistants" and only eight Indian, 111 European produce dealers to 34 Indian, but 658 European storekeepers (general) to 1,260 Indian. That the Indian hawkers outnumbered the European 1,487 to 19 is not surprising.[53]

But it was not merely a question of the numerical total of Indian entrepreneurs. With the appearance of the "Arab" in Natal, a more self-confident and ambitious Indian element was introduced into the colony. Under their leadership, In-

[51] *Natal Blue Book,* 1880.   [52] *Ibid.,* 1885.
[53] According to the Transvaal census of 1904, of the 12,320 "mixed and coloured" listed (9,986 Indians), 5,101 were designated "mercantile persons."

dians for the first time vented their feelings of discontent in a petition sent to the secretary of state for the colonies. They resented not being allowed on the streets of Durban and Pietermaritzburg after 9 P.M., and they requested that shops be allowed to remain open on Sunday, which was the only day on which indentured Indians could make their purchases. They complained about police brutality and the lack of interpreters and Indians on juries in the supreme court.[54] The Indian memorial brought an immediate reaction from London and Calcutta, and dispatches flowed into Pietermaritzburg demanding a prompt reply.[55]

The first stirrings of Indian political activity and the beginnings of commercial competition aroused the petty bourgeois establishment which held sway in Natal's towns and cities and which controlled the power to influence the course of events in the council chambers of the colonial capital. Indian merchants were falsely accused of contributing nothing to the community because they supposedly sent all their profits to India,[56] and of succeeding in business as a result of living in squalor and off the smell of the proverbial "oiled rag." A magisterial report from the Inanda division, in 1884, delineated the growing problem as the white community saw it: "A few more Indian stores have opened in the town of Verulam during the year, and two European stores have been closed for want of support, the Indians have entirely absorbed the petty trade, as well as that with Indians and Natives." [57] In 1885, a report from the Lion's Head division

[54] NAI, Nov. 1884, procs. 9–10, "Memorial from the Indian Residents in Natal Relative to Certain Grievances Under Which They Represent Themselves to be Suffering in that Colony."

[55] *Ibid.*

[56] In contrast to the Indians of East Africa, those in Natal and the Transvaal kept few commercial connections with India and virtually none lasted past 1925. No figures are available concerning transfer of capital from South Africa to India, but any large exodus of funds would seem highly unlikely.

[57] Palmer, *op. cit.,* 46.

read similarly: "Complaints continue to be made of the increasing number of Indian traders and hawkers in the district. These people render it impossible for small European store-keepers to make a living, and all the Native trade of the Colony is getting into the hands of the Free Indians." [58]

Two rival camps now faced each other—on the one side, the white settlers, arrogant members of what Joseph Chamberlain called, "the greatest governing race the world has ever seen;" [59] on the other, the Indians, mostly of humble Hindu origin but leavened by a sprinkling of Muslim merchants of higher standing. What would normally have been a far from cohesive community was progressively forced toward cooperation, at least in the political sphere, by a common set of disabilities. Largely deprived of civil and political rights, the Indians aspired to equality under the law, but they were just as convinced of the superiority of their own cultural heritage as the white man was of his. Indians were determined to maintain their own identity as British Indian subjects settled in South Africa. At many levels they did not wish to assimilate with the Europeans, who, although they wanted no part of their colored neighbors, were still confused and in a sense annoyed by the Indians' failure to wait, hat in hand, outside the temples of Victorian Anglo-Saxonism.[60]

And the whole drama was to be played out without any reference to the silent and essentially unnoticed majority of the population—the Africans, who in 1911 accounted for more than 82 per cent of the total population of South Africa.[61] For if the Indian and the European differed on many

[58] *Ibid.*

[59] R. A. Huttenback, *The British Imperial Experience* (New York, 1966), 90.

[60] Union of South Africa census, 1951. The census listed English as the home language of only 5.71% of the Indian population and Afrikaans of another 0.02%.

[61] *Ibid.*, 1911.

points, they shared a similar view of the native African. To the average Indian, blackness connoted inferiority. Lightness of skin was associated with a high caste status attained through virtue in previous journeys along life's path. Darkness of pigmentation implied low caste and untouchability; the result of the soul's less worthy history. It should be remembered that the indentured Indians on Henry Shire's estate in Umhlanga particularly resented being whipped by an African, and any classification of Indians with Africans by the white governments of South Africa immediately brought bitter cries of outrage.[62]

The story that will unfold in subsequent pages, therefore, concerns a confrontation between the brown man and the white man, the black man not being deemed worthy of involvement by either of the protagonists.

[62] Gandhi, who was after all an orthodox Gujerati Hindu of the Vaishya caste, shared this attitude (see p. 138 and n. 35, Chap. V). His ecumenical egalitarianism emerged slowly as he grew and developed.

III / The Advent of a Champion

THIRTY-THREE years after the first indentured Indian had set foot in Natal, the colony was granted responsible government. It was 1893, and the white settlers were united on four points vis-à-vis their Indian neighbors. They agreed that Indian laborers should no longer be permitted to remain in Natal at the conclusion of their contracts. They were determined to prevent Indians from voting. And they sought to impede the future immigration of free Indians, as well as the licensing of Indians to conduct business in Natal. The attainment of these objectives was now a distinct possibility, for responsible government deprived the British Government of much of its control over legislation passed in Natal. The right to review and disallow acts of the legislature still remained, but constitutional common law all but prohibited its use in purely internal affairs.

As a first step toward the desired goals, a Natal delegation visited India in 1894 and attempted to induce Calcutta to agree to the termination of all indentures in India. The mission failed in its main objective, but the delegates did gain the Government of India's approval for the passage through the colonial legislature of a particularly pernicious measure —a three-pound tax to be levied annually on formerly indentured Indians who would not return to their native land at the conclusion of their contracts. This law [1] was never successful in achieving its objective of inducing ex-indentured

[1] Natal Act 17 of 1895.

Indians to leave Natal. On the other hand, the fee was collected not only from adult males but from female dependents above the age of thirteen and boys who had passed their
sixteenth birthday. For a family with an average annual income of twelve to sixteen pounds, the burden was almost
unbearable.

The Indian position if not yet desperate was steadily deteriorating. Natal was becoming increasingly more hostile to
natives of the subcontinent and more antagonistic to men
whose skins were other than white. As the gloom gathered
and the atmosphere became more volatile and menacing,
there stepped onto a Durban quay a young Indian lawyer,
immaculately groomed and just five years removed from his
call to the bar at the Inner Temple. His name was Mohan-
das Karamchand Gandhi, and he had been driven by dissatisfaction at the progress of his legal career in India to accept
a year's contract in South Africa in connection with a
£40,000 civil suit. As he landed on Durban's wharf in May of
1893, Gandhi did not expect to spend twenty-one years away
from home nor to develop during this time a dramatically
different approach to the problems of dissent and social
change.

Gandhi immediately encountered the wall of anti-Indian
feeling in Natal, but being a man of considerable pride he
fought back. On his first day in court he wore a *pugri* (tur-
ban) and was ordered to remove it by the judge. He refused
to do so and left the chamber in protest. But worse was to
come. He bought a first-class train ticket to Pretoria, only to
be forced out of his compartment by a constable who wanted
him to sit in the baggage car. Rather than accede, Gandhi
spent the night in the unlit, ice-cold station at Pietermaritzburg. The next day, at Charlestown, he boarded a stage for
Standerton and was at first given a seat next to the driver.
He was, however, soon ordered to move to the footboard;
but again he would not comply and was roughly handled as
a consequence of not submitting to an "insult [which] was

more than I could bear." [2] Gandhi was in South Africa for purely professional reasons and could easily have returned to India. But these indignities forced him to consider his position more deeply. "I began to think of my duty," he later wrote.

> Should I fight for my rights or go back to India, or should I go on to Pretoria without minding the insults, and return to India after finishing the case? It would be cowardice to run back to India without fulfilling my obligation. The hardship to which I was subjected was superficial—only a symptom of the deep disease of colour prejudice. I should try, if possible, to root out the disease and suffer hardships in the process. Redress for wrongs I should seek only to the extent that would be necessary for the removal of the colour prejudice.[3]

The colony of Natal constituted a very small arena for a man of Gandhi's ability, for he was not just another canny Gujerati lawyer bearing the credentials of a British legal education. He was deeply introspective—a moralist and ideologue who all his life wrestled with conscience and the spirit, Truth and Right. These preoccupations spawned a complex mentality which allowed Gandhi to think little of personal discomfort, to eschew the shackles of ego and ambition, and, concomitantly, rarely to harbor resentment or rancor against others. In his autobiography, Gandhi recalled an incident in the first year of high school when the education inspector had come to examine him and his classmates. Mohan, as his contemporaries called Gandhi, was asked to spell "kettle" and was unable to do so.

> The teacher tried to prompt me with the point of his boot, but I would not be prompted. It was beyond me to see that he wanted

[2] M. K. Gandhi, *The Story of My Experiments with Truth* (Boston, 1957), 113.

[3] *Ibid.*, 112. Gandhi had been promised £105 under the terms of the year's contract which had brought him to Natal. After his decision to remain in South Africa, his earnings soon reached a peak of £5,000 per annum.

me to copy the spelling from my neighbour's slate. . . . The result was that all the boys, except myself, were found to have spelt every word correctly. Only I had been stupid. The teacher tried later to bring this stupidity home to me, but without effect. . . .

Yet the incident did not in the least diminish my respect for my teacher.[4]

Not that Gandhi developed his personal philosophy and code of ethics easily, or ever saw the process as complete; truth to him was never monolithic or simple, and he spent his life in what he, himself, called "experiments with truth." His metaphysical probings were to lead him often from one extreme to another. Upon encountering Gandhi in Piccadilly Circus, Sachchidanand Sinha, a fellow Indian, described the twenty-one year old fledgling barrister:

He was wearing a high silk hat burnished bright, a Gladstonian collar, stiff and starched, a rather flashy tie displaying almost all the colours of the rainbow under which there was a fine striped silk shirt. He wore as his outer clothing a morning coat, a double-breasted vest, and dark striped trousers to match and not only leather boots but spats over them. He carried leather gloves and a silver-mounted stick.[5]

What a far cry from the more familiar figure, garbed only in the abbreviated *dhoti* of the poorest Indian cultivator!

As in dress, likewise in food, philosophy, and religion; a short period of meat eating gave way to devout vegetarianism and the realization that control of the palate and carnal appetites in general led to the sublimation of materialism and the physical self and the attainment of real freedom. Gandhi's dietary experiments, which were at first dictated by imperatives of health and economy, were to become part of his religious and spiritual evolution. It is not hard to see the connection of vegetarianism to the Hindu concept of *ahimsa* (literally nonhurting, nonviolence) which was to become the basis of so much of Gandhi's thinking. It was through some

[4] *Ibid.*, 6.   [5] B. R. Nanda, *Mahatma Gandhi* (London, 1958), 28.

vegetarian friends that Gandhi was first introduced to the Bible, and commenced a lifelong practice of conjecturing on the meaning of the Christian New Testament and the Hindu epics, especially the *Gita*.

The evolution of what was later often referred to as "Gandhiism" was, of course, only in its earliest stages when Gandhi landed in South Africa. Still, it was inevitable that he would soon attract considerable public attention. Probably the first intimation the European population of Natal received of the arrival of its new adversary was a letter Gandhi wrote to the *Natal Advertiser* in answer to an editorial attacking Indian traders as unethical, semibarbarous, and an undesirable element in the colony. Natal was not accustomed to such literacy and sophistication from an Indian.

But you say these wretched Asiatics [6] live a semi-barbaric life. It would be highly interesting to learn your views of a semi-barbaric life. I have some notion of the life they live. If a room without a nice, rich carpet and ornamental hangings, a dinner table (perhaps unvarnished) without an expensive tablecloth, with no flowers to decorate it, with no wines spread, no port or beef *ad lib,* be a semi-barbaric life; if a white comfortable dress, specially adapted to a warm climate, which, I am told, many Europeans envy them in the trying heat of summer, be a semi-barbaric life; if no beer, no tobacco, or ornamental walking stick, no golden watch chain, no luxuriously-fitted sitting room, be a semi-barbaric life; if, in short, what one commonly understands by a simply frugal life be a semi-barbaric life, then, indeed, the Indian traders must plead guilty to the charge, and the sooner semi-barbarity is wiped out from the highest Colonial civilization, the better. . . .

It seems, on the whole, that their simplicity, their total abstinence from intoxicants, their peaceful and, above all, their businesslike and frugal habits, which should serve as a recommendation, are really at the bottom of all this contempt and hatred of the poor Indian trader. And they are British sub-

[6] Whereas the term "Asiatic" was customary in the 19th and early 20th centuries, modern usage prescribes the designation "Asian."

jects. Is this Christian-like, is this fair play, is this justice, is this civilization? I pause for a reply.[7]

Ten days later Gandhi again wrote to the *Advertiser*, this time on the subject of the Indian franchise.[8] The fear that the Indian vote would soon swamp the European, he contended, was merely a chimera, for there would never be an appreciable number of Indians possessed of the necessary qualifications for registration on the voters' roll. As to Indians not being sufficiently civilized to vote, Gandhi pointed to the numbers of Indians holding high positions in the Government of India. Finally, he invoked what he called, "The Magna Charta of the Indians"—the Queen's Mutiny Proclamation.[9]

Letters to the newspapers were followed by petitions to the assembly and exchanges with Natal government officials. On June 28, 1894, the Indians of Natal, led by Gandhi, petitioned the legislature for the maintenance of the Indian franchise, emphasizing in persuasive terms that India had an ancient tradition of municipal and local government.[10] On the following day, Gandhi addressed the prime minister of Natal on the same subject.[11] Petitions to the governor and the legislative council now flowed from his pen in rapid succession, culminating in a great document on the Indian franchise sent to Lord Ripon, the secretary of state for the colonies, over the signature of some 10,000 Indians.[12] Gandhi felt particularly close to Dadabhai Naoroji, then a member of the British Parliament, and enlisted his aid in the cause of South Africa's Indians.

"A word for myself and I have done," Gandhi wrote in the conclusion of a letter to the "Grand Old Man of Indian Politics":

[7] *Works*, 1, 75–76; Gandhi to *Natal Advertiser*, Sept. 19, 1893.

[8] *Ibid.*, 78–80; Gandhi to *Natal Advertiser*, Sept. 29, 1893.   [9] *Ibid.*

[10] Gandhi used the Panchayat (village council), whose members were elected by the village, as an example.

[11] *Works*, I, 97–99.   [12] *Ibid.*, 117–128.

I am inexperienced and young, and, therefore, quite liable to make mistakes. The responsibility undertaken is quite out of proportion to my ability. So you will see that I have not taken the matter up, which is beyond my ability, in order to enrich myself at the expense of the Indians. I am the only available person who can handle the question. You will, therefore, oblige me very greatly if you will kindly direct and guide me, and make necessary suggestions which shall be received as from a father to his child.[13]

One month later Gandhi founded the first major Indian political organization in South Africa, whose secretary he became, and which he named the Natal Indian Congress in honor of Naoroji, who had presided over the Indian National Congress in 1893. Under the auspices of the Natal Indian Congress, Gandhi was to conduct his future struggle for Indian rights in Natal.

A stream of correspondence on every subject deluged the newspapers and government offices of Natal. They maintained a very high level of erudition. Gandhi was not loathe to quote Max Müller, Schopenhauer, or Victor Hugo in support of the Indian position—surely a unique experience for the recipients of his letters. Although Gandhi had at first been identified as an unwelcome stranger, both the *Natal Mercury* (the planter newspaper) and the *Natal Witness* (representative of up-country opinion) wrote frequent editorials lauding him. The *Witness* conceded that

there are many Indians of the stamp of Mr. Gandhi who are doubtless eminently qualified to exercise the fullest possible franchise in any self-governing community. But with all possible deference to such authorities as Schopenhauer, Macaulay, and Max Müller, the fact remains that for Natal to admit an equality which does not exist in fact and could not be safely admitted even if it did, would be foolish.[14]

[13] Nanda, *op. cit.,* 44.
[14] *Natal Witness* (quoting the Johannesburg *Star*), Jan. 4, 1895.

The *Mercury,* for its part, was unstinting in its praise. "What we want," the paper explained, "is a European Mr. Gandhi to come forward and put life and movement into the dry bones of our political ideas. It is all the more necessary that we should have something of the kind, when we have an example like the Indian Congress before us." [15] On another occasion, the *Mercury* delivered itself of the opinion that,

Mr. Gandhi writes with calmness and moderation. He is as impartial as any one could expect him to be, and probably a little more so than might have been expected, considering that he did not receive very just treatment at the hands of the Law Society [which had opposed Gandhi's admission as an advocate to practice before the supreme court] when he first came to the Colony.[16]

Gandhi was not only attracting attention in the colonial press, he was arousing active animosity in the legislature. During the assembly debate on the Franchise Law Amendment Bill, one representative (Maydon) remarked that Gandhi was only opposing the bill for personal political advantage. "He is a discredited person," the honorable member stated, "among the class which he is seeking to benefit, and beyond that he loses if he fails to fight the battle, the direct personal gain of receiving reward for the battle which he fights, consequently whether he wins or loses, he has everything to gain by fighting." [17]

In 1896, Gandhi, now twenty-six years of age, returned to his native land to inform his fellow countrymen about the indignities to which Indians were subjected in South Africa. He went as the official representative of the Natal Indian community, and the five months he spent in India were filled wth activity. He frequently addressed large audiences. He wrote numerous articles, and he published a pamphlet entitled *The Grievances of the British Indians in South Af-*

---

[15] *Natal Mercury,* June 6, 1896.   [16] *Works,* II, 36.
[17] Natal *Hansard,* May 11, 1896.

rica which quickly went through two printings. In it he detailed the sufferings of the Indians in Natal. They were reviled as "Ramysamy," "Mr. Samy" (both corruptions of "swami"), or "Mr. Coolie," and they were referred to as "the Asian dirt to be heartily cursed," or "a thing black and lean and a long way from clean." Indians were damned, spat upon, pushed off public footpaths and out of trams, railway compartments, and hotels. In Dundee, during Christmas 1895, Gandhi revealed, "a gang of White men set fire to the Indian stores without the slightest provocation, in order to enjoy themselves." Justice applied only to white men and not to Indians. False arrests without subsequent recompense were common. Gandhi quoted a member of the legislative assembly who, upon the passage of the Immigration Bill of 1894, had said that "the intention of the Colony [is] to make the Indian's life more comfortable in his native land than in the Colony of Natal." Gandhi did not limit his comments to the situation in Natal; he also discussed the difficulties being faced by Indians in Cape Colony, the Orange Free State, the South African Republic (Transvaal), and the Chartered Company's territory (Rhodesia). Finally, he expanded on the inequities of the pass system, the three-pound tax, and the restrictions imposed on Indians desiring to purchase property in Zululand. The protector of Indian immigrants, Gandhi implied, was a kept man.[18]

When Gandhi left India at the end of 1896, he had spread word of the Indian dilemma in South Africa far and wide and through every level of Indian society. Had it not been that the growing intensity of anti-Indian feeling in Natal required his presence in the colony, Gandhi might have stayed in India longer. As it was, he sailed aboard the *Courland,* which anchored in Durban harbor on December 18, 1896. Another vessel, the *Naderi,* bearing some four hundred Indian passengers, arrived in port at the same time. Neither ship was permitted to proceed beyond the outer anchorage,

[18] *Works,* II, 1–52.

however, because it had sailed from Bombay, which was, the Durban authorities claimed, infected with plague. A mild form of bubonic plague had indeed been raging in certain parts of Bombay when the *Courland* and the *Naderi* sailed, but the two ships had been granted clean bills of health. Nevertheless, they flew the quarantine flag as they approached Durban, and the port's health officer placed them in quarantine, "until 23 days had elapsed since leaving Bombay." [19] On December 22, the quarantine expired, but the vessels were still not permitted to enter the harbor. They were rather told to burn bedding, to destroy food, and in other ways to cleanse the ships—processes they were ordered to repeat several times. Meanwhile, the ship owners were incurring expenses of £150 a day, and the ships themselves began to run low on supplies. The Government of Natal was clearly using this quarantine as an excuse to delay the entry of the vessels at a time when public opinion on the Indian question was at the flash point.

Under extended quarantine the unfortunate passengers languished at the mercy of the colonial government, while on shore agitators were stirring up large-scale opposition to the landing of the Indians, which they termed an "Asiatic invasion." Throughout the period of Gandhi's visit to India, steamers bearing large numbers of Indians had continued to arrive in Natal. The colonial artisans felt increasingly threatened and the organization of anti-Indian societies had burgeoned.[20] The news that Gandhi was on board the *Cour-*

[19] *Ibid.*, 193. Bombay was declared an "infected port" on Dec. 19, the day after the vessels had arrived in Durban.

[20] A European Protective Association was formed in Pietermaritzburg on Sept. 18, 1896. Its chief aim was to force the expulsion of the Indians from Natal. On Nov. 26, a similar organization, the Colonial Patriotic Union, was established in Durban, with the object of preventing the further influx of Asians into Natal. The Union, however, was willing to sanction the continued importation of indentured labor into Natal, as long as Indians introduced into the colony in this way were returned to India upon the expiration of their contracts.

land, and a conviction that most of the Indians awaiting permission to land were skilled workers, greatly exacerbated the situation. Gandhi attempted to counteract the growing hysteria by granting an interview to some reporters from the *Advertiser* on January 13, 1897—the twenty-seventh and, as it turned out, the last day of the quarantine. He pointed out that there were only 600 passengers on the two ships—not the 800 that the citizens of Durban thought were aboard. Of this number, Gandhi emphasized, only 200 were planning to disembark at Durban, and no more than 100 (including 40 women) were new immigrants to the colony.[21]

As time went on, a large, increasingly hostile throng gathered on shore. Indians on the immigrant vessels were strongly urged to return home, and Gandhi was threatened with tar and feathers or lynching should he land. The white colonists were particularly incensed at Gandhi, for Natal had received a very inaccurate report on the contents of Gandhi's pamphlet. Reuters had telegraphed that Gandhi had claimed Indians were robbed and assaulted in Natal, and this information, combined with rumors concerning the meetings Gandhi had addressed in Bombay and Madras, enraged the settlers. In actual fact, the pamphlet contained nothing that Gandhi had not stated many times in Natal itself. The editors of the *Mercury,* after actually reading it, admitted that

Mr. Gandhi, on his part and on behalf of his countrymen, has done nothing that he is not entitled to do, and from his point of view, the principle he is working for is an honourable and legitimate one. He is within his rights, and so long as he acts honestly and in a straightforward manner, he cannot be blamed or interfered with. So far as we know, he has always done so, and his latest pamphlet, we cannot honestly say, is an unfair statement of the case from his point of view. Reuter's cable is a gross exaggeration of Mr. Gandhi's statement.[22]

[21] *Works,* II, 162. The 60 men were storekeepers' assistants, traders, and hawkers.

[22] *Natal Mercury,* Sept. 18, 1896.

Most of the colonists preferred, however, to believe Reuters.

While the *Courland* and the *Naderi* were riding at anchor, a local butcher, Harry Sparks, captain of the Natal Mounted Rifles of the Volunteer Force, published a notice over his signature, calling upon "every man in Durban to attend a public meeting to be held . . . on Monday the 4th January . . . for the purpose of arranging a demonstration to proceed to the Point to protest against the landing of Asiatics." [23] A large assemblage gathered in the Durban town hall on the stipulated date, and it was resolved that the government should return the Indians in the harbor to India at its own expense and "that every man at this meeting agrees and binds himself, with a view to assisting the Government to carry out the foregoing resolution, to do all his country may require of him, and with that view will, if necessary, attend at the Point at any time when required." [24] A chief speaker at the meeting was Dr. MacKenzie, one of the physicians appointed by the government to determine the quarantine period. As reported in the *Natal Advertiser,* to cries demanding the readying of tar and feathers, the good doctor said:

Mr. Gandhi, (prolonged hissing and hooting) that gentleman who came to Natal and settled in the borough of Durban. He was received here freely and openly; all the privileges and advantages which the Colony could afford him were at his disposal. No contracting or circumscribing influence was brought to play upon him any more than on the audience or himself (the speaker), and he had all the privileges of their hospitality. In return, Mr. Gandhi had accused the Colonists of Natal of having dealt unfairly with Indians, and of having abused and robbed and swindled them. (A voice, "you can't swindle a coolie.") He (the doctor) quite agreed with that. Mr. Gandhi had returned to India and dragged them in the gutter, and painted them as black and filthy as his own skin. (applause). And this was what

[23] *Works,* II, 197.
[24] *Ibid.,* 173; Gandhi to Sir William Hunter, Jan. 29, 1897.

they might call, in Indian parlance, an honourable and manly return for the privileges which Natal had allowed him.[25]

The meeting also called for the extension of the quarantine on the two ships, and when the government indicated that it could not act in the manner desired, a second meeting was convened. J. S. Wylie, a Durban solicitor and a captain in the Durban Light Infantry, spoke. "If the Government did nothing," he said, "Durban would have to do it herself and go in force to the Point and see what could be done." [26] Dr. MacKenzie again harangued the crowd. "The Indian Ocean was the proper place for those Indians," he stated.

They were not going to dispute their right to the water. But they must be careful not to give them the right to land adjoining that ocean. . . . He heard a naval volunteer say last night that he would give a month's pay for a shot at the ship; was every man present prepared to lay down a month's pay to carry out the object of that meeting? (applause, and cries of assent). Then the Government would know what they had behind them. One of the objects of the meeting was to convey to the Government the wish that they wanted a special session of Parliament to extend the quarantine. (applause) [27]

An ultimatum was at this point sent to the captain of the *Courland*, demanding the return of his passengers to India and threatening the resistance of thousands of Durban citizens should any attempt be made to land them.

When the quarantine was finally lifted on January 13, a mob duly gathered and advanced to the Point to oppose the Indians' disembarkation.[28] Once arrived at its destination, it was met by Harry Escombe, Natal's attorney-general and

[25] *Ibid.*, 198; *Natal Advertiser,* Jan. 5, 1897.   [26] *Ibid.*, 174.

[27] *Ibid.*, 201; Indian Memorial to Chamberlain, March 15, 1897.

[28] The crowd included 900 to 1,000 railwaymen, 150 men from the yacht and rowing clubs, 450 carpenters and joiners, 80 printers, 400 shop assistants, 70 tailors and saddlers, 200 bricklayers and plasterers, and 500 natives led by a dwarf, as well as members of the general public. *Ibid.*, 207–208; *Natal Advertiser,* Jan. 16, 1897.

minister of defense. Escombe commended the demonstration
committee for bringing its grievances to the government's attention. But he urged the crowd to remember that

you belong to an Empire presided over by probably the grandest
Sovereign and the grandest woman who has ever impressed her
influence on the page of history. This is the 60th year of Victoria's reign, and in the autumn of her life—which I hope will be
long prolonged—it should never be said that anything that took
place in Natal caused the least sorrow or sadness in the heart of
that great Sovereign, because, with loyalty to Her Person and
Throne, all will come right if you only go the right way to work.
I ask you to trust the Government as we have trusted you, and
join with me in saying, God save the Queen.[29]

The mob muttered. Cries of, "Why don't you bring Gandhi
ashore," and "Get the tar and feathers ready," demanded action.[30] The ubiquitous Dr. MacKenzie shouted that he was

[29] Natal leg. assem. sess. paps., 5th sess., 1st parl., 1897, L.A. no. 1,
copies of corres. re. Ind. imm., gov. to sec. of state, Jan. 15, 1897.
Harry Escombe was without doubt one of the more able political figures in late-19th-century Natal. He had a much more balanced view of
the Indian question than most of his colleagues in the legislative assembly, and he frequently gave speeches defending the right of Indians
to be citizens of Natal. Escombe was politically ambitious, however,
and as his fortunes rose, his opinions, or at least his speeches, began to
resemble more closely those of the other members of the legislative assembly. Upon assuming the premiership in 1897, he continued to bow
to public sentiment whenever it seemed expedient. (Vide *Speeches of
the Late Right Honourable Harry Escombe,* ed. J. T. Henderson, pri-
vately printed, Pietermaritzburg, no date.) After his term as prime
minister, Escombe tended to return to his more moderate position; the
fact that he acquired, when once more a lawyer in private practice,
several wealthy Indian clients is probably not beyond the point.

Escombe had made political use of Indian clients before he ever became prime minister. Pyarelal, *Mahatma Gandhi,* I (Ahmedabad,
1965), 395, traces much of the animosity toward the Indian franchise to
an election, circa 1882, which Harry Escombe won, it was claimed, by
convincing several wealthy Indian traders to enter their names on the
voters' roll and to vote for him.

[30] *Works,* II, 209; Indian memorial to Chamberlain, March 15, 1897.

"just as game as anybody to take a coolie by the neck and throw him overboard." [31] Still Escombe's speech had the desired effect, and the mob of several thousand [32] dispersed, having first cheered the Queen.

The Government of Natal was not totally displeased with the demonstration. In fact, it was accused, in the colonial press, of having encouraged it. The *Times of Natal* reported an interview between the demonstration committee and the attorney-general.

The Committee proposed to do what was illegal, and added: "We presume that you, as representing the Government and good authority of this Colony, would have to bring force to oppose us?" To this Mr. Escombe is represented to have replied: "We will do nothing of the sort. We are with you, and we are going to do nothing of the sort to oppose you. But if you put us in such a position we may have to go to the Governor of the Colony, and ask him to take over the reins of this Colony, as we can no longer conduct the Government—you will have to find some other persons." According to this account [Wylie's], the Government have made a confession of most deplorable weakness. A Minister, on being informed that a body of people propose doing what is unlawful, should without a moment's hesitation, inform his interviewers that the course of law will in no degree be interfered with, and if the occasion calls for it, that Minister should say out bluntly that the law, at all costs, will be supported by all available resources. Mr. Escombe, on the other hand, said in effect, that the Government would do nothing to oppose the unlawful action proposed. This playing into the hands of men who speak publicly of the Indian Ocean as being the proper place of Indian immigrants, shows regrettable weakness in a member of the Government in Office.[33]

The demonstration strengthened the prime minister, Sir John Robinson, in his efforts to prevent the immigration of free Indians into Natal; for he was quite willing to use the

[31] *Ibid.*   [32] 5,000 is the usual estimate.
[33] *Works,* II, 229–230; *Times of Natal,* Jan. 1897. Quoted in memorial to Chamberlain, March 15, 1897.

threat of plague and the danger of violence as a lever. He even asked the Colonial Office to inform the Government of India that "in the interests of order it is desirable that the emigration from India of free Indians to Natal should be arrested." [34] The Government of Natal did not, however, want the violence which, despite Escombe's efforts, was not totally avoided. Although most of the Indians disembarked peacefully and in safety, Gandhi, the chief object of white hatred, was not so fortunate. The Natal Government described the incident to the secretary of state when it was pressed for information.

One untoward incident occurred. Mr. Gandhi, a Parsee [35] lawyer, who had been prominent in the agitation which took place amongst the Indians against the recent franchise legislation, and the author of a pamphlet on the subject of the treatment of Indians in South Africa, some statements in which were resented here, landed at the regular landing place, but within the limits of the Borough of Durban, and was recognised by some disorderly persons, who mobbed and ill-treated him. Ministers have formally expressed to me their regrets at the incident, for which, however, they cannot be held responsible, as the police arrangements within the Borough of Durban are not under their control. I am glad to say that Mr. Gandhi was not seriously hurt. I learn that Mr. Gandhi, in coming ashore at so inopportune a

[34] Natal leg. assem. sess. paps., 5th sess., 1st parl., 1897, L.A. no. 1, copies of corres. re. Ind. imm., prime minister to gov., Jan 14, 1897.

The Government of India replied: "Indian Law does not restrict emigration unless emigrant is already under agreement to labour, and Government of India cannot prohibit departure to any port of India of any other class of Her Majesty's subjects who pay their own passages and embark without specific contract, nor could they possibly propose to their legislators to take such power, but they are taking steps to warn intending emigrants that their landing in Natal is likely to arouse strong popular feeling as regards Bubonic Plague." *Ibid.*, viceroy to gov. of Natal, tel., Jan. 16, 1897. All emigrants were, however, rigorously inspected by the Indian authorities for signs of Bubonic Plague. *Ibid.*, India Office to Colonial Office, Feb. 9, 1897.

[35] Gandhi was, of course, not a Parsi but a Gujerati Vaishya Hindu.

moment, when ill-disposed persons were angry at the peaceful issue of the demonstration and before passions had had time to cool, acted on advice which he now admits to have been bad, and accepts the responsibility of his action in the matter.[36]

The Natal Government's description of the event was something of an oversimplification. F. A. Laughton, the lawyer who had accompanied Gandhi ashore, but who was no particular friend of the Indians in Natal, explained that Gandhi had only chosen to land at that time because of the accusations of cowardice and calumny which had been leveled against him.

To vindicate himself before the public then, it was decided that he should not give his enemies an opportunity of saying that he was "funking it" on board the "Courland," where he could have stayed for a week, if he had chosen; that he should not sneak into Durban like a thief in the night, but that he should face the music like a man and like a political leader, and—give me leave to say—right nobly did he do it. I accompanied him simply as a member of the Bar, to testify, by so doing, that Mr. Gandhi was an honourable member of an honourable profession, in order that I might raise my voice in protest against the way in which he was being treated, and in the hope that my presence might save him from insult.[37]

But Laughton's efforts were all in vain. Gandhi landed at about five o'clock in the afternoon. He was recognized by some boys who followed him as he made his way down West Street, the main street of Durban. Soon a crowd began to gather. As it grew in size, Laughton was separated from Gandhi. The crowd, now a mob, became increasingly menacing, and Gandhi was soon the target of stale fish and other pro-

[36] Natal leg. assem. sess. paps., 5th sess., 1st parl., 1897, L.A. no .1, copies of corres. re. Ind. imm., gov. to sec. of state for the colonies, Jan 15, 1897. In a telegram to the secretary of state of the same date, Hely-Hutchinson had described Gandhi as "an individual who, by his actions as an agitator, has made himself specially obnoxious." *Ibid.*

[37] *Natal Mercury,* Jan. 16, 1897.

jectiles. Encouraged, the rabble began to whip its victim—his hat was knocked off, and he was cut extensively on the neck, ears, and around the eyes. Only the intervention of Mrs. R. C. Alexander, the wife of Durban's police chief, saved Gandhi from severe injury. She protected him with her umbrella and, with the aid of some policemen who had been attracted to the scene by the commotion, assisted him to the house of an Indian who lived nearby. The mob was not discouraged, however, and in the gathering darkness, laid siege to the residence. As it increased still further in size, the chief of police became concerned about Gandhi's safety. The tension did not abate until Gandhi was smuggled out of the house and into the security of a police station, disguised as a constable.

Characteristically, when the secretary of state cabled the Natal Government to prosecute Gandhi's assailants, Gandhi informed the attorney-general that he did not wish to press charges. Rather he begged to thank Escombe

and the government for the kind enquiries made about me and the kindness shown to me by the officials of Durban after the incident that happened on Wednesday last.

I beg to state that I do not wish that any notice should be taken of the behaviour of some people towards me last Wednesday, which I have no doubt was due to misapprehension on their part as to what I did in India with reference to the Asiatic question.

It is due to the Government to state that, although under instructions from you, the Superintendent of Water Police offered to take me to town quietly at night, I proceeded to the shore with Mr. Laughton on my own responsibility without informing the water police of my departure.[38]

The Indian community of Durban gave Police Chief R. C. Alexander a gold watch for "saving the life of one whom we delight to love." [39] Mrs. Alexander was presented with a

[38] *Works,* II, 166.
[39] *Ibid.,* 284; Indians to R. C. Alexander, March 24, 1897.

chain and inscribed locket for an "act which will ever be a pattern of true womanhood." [40]

Indentured Indians were the particular responsibility of the Indian Government, and the Natal authorities were most careful to avoid a confrontation that would endanger the vital supply of Indian labor. The "Arabs," on the other hand, came to Natal of their own volition, and were not covered by most of the protective legislation passed on behalf of the indentured Indians in India and Natal. The colonial government had therefore only to keep in mind the general imperial responsibility of the Colonial Office in moving against them.

Natal's main objective was to inhibit the ease of entry into the colony enjoyed by free Indians. Initially the legislative assembly wanted to pass an act specifically excluding all but indentured Indians from the colony, but the Colonial Office would not permit it. [41] As a result, Act 14 of 1897, "To place certain restrictions on Immigration," was technically nonracial. Qualifications for entry into Natal were based on property (£25) [42] and knowledge of a European language. [43] Although the Governor of Natal, Sir Walter Hely-Hutchinson, clearly stated to Joseph Chamberlain, the secretary of state for the colonies, that "the main object of the proposed law is to prevent Natal from being flooded by undesirable Immigrants from India," [44] Chamberlain was able blandly to inform the Indians of Natal that "the Immigration Restriction Act . . . does not affect British Indians, as such." [45] The sec-

[40] *Ibid.*, 285; Indians to Mrs. R. C. Alexander, March 24, 1897.

[41] Natal leg. assem. sess. paps., speech by the prime minister on the immigration act, L.A. no. 5, 1st sess., 1st parl., 1897.

[42] The property qualification was later made less specific. Rather than prospective immigrants with less than £25, paupers and those liable to become a public charge were excluded from Natal.

[43] Linguistic competence was proved through the ability to write out and sign an application to enter Natal in a European language.

[44] NA, Natal no. 23, gov. to sec. of state, Feb. 26, 1897.

[45] *Ibid.*, no. 99, sec. of state to gov., Nov. 12, 1897.

retary of state's real view of the matter was reflected in a memorandum sent by the Colonial Office to the India Office: "Some form of legislation in restriction of Indian Immigration was inevitable in Natal; and the Secretary of State was of opinion that it was desirable that a law should be passed in that colony in a form which was not open to the objection that it persecuted persons of a particular colour." [46]

The Immigration Restriction Act of 1897 was consequently not disallowed by the British Government, and it was administered in such a manner that most Europeans were judged eligible to enter Natal while virtually all Indians were not.[47] As the prime minister of Natal told the legislature, "it never occurred to me for a single minute that [the act] should ever be applied to English immigrants. . . . Can you imagine anything more mad for a Government than that it should apply to English immigrants? The object of the bill is to deal with Asiatic immigrants." [48] To further calm the nerves of the Colonial Office, the act provided that exemptions from its workings could be granted by the governor. But during the first year the act was in operation, only twelve Asians were so exempted—five Indian servants of the 5th Lancers, three Indian teachers, three Mauritius Creole servants, and one Indian servant for the Addington Hospital.[49]

The British Government found itself in a most difficult position. It had the right to disallow all legislation passed by the British colonies in South Africa, regardless of their state of constitutional development, but, in practice, after a colony attained responsible government, the Colonial Office

[46] *Ibid.*, Indian collection, under-sec., Col. Off., to under-sec., Ind. Off., Oct. 2, 1897.

[47] *Ibid.*, Ind. coll., Govt. House papers, Ind. Off. to Col. Off., July 21, 1897.

[48] *Vide* n. 41.

[49] Natal leg. assem. sess. paps., L.A. 19, 2nd sess., 2nd parl., 1898, July 7, 1898.

only interfered in matters having imperial implications. Despite an official philosophy dedicated to the equality of all British subjects, regardless of race, the British Government found itself hard put to interfere with the will of a white colonial government discriminating against nonwhite British subjects, even if that government represented only a small minority of the total population of the colony. Natal's position was less uncertain. The prime minister had no doubt as to what the British Government's attitude should be on the question of free Indian immigration:

If it became a question as between the colonial Empire and the Indian Empire, then I say, without the least reserve, that the interests of those of British extraction must be preferred to the interests of those of Indian extraction. . . . If you allow them [the Indians] to make it [Natal] a paradise for Indians, you will find that, as far as Europeans are concerned, it is an exact antipode of paradise. . . . We mean to preserve this fair land, as far as we can, for those who are now in the Colony, to maintain it, as far as it is possible, as a British Colony, and not to have the whole of the conditions of the country submerged under an Asiatic wave of immigrations.[50]

Although the Government of India could, on its own initiative, stop the immigration of indentured Indians to any part of the empire, it could not actually interfere with legislation passed in other British possessions. The viceroy did, however, often call to the attention of the Colonial Office laws, such as the Natal Immigration Restriction Act, which he considered detrimental to the welfare of overseas Indians. But the Indian authorities' chief concern remained the indentured Indian, and they were reluctant to take a firm position in defense of the rights of voluntary immigrants. Besides, within the Indian Government itself there were many who sympathized with the attitudes of the white settlers in Natal. When the Natal Immigration Restriction Act came

[50] *Ibid.*, L.A. no. 5, 5th sess., 1st parl., 1897; speech by the prime minister, March 25, 1897.

up for discussion in the viceroy's council, J. Westland, the finance member, defended the colony's position. "We must recognise the fact," he wrote,

that it will be an utter reversal of the whole colonial policy of Britain, if we expect the Home Government to interfere in the details of colonial self-government in laying down for a colony the lines along which it is to develop itself. From an English point of view, it is not the question of which is the higher or the nobler line to take, but it is the question why the colonist should be interfered with in judging for himself what is best for himself, even though the Home Politicians may not agree with him as to the ultimate advantage.

I must say at once that in these matters I take the colonists' side.[51]

Westland, like the Natal colonists, would resent the arrival of new immigrants, "to contest with me the right to reap the profits and advantages of the country that I had made habitable." [52] He did not believe that "a British subject, as such, has an inherent right to go and make his living on his own terms, in any portion of the dominions of Her Majesty," [53] and he felt that Europeans, when they had conquered a wilderness, should not be forced to accept aliens. "I cannot see any reasonable foundation for the doctrine that when we conquer a race or nation by the force of arms, the people of that nation acquire rights as against members of the conquering race who happen to have cast their lot in tropical or sub-tropical colonies." [54]

J. Woodburn, another member of the council, took a view similar to Westland's. It was his opinion that if Indians "were admitted [to Natal] on terms of absolute equality, the British would be elbowed out." [55] In consequence of the tone of the discussions in the council, the Government of

[51] NAI, Aug. 1897, proc. 12, minute by J. Westland, June 11, 1897.
[52] *Ibid.*   [53] *Ibid.*   [54] *Ibid.,* note by J. Westland, Oct. 26, 1897.
[55] *Ibid.,* note by J. Woodburn, March 15, 1897.

India limited its opposition to the Natal Immigration Restriction Act largely to an effort to ensure that Indians already living in Natal, who left the colony temporarily, would not, upon their return, be excluded as "prohibited immigrants," a contingency which, given the wording of the law, was not totally unlikely.[56]

Both the British and Indian governments were intimately concerned with the growing Indian problem in South Africa. For if the empire stood for equality, any attack on a particular group of the Queen's subjects by other members of the British family struck at the very roots of the imperial philosophy. The situation was, however, fraught with emotional ambivalence, for it must have been difficult for Englishmen in the nineteenth century, not the most tolerant of ages, to feel in their hearts that Africans and Indians were really the equals of white men. Joseph Chamberlain manifested some of this ambivalence when he said:

We quite sympathise with the determination of the white inhabitants of these Colonies which are in comparatively close proximity to millions and hundreds of millions of Asiatics that there shall be no influx of people alien in civilisation, alien in religion, alien in customs, whose influx, moreover, would most seriously interfere with the legitimate rights of the existing labour population. An immigration of that kind must, I quite understand, in the interests of the Colonies, be prevented at all hazards, and we shall not offer any opposition to the proposals intended with that object, but we ask you also to bear in mind the tradition of the Empire which makes no distinction in favour of, or against race or colour; and to exclude, by reason of their colour, or by reason of their race, all Her Majesty's Indian subjects, or even all Asiatics, would be an act so offensive to those peoples that, it would

[56] *Ibid.*, Nov. 1897, procs. 8–20, Ind. Off. to Col. Off., July 21, 1897. The India Office, as a consequence, wanted the word "domiciled" in the law changed to "resident." CO 179/202, Ind. Off. to Col. Off., Nov. 2, 1897. NA, Natal Ind. coll., Govt. House, Col. Off. to Ind. Off., July 21, 1897.

be most painful, I am quite certain, to Her Majesty to have to sanction it.[57]

The British Government was caught between increasingly anti-Asian white minority governments in South Africa, liberal opinion in Britain, and national indignation in India. The *Times* felt that Natal Indians had been persecuted by the colonial legislature. "They have been wantonly assaulted in the streets and been unable to obtain redress from the courts. They have been robbed and outraged and reviled for presuming to exist at all . . . and they have been persistently denied the status of citizens." [58] On September 6, 1895, the *Times* again editorialized:

Our Indian subjects have been fighting the battles of Great Britain over half of the old world with a loyalty and courage which have won the admiration of all British men. . . . It would be a violation of the British sense of justice to use the blood and courage of these races in war and yet to deny them the protection of the British name in enterprises of peace. . . . The necessity has now arisen of protecting the Indian labourer . . . and for securing to him the same rights as other British subjects enjoy.

Frequent questions and debates occurred in Parliament on the subject of Indians in South Africa, and as if to underline the curious complexity of the empire, the attack was often led by Indian members of Parliament.[59] On October 11, 1897, Dadabhai Naoroji, in a letter to Chamberlain, remarked that

we are repeatedly told that we are British subjects, quite as much as the Queen's subjects in this country, and not slaves and I always look forward with hope to a fulfillment of these pledges and Proclamations . . . and I pray that it may be a reality and not remain a romance.[60]

[57] NA, Natal no. 102, sec. of state to gov., Nov. 12, 1897. Quoted in encl., Natal Indians to Dadabhai Naoroji, Sept. 18, 1897.

[58] The *Times,* Aug. 27, 1894.   [59] *Hansard,* XCLX, Aug. 16, 1900.

[60] NA, Ind. coll., no. 102, sec. of state to gov., Nov. 13, 1897, encl., Naoroji to Chamberlain, Oct. 11, 1897.

Perhaps the British dilemma was summarized most concisely in a Colonial Office minute dealing with the Natal Indian question.

The whole subject is perhaps the most difficult we have had to deal with. The Colonies wish to exclude the Indians from spreading themselves all over the Empire. If we agree, we are liable to forfeit the loyalty of the Indians. If we do not agree we forfeit the loyalty of the Colonists.[61]

Embarrassed and frustrated, the British Government compromised. It insisted that the letter of any particular law be nondiscriminatory but cared little about the spirit. Such was the case with the Immigration Restriction Act; with Natal Act 38 of 1896, which further restricted the sale of intoxicating liquor to Indians by stipulating that they could drink only on licensed premises and then only if the liquor were served to them in glasses; and with Act 2 of 1897, "An Act to Amend the Laws Relating to Quarantine." On the surface, the Quarantine Act looked like a perfectly reasonable piece of legislation designed to prevent persons from areas infected with disease from landing in Natal, but section 2 of the law convinced the Indians that it was just another legislative stratagem designed to prevent Indians from entering Natal. The offending clause allowed the colonial health authorities to prevent the landing of healthy Indians who had not been exposed to infection. A quarantine order, the law read, "shall extend to a ship having on board passengers who have come from a proclaimed place, notwithstanding that they may have embarked at some other place, or that the ship has not touched at the proclaimed place." [62]

A more sympathetic attitude toward the Colonial Office's obvious predicament might be possible if greater evidence were available that, when unimpeded, the secretary of state and his associates strongly and genuinely favored an empire

[61] CO, 179/202, Col. Off., domestic, no. 4900, received March 6, 1897, minuting by F. S., June 17, 1897.

[62] Natal Act 2, 1897, section 2.

where all subjects, regardless of race, received equal treatment under the law. Unfortunately, the course of events in Zululand, a province under the Colonial Office's immediate supervision, and hence not subject to the jurisdiction of a colony enjoying the rights of responsible government, tends to point to an opposite conclusion.

By the early 1890's, Indian traders had filtered into Zululand from neighboring Natal to be greeted with familiar hostility by the few white colonists of the region. Between 1891 and 1893 proclamations were issued by the Zululand administration curtailing the rights of Indians to live and trade in towns and to take out mining licenses.[63] Governor Sir Charles Mitchell of Natal, the officer charged with the supervision of Zululand affairs, was

anxious to avoid the difficulties and troubles that are created in Pietermaritzburg and Durban as well as in the small townships of this Colony [Natal] by the Banyan Indian trader. The presence of these men in a young community is of doubtful advantage to anyone, and in my opinion, of absolute disadvantage to the Native population, and I should be glad, if Your Lordship [Lord Knutsford, the secretary of state for the colonies] sees no objection to restrict them from doing so for some time to come.[64]

The Colonial Office was well aware of the potential embarrassment of the situation. The British Government was strongly defending the rights of British Indians in the South African Republic against the very same type of legislation its minions were proposing for Zululand. Edward Wingfield, one of the assistant undersecretaries, conceded that "it is hardly for the British Govt. to cast the first stone at the Boers in the matter of anti-Indian legislation." [65] Frederick

[63] CO, 427/12, proclamations V and VII of 1891 (Regulating Sale of Liquor to Indians) and CO, 427/27, proclamations III and IV of 1897, Eshowe and Nondweni mun. regs.

[64] CO, 427/15, Zululand no. 92, Mitchell to Col. Off., Aug. 7, 1891.

[65] CO, 427/16, Zululand no. 52, Mitchell to Col. Off., June 12, 1893, minuting by Edward Wingfield, asst. undersec., Aug 3, 1893.

Graham, a ranking first class clerk,[66] admitted: "This is awkward. We have been fighting the battle of these Indians in the Dutch Republics, and now the Government is asked to impose difficulties on them in a purely Crown Colony." [67]

Shedding considerable light on one of the stances assumed by the Colonial Office when necessity demanded it, Graham admitted that "the question [is] rather more awkward than the Chinese question in Australia where we could shelter ourselves behind the stablished fact of Responsible Government." [68] Besides, he continued, "the greatest difference between the two questions is that in the one case we had to deal for the most part with the subjects of a foreign power, while here we have to deal with British subjects who appeal for protection to the Secretary of State for India and to Parliament." [69] Nevertheless, Graham concluded on the by now customary note of rationalization. "I don't see," he wrote,

how it will be possible to refuse assent to the Proclamation [for creating Indian locations at Eshowe] nor will it be possible to oppose the strong popular feeling in S. Africa against the Indians. After all their grievance is a very small one, they are not like the natives, they need not go there unless they like, and in the case of Zululand they have not yet acquired vested interests as they have in the Transvaal. Perhaps on this ground *and for this reason* the Proclamation might be approved without delay and Sir Charles Mitchell asked to make out the case against them [the Indians] later.[70]

In a more specific vein, Hartmann Just, another first class clerk, suggested that Indians and other non-Europeans could

[66] The title "clerk" did not necessarily connote a menial in the Colonial Office. The upper reaches of the civil service hierarchy after the permanent undersecretary consisted of the assistant undersecretaries followed by the principal and the first-class clerks.

[67] CO, 427/16, Zululand no. 52, Mitchell to Col. Off., June 12, 1893, minuting by Graham, Sept. 4, 1891.

[68] *Ibid.*   [69] *Ibid.*   [70] *Ibid.*

be excluded from land ownership by the administrative expedient of not approving their applications to bid on or occupy real estate. Thus there was no need to mention them in the proclamation at all. "If the present position is to be justified to Mr. Bhownaggree and Mr. Naoroji," he concluded,

> we must take refuge in the argument that the Zulus and other non-Europeans also are not allowed to hold land, but it is not a good argument, because the Zulus are excluded on the ground that land is held by them tribally and it is not in accordance with their custom and organisation for individuals to possess private property in land.[71]

Chamberlain adopted his subordinate's suggestion and informed the Zululand administration that he would

> be glad if you would consider whether the exclusion of undesirable persons, whether Indians, Natives or others, from holding land, could not be secured by administrative action either by withholding approval from applications made by such persons for leave to bid for erven [town lots] . . . or by stipulating that any one who occupies an erf must receive a permit to do so, as a suitable and desirable resident, or by any other suitable method, which would not be open to the criticisms made against the present regulations.[72]

On the question of the issuance of trading licenses, magistrates were left absolute discretion without the right of appeal.[73]

Both Lord Knutsford and Joseph Chamberlain, as secretaries of state, in essence agreed to the establishment of a policy of Indian exclusion and restriction for Zululand.[74]

[71] CO, 417/24, Zululand no. 22, Hely-Hutchinson to Col. Off., April 6, 1896, minuting by H. W. Just, May 26, 1896.

[72] *Ibid.*, draft, Col. Off. to Hely-Hutchinson, June 24, 1896.

[73] CO, 427/16, Zululand no. 52, Mitchell to Col. Off., June 12, 1893, minuting by Graham, Aug. 8, 1893.

[74] CO, 427/12. On the question of Indian rights in Zululand, the Colonial Office took the unusual step of not informing the India Office. As Edward Fairfield, an assistant undersecretary, minuted: "No. It

As the former minuted, "The case of Zululand is very peculiar, and it is important to prevent, as far as possible, the introduction of settlers likely to create complications and difficulties." [75]

In Natal, even the most overtly offensive laws and practices were frequently condoned by the Colonial Office. It has already been noted that "coolies" were required to register when in a town on the basis of their belonging to an "uncivilised race"; [76] and that Law 15 of 1869 had not been disallowed even though its second section stated that "every coloured person [77] found wandering abroad in a Borough after and before such hours as the Corporation may fix, and not giving a good account of himself or herself, is liable on conviction, to hard labour not exceeding three months, or to a fine not exceeding £5." [78] In addition, Indians were usually excluded from government high schools,[79] and made liable to arrest unless in possession of a pass.[80] The pass law was ostensibly enacted to protect free Indians from being apprehended in error. It stipulated that a free Indian was entitled to a pass which would protect him from arrest as an absconding indentured laborer. In providing the police protection from suits for false arrest, should they take into custody a free Indian without a pass, the act's chief effect was to make it mandatory for free Indians to obtain passes. Considerable pressure from the British and Indian governments resulted in the passage of Natal Act 18 of 1898, under the provisions of which an arresting officer was only protected from a suit

---

is no use stirring things up. They are too fond of protesting in favour of their Arabs as it is." CO, draft (Zululand no. 54) to Mitchell, c. Nov. 1891.

[75] *Ibid.,* minuting by Knutsford, Sept. 24, 1891.

[76] Natal Law 21, 1888.   [77] A designation which included Indians.

[78] NA, gen. conf. desps. from Natal, gov. to high comm., Cape Town, Aug. 24, 1898.

[79] *Ibid.,* Natal no. 7, gov. to sec. of state, Jan. 13, 1909.

[80] Natal Act 28, 1897.

for false arrest if he apprehended an Indian without a pass, "under a bona fide belief or suspicion that he is an indentured Indian." But the act was essentially meaningless, for to prove that such a suspicion was not present at the time of arrest was, of course, impossible.

In the sphere of major legislation, the Immigration Restriction Act was only part of Natal's attack on the "Arabs." The removal of Indians from the colony's electoral rolls was still considered a matter of equal urgency.[81] In 1894, a bill making all Indians ineligible to vote in Natal parliamentary elections was read a second time in the legislative assembly, but the Colonial Office informed the Government of Natal that "to assent to this measure would be to put an affront upon the people of India as no British Government could be a party to." [82] Debate on the measure nevertheless continued to rage for many months in the legislative assembly. Asiatics, it was claimed, had no experience in voting, and even the most sophisticated Indians in Durban were said to have become confused by the voting procedure. The prime minister thought that there were so many Indians in Natal that the white man might be swamped at the polls.[83] The fact that all voters had to be possessed of £50 in property or to pay £20 annual rent—qualifications which excluded virtually all Indians from the franchise—seemed to have been conveniently forgotten.[84] The prime minister even attempted to use the vast petition of protest sent by Gandhi to the secretary of state for the colonies to his advantage. "There are only 10,-279 electors already on the rolls of the Colony," he wrote. "Consequently had the Petitioners their desire, at this moment they would form nine-tenths of the electorate." [85]

[81] In fact, the act "to amend the Law relating to the Franchise" was actually passed several months before the Immigration Restriction Act.

[82] NA Natal no. 27, sec. of state to gov., Sept. 21, 1895.

[83] Natal leg. assem. sess. paps., 1896, L.A. no. 6, April 21, 1896, corres. re. the franchise law, ministers to gov., July 27, 1894.

[84] There were at the time 251 Indians on the voters' roll as compared to 9,650 Europeans—a ratio of 1:38.

[85] *Vide* n. 83.

Looking to the future, the prime minister felt that the restriction of the franchise was "a duty we owe not only to ourselves, the Colonists of Natal, but to South Africa." [86] To an Indian delegation that approached him, the prime minister disingenuously averred that, "the very fact that their people were to be disqualified in the Bill from exercising the franchise was in itself an absolute guarantee that the Government would consider itself under a special obligation to promote their interests." [87]

From the very first, the governor of Natal, Walter Hely-Hutchinson, accurately conveyed his minister's feelings (and for that matter his own) to the Colonial Office. He reiterated the views of the prime minister in claiming that the Indians of the colony, if left in possession of the franchise, "would all vote together; and would thus control 40,000 Europeans and 450,000 natives." [88] Of greatest significance, however, was his clear delineation of the basic issue as the Natal cabinet saw it.

The question is really, whether Natal is to be governed, in future, by persons of European descent or whether persons of Asiatic descent are to be allowed a voice, which would later become a preponderant voice in the Government of the Colony. Public opinion in Natal conceives that there is only one reply to that question; and that it can best be solved in that sense by the law to which the petitioners object.[89]

[86] Natal *Hansard,* June 20, 1894.   [87] *Ibid.,* July 2, 1894.

[88] Natal leg. assem. sess. paps., 1st sess., 1st parl., 1896, L. A. no. 7, Natal no. 66, gov. to sec. of state, July 31, 1894.

[89] *Ibid.,* Natal actually considered the bill in its final form a concession to the Colonial Office. The colony's government would have preferred a more extreme measure. Hely-Hutchinson, in urging the bill's prompt ratification by the British Government, wrote to Chamberlain (Chamberlain Papers, JC 10/17/34) on August 19, 1896, that "the Natal Ministers practically adopted a private suggestion which emanated from the Colonial Office." The governor felt that any further modification of the bill or any undue delay in its passage would cause the government to fall as "they would be altogether discredited."

It did not take long for the white colonists of Natal to discern the Colonial Office's attitude toward racial discriminatory colonial legislation with all its dangerous imperial implications. Only two years after the repulse of its original franchise act, Natal was able to disenfranchise for the future all Indians, regardless of qualifications, who were not at that time on the voters' rolls. The colonial legislators merely stipulated that those "who (not being of European origin) are Natives or descendants in the male line of Natives of countries which have not hitherto possessed elective institutions," unless exempted by the governor in council, could not vote in parliamentary elections.[90]

Once the specific racial terminology was removed from the franchise law, the Colonial Office's opposition essentially evaporated. Edward Wingfield, Chamberlain's chief aide, although he personally deplored all legislation directed against Indians, concluded that "in the present state of colonial opinion . . . it is impossible in the self-governing colonies to require that British Indians shall be placed in exactly the same position as European British subjects." [91] The secretary of state himself wrote to Natal, "It is manifestly the desire and intention of your Government that the destinies of the Colony of Natal shall continue to be shaped by the Anglo-Saxon race and that the possibility of any preponderant influx of Asiatic voters be averted." [92] As this position was one with which Chamberlain had previously indicated agreement,[93] he was "not prepared to advise Her Majesty to exercise her powers of disallowance . . . [although he was] in communication with the Government of Natal on the subject of preserving the rights of those of Her Majesty's Indian subjects who were already resident in Natal." [94] There was, after all, little reason for objection, Chamberlain contended.

[90] Natal Act 8, 1896.   [91] *Vide,* p. 64 and n. 46.
[92] Quoted in Natal *Hansard,* May 6, 1896.   [93] *Vide* n. 46.
[94] NA, Ind. coll., Govt. House, Col. Off. to Naoroji, Nov. 13, 1897.

The Act is general in its terms and does not exclude British Indian or any other non-European race, co-nominee, but natives (not being of European origin) or descendants of Natives of countries which have not hitherto possessed elective representative institutions founded on the parliamentary franchise, who are, therefore, presumably not qualified for the exercise of the franchise. The act, it will be observed, saves the right of all electors already enrolled and provides for the possibility of exemption from the operation in special cases.[95]

At first, the Indian Government took strong issue with the franchise law. It duly pointed out that natives of India and Englishmen stood on a similar footing when voting in Indian municipal, provincial, and supreme council elections.[96] But in the long run, the Government of India also conceded. It again decided that its primary responsibility was to the indentured Indians, and that it could not do much about popular sentiment in Natal in any case.[97] The Indian authorities were willing to sacrifice the rights of future free immigrants to Natal and to devote their efforts to preserving the position of Indians already in the colony.[98] But they were not willing to go too far even on this front. The Natal Indians, the viceroy felt, should do what they could to obtain the removal of insidious distinctions, but the Government of India, itself, should be careful about interfering with Natal authorities. "It would be a mistake," he concluded, "to press them on points like the franchise." [99]

Objectionable as the immigration restriction and franchise acts were, by far the most insidious piece of legislation passed in the period 1896–1897 was Natal Act 18 of 1897, "To amend the law relating to licenses to wholesale and

[95] Quoted in Iqbal Narain, *The Politics of Racialism* (Ahmedabad, 1957), 127.

[96] CO, 179/202, GOI, dept. of rev. and ag. (em.), no. 22, viceroy in council to sec. of state, March 31, 1897.

[97] NAI, Aug. 1897, proc. 12.

[98] CO, 179/202, Ind. Off. to Col. Off., Nov. 21, 1897.

[99] NAI, Aug. 1897, proc. 12, note by Elgin, March 19, 1897.

retail dealers," which made all applicants for trading licenses or renewal of trading licenses subject to municipal licensing officers to be appointed by the corporations. By means of this act the municipalities of Natal expected to rid themselves of merchants whom they accused, on the one hand, of underselling Europeans as a consequence of the low wages they paid, and whom they belabored, on the other hand, for offering salaries "so handsome that several lady assistants in the large drapery establishments in town express a determination to put their pride in their pockets and suffer the indignity of being in the employ of an Arab." [100] Equally contributing to the advantage the Arab enjoyed in commerce, the European press insisted, was the inexpensive filth and misery in which the Indian merchants lived. Yet a writer in the *Witness* intoned:

These Arabs are becoming luxurious. The other day I saw a fine sight, in the shape of an Arab, with his long-skirted, turbaned family, lolling on the cushions of a large open carriage drawn by a pair of good horses. The white aristocrats of this town revel in coolie coachmen. Soon we will find our Arab friends employing white men to sit on the box decked out in all the glory of boots, buttons and breeches.[101]

The act stipulated that all books were to be kept in English and that commercial premises should be maintained in a sanitary condition. The licensing officer was to determine whether these conditions were being met or not. Appeals were to be allowed to a board to be made up of municipal officials, but not to the courts of the land.

From the first, the Indian Government had opposed the licensing act. It had insisted that Indians be permitted an appeal to the supreme court in licensing cases. As had been the case with the franchise act, however, the Indian authorities began to vacillate and eventually retreated to their usual

---

[100] Pyarelal, *op. cit.,* 475.   [101] *Ibid.,* 475–476.

position. The indentured Indians and free Indians already established in Natal, they claimed, were their main responsibility. If the proposed law were only to affect new arrivals, they would after all be entering the situation with their eyes open.[102] The British Government was, of course, in a better position to object to the licensing act than the Indian Government, but it approved the measure with little hesitation, again on the grounds that it contained nothing specifically discriminatory to Indians, and because it naïvely accepted the Government of Natal's assurance that the law would be fairly administered.[103]

In actual fact, the municipalities, urged on by European protective societies that sprang up in many towns, and checked neither by the courts nor by the colonial administration, looked upon the law as a mandate to remove all the Indians from their midst. When appeals were lodged with the licensing boards, they were nearly always laughingly dismissed, regardless of the evidence.[104] The actions of the municipal licensing boards were too blatant for even the Colonial Office, and in 1899 Chamberlain addressed Hely-Hutchinson on the question:

I am led to the conclusion that in view of the attitude adopted by certain municipalities, unless an appeal is given from the Town Councils who have the power of refusing licenses under Act No. 18 of 1897, grave injustice is likely to be done to the Asiatic traders.

3. When the Act in question was submitted for the signification of Her Majesty's pleasure, I did not consider that I could properly advise Her Majesty to interfere with the Colonial Legislation in regard to the provision for making final the decision of the Town Council.[105]

[102] NA, Ind. coll., Govt. House, Ind. Off. to Col. Off., Nov. 2, 1897.

[103] *I.e.,* that Indians' vested interests would be protected. CO 179/204, Ind. Off. to Col. Off., July 14, 1898.

[104] NA, Natal conf. no. 1, gov. to sec. of state, May 18, 1907.

[105] *Ibid.,* Ind. coll., Natal no. 45, sec. of state to gov., May 19, 1899.

The secretary of state claimed that he had been assured that the act would not be harshly enforced, and that the vested interests of Indians would be respected. As the law had not so been administered, unless the act were amended to allow for an appeal to the supreme court, indentured Indian immigration to Natal would probably come to an end.[106] Had Chamberlain read the legislative assembly debates on the act, he might have made a more realistic assessment of the situation at the outset. "This Bill," a leading member of the assembly (Tatham) had proclaimed,

is a Bill which is intended by an indirect method, to get at a direct evil. Let there be no mistake about that at all. We may as well face the fact and if the Bill passes a second reading it is no use calling it un-English or un-British because it is an indirect method of accomplishing your end, because even every member of this Assembly knows full well that the object of this Bill is to get at the Asiatic trader. The term "Asiatic trader" is not mentioned in the Bill and yet the meaning is to get at the Asiatic trader; although you do not mention the name.[107]

Natal's two major newspapers, the *Mercury* and the *Witness,* combined to support the three major acts passed by the legislative assembly in 1896–1897: the Immigration Restriction Act, the franchise act, and the licensing act. The *Mercury* wrote that "the awakening of the Colonists to the danger of being swamped by a low-class population was only the first practical step toward the complete solution of a question that must of necessity be transmitted to the next generation." [108] The *Witness* emphasized the colonists' prior responsibility to the native population:

The Indian rubbish which is being shot upon these shores is more and more appropriating the charitable funds of this country and matters have reached the stage at which we are turning out our own family, in which we include the native aboriginal

[106] *Ibid.*   [107] Natal *Hansard,* March 31, 1897.
[108] *Natal Mercury,* Jan. 29, 1895.

population, to starve in order to make room for and entertain those who have no claim upon us.[109]

Early in 1897, the *Witness* urged the establishment of separate locations for Indians and claimed that the Immigration Restriction Act did not go far enough.[110]

It would appear that the Indians in Natal were falling into an increasingly desperate position. As a petition to Sir Mancherjee Bhownaggree, one of the Indian members of Parliament, stated:

The Indian question in this Colony has reached the critical point. It affects not only Her Majesty's Indian subjects residing in the Colony but the whole population of India. It is pre-eminently Imperial in its aspect. "May or may they not," as the Times puts it, "go freely from one British possession to another, and claim the rights of British subjects in allied states." European Natal says they shall not, so far as she is concerned.[111]

The presence of Gandhi was apparently the one ray of hope for Natal's Indians, and after his return from India his life became even more hectic. Among other things he organized a relief committee to raise funds to help victims of the famine that was sweeping India—soliciting European as well as Indian aid. Gandhi was also becoming convinced that the Natal authorities were determined to drive all the Indians in the colony back to India, to deprive Indians of their rights as British subjects. He felt that the events of January 13, 1896 (the date of the attack on him in Durban), were significant chiefly in this context, and he used them as the basis of a long memorial to the secretary of state, in which he again outlined the disabilities under which Indians labored in Natal.[112] Gandhi quoted from the minutes of an anti-Indian

[109] *Natal Witness,* March 25, 1893.   [110] *Ibid.,* Jan. 7, 1897.

[111] NA, Ind. coll., Govt. House, 877, C. 92/1897, conf. minute paper, Nov. 19, 1897, Natal conf., sec. of state to gov., Nov. 19, 1897, encl. 43, Natal Indians to Sir M. Bhownaggree, March 27, 1897.

[112] *Works,* II, 187; Indian memorial to Chamberlain, March 15, 1897.

meeting held at Pietermaritzburg, where Indians were referred to as "black vermin," were described as being able "to
live on the smell of an oil rag," and were accused of breed-
ing like rabbits. One speaker said, "The worst of it is that we
can't shoot them down." [113]

Yet until 1919, Gandhi believed that the British Government was sincere in its support of an imperial philosophy
based on the equality of all British subjects—after all, despite all of his disappointments, he did urge Indians to join
the army and fight for Britain during World War I! It was
at least partly because of this faith that he continued to bom-
bard the Colonial Office with memorials and petitions.
When the Queen's Diamond Jubilee approached, Gandhi
was still sufficiently enamored of the British Empire to write
a warm message of felicitation.

Most gracious Sovereign and Empress . . . In token of our joy at
the approaching of the completion of the 60th year of your glorious and beneficent reign, we are proud to think that we are
your subjects, the more so as we know that the peace we enjoy in
India, and the confidence of security of life and prosperity which
enables us to venture abroad, are due to that position. We can
but re-echo the sentiments of loyalty and devotion which are finding expression among all your subjects and in all parts of your
vast dominions on which the sun never sets. That the God Al-
mighty may spare you in health and vigour for a long time to
come to reign over us, is our devout wish and prayer.[114]

The address was inscribed on a silver shield and bore twenty-one signatures, the last being Gandhi's. As a further trib-
ute, Gandhi inspired the founding of a Diamond Jubilee Library to be supported by the Indian community.

Expressions of loyalty to the Queen did not mean that
Gandhi would relax his efforts to protect the Indians of
Natal from legislation that would be to their detriment. On
July 2, 1897, Gandhi, on behalf of the Indian community,
composed another long memorial to Chamberlain protesting

[113] *Ibid.*   [114] *Ibid.*, 316–317.

the quarantine, immigration restriction, and licensing bills. It was an artful piece of prose, for Gandhi succeeded in convicting the white colonists largely through their own words. In reference to the anti-Indian nature of the quarantine act, he quoted the *Mercury* of March 30, 1897:

We had not the slightest objection to take a mean advantage of the provisions of the Quarantine Bill. To prevent the landing of Indian immigrants in Natal, on the ground that they came from a country infected with dangerous infectious disease within a thousand miles of the district they came from, is just as disingenuous as the operations of the Immigration Restriction Bill.[115]

On the Immigration Restriction Act, Gandhi invoked the prime minister:

As to Immigrants being in possession of twenty-five pounds, when those words were introduced it never occurred to him that it would be applied to Europeans. It could be applied if the Government were foolish enough. The object, however, was to deal with the Asiatics. Some people said they liked an honest straightforward course. When a ship was heading against a wind, she had to tack, and bye and bye she accomplished her goal. When a man met difficulties, he fought against them, and, if he could not knock them over, he went around them instead of breaking his head against a brick wall.[116]

When it came to the licensing act, Gandhi again referred to a statement by the prime minister:

They asked that powers be given to each municipality in excess of its present powers to control the issuing of licenses, and there need be no hesitation in saying what their object was. It was to prevent persons who competed with Europeans from getting licenses to trade. . . . It would not be possible to pass this Bill

---

[115] *Ibid.,* 327.

[116] *Ibid.,* 328. In actual fact, Gandhi did not so much object to Indians not being allowed into South Africa in the first place (he was not even too critical of the Australian law excluding Asians from the continent) as he was determined that they be treated fairly if admitted.

without appearing to take away a part of the liberty of the subject, because the subject now had a right to a license as a matter of course, and if this Bill were passed into law, the subject would no longer have the right. He would only have the right if the licensing authority thought fit to grant it. This Bill interferes with the course of law, because the Bill would be defeated in its object if the Courts had jurisdiction. The Town Councils would be responsible to their constitutents, and there would be no appeal from their decisions, as regards the granting of licenses, to a Court of Law.[117]

Gandhi also objected to the act designed to protect uncovenanted Indians from arrest, as it essentially forced free Indians to take out passes when the law made no such requirement, and because the act, although it was supposed further to protect Indians, really afforded the police license to arrest them with impunity.[118]

The failure of the British Government to disallow the four measures which Gandhi chiefly opposed forced the battle into an essentially different context. Although Gandhi began to defend more actively the position of the Indians in the Transvaal, his main effort was directed against the application of the licensing act to the detriment of Indian traders, most of whom came from his own part of India. He involved himself in many cases in which he sought to save the licenses of Indians to whom renewals had been denied. But his efforts rarely met with success, despite the firm evidence he presented. On December 31, 1898, Gandhi and several other Indians, mostly Muslims, addressed a strongly worded petition on the subject of licensing abuses to the secretary of state. When Indian soldiers were fighting Britain's battles and Indian laborers were opening new fields for colonization, was it fair, Gandhi asked, that their fellow countrymen in Natal were being denied a fair opportunity to make a living? [119] The licensing officer, Gandhi claimed, was appointed by the town council with the one prerequisite that

117 *Ibid.*, 334.   118 *Ibid.*, 337.   119 *Ibid.*, III, 27.

he be staunchly anti-Indian. He cited the case of Somnath Maharaj of Durban, who, despite his adherence to all the sanitary standards and the hiring of a European bookkeeper, was refused a license in a case described by Mr. Justice Mason of the Natal Supreme Court as "a disgrace to the Town Council." [120]

The case of Dada Osman was similar. He had been resident in Natal for fifteen years and spoke and wrote English fluently. Osman already operated two businesses in the colony, and he now wished to move to Durban with his wife and children, whom he had just brought from India. Just before his arrival in Durban, he had rented a spacious building for £11 a month and had spent over £100 on furniture. Osman's premises were sanitary, his books were kept in English, and he was able to present strong testimonials from European businessmen who had dealt with him over the years. Yet his application for a license was denied by the licensing officer, and his appeal against the decision was unanimously turned down by the town council acting in the capacity of a licensing board. One member of the board, Councilor Collins, defined the true nature of the problem:

He believed that the license would be refused, and the reason was not because the applicant or the premises were unsuitable but because the applicant was an Indian. What Mr. Gandhi [who was Osman's lawyer] had said was perfectly true, and he (Mr. Collins) felt some relief in saying that most of these licenses had been refused principally on the ground of the applicants being Indians. The Council was placed in a very unhappy position in having to carry out a policy which in the discretion of Parliament was considered necessary. Parliament, representing the community of Natal, had come to the conclusion that it was undesirable that the Indians should increase their hold on the trade of Durban. And it was on that account that they were practically called upon to refuse the licenses which were not otherwise objectionable. Personally, he considered the refusal of the license a

[120] *Ibid.*, 29; *Times of Natal,* March 30, 1898.

grievance to the applicant who was a most suitable person to appear before the Council to ask for a license. But it had been found expedient as a matter of Colonial policy, that these licenses should not be increased.[121]

In Newcastle, the licensing officer, as a matter of course, refused to renew the licenses of all eight Indian traders who had held licenses in the previous year. Gandhi pointed out that the Newcastle licensing officer was also the town clerk, and consequently also the clerk of the court when the town council sat to hear appeals against the decisions of the licensing officer.[122] The situation in Dundee was not much different. C. G. Wilson, the chairman of the local board, frankly stated that "it was their endeavour, if possible, to rid the town of the Asiatic curse. They were not only a curse here, but to the whole Colony of Natal." [123] Gandhi made it clear that more liberal opinion in the colony had wanted the act only to discourage the influx of more Indian traders and not to work to the detriment of those already established. As the *Times of Natal* stated on December 21, 1898, "The Act was passed, not so much with a view to enabling the licensing bodies to deal with the Indians already trading in the Colony, as to prevent others coming here to trade." [124]

Gandhi devoted most of his energy to the licensing issue because it struck at the very roots of Indian survival in Natal, but he still had time for several other problems. Indian education in Natal was deplorable, he claimed. Ordinary public schools were closed to Indians, and the subsidy available for Indian education was totally inadequate.

---

[121] *Ibid.*, 31–32; *Natal Advertiser*, Sept. 13, 1898.   [122] *Ibid.*, 33–34.

[123] *Ibid.*, 35; *Natal Witness*, Nov. 26, 1896.

[124] *Ibid.*, 37. Gandhi estimated that there were over 300 store or shopkeepers' licenses and 500 hawkers' licenses issued to Indians in Natal. These 800 license-holders were part of an Indian community of 4,000 "Arabs." There were about 50,000 Indians who were either indentured, formerly indentured, or descendants of those who came to Natal under contract. *Ibid.*, 122; article on Indian traders in Natal written for the *Times of India,* Durban, Nov. 18, 1899.

School buildings were less than marginal, and teachers received no more than two to four pounds a month.[125] Although Gandhi could no longer request the British Government to disallow the Immigration Restriction Act, he could and did draw attention to the inequities of its application. Immediately after the passage of the act, Gandhi asserted, the Government of Natal informed steamship companies of the heavy penalties they faced should they bring an illegal immigrant to Natal, and this threat, combined with the strictures of the quarantine act, made the companies very reluctant to carry any but indentured Indians to Natal. To further inhibit any free Indian ingress, all Indians who wished merely to visit Natal had to leave a deposit of £50 or more, and endure a long delay. Eventually, this figure was reduced to £10 for Indians either passing through Natal or staying up to six weeks. In both cases, however, a one-pound fee was charged. The fee and deposit schedule was so high that it was almost impossible, until the suspension of the charges during the Anglo-Boer War, for Indians even to cross Natal when on their way back to India from the Transvaal.[126]

Gandhi's many articles and letters on the abuses associated with the administration of the Immigration Restriction Act so aroused Lord Curzon, the viceroy of India, that he wrote a lengthy and impassioned dispatch on the matter to Lord George Hamilton at the India Office. Curzon was chiefly concerned about the Indians domiciled in Natal, who had been to India for a visit. To convince the appropriate officials that he was indeed a bona fide resident of the colony, such an Indian had to hire a lawyer to draw up an affidavit attesting to the fact that he had been in business for at least two years before the passage of the act. If the Indian were

[125] *Ibid.,* 82–86; *Times of India* (weekly edition), Aug. 19, 1899.

[126] *Ibid.,* 115–120; *Times of India* (weekly edition), Sept. 12, 1899. The degree to which the fee and deposit were prohibitive can be ascertained by the fact that a deck passage to Natal from India cost from two to five guineas.

successful in this endeavor, he could then obtain a certificate of domicile for 2/6. Curzon strongly urged that the act be administered in accordance with the guarantees offered by the Colonial Office to the India Office. He had been led to believe that a domiciled Indian, under the terms of the act, was one who had been born and bred in the colony, or who was resident there at the time of its passage, and he insisted that this protection of the vested interests of Indians in Natal be preserved.[127]

It is hard to imagine what would have been the lot of Natal's Indians without the presence of Gandhi. Not that he materially changed the course of colonial legislation, but his eloquence and sheer literary fecundity kept the Government of Natal under the merciless scrutiny of liberals and humanitarians in Britain,[128] in India, and, for that matter, in South Africa itself.

[127] NAI, July 1900, proc. 4, no. 36, viceroy to sec. of state, July 12, 1900.

[128] The Indians of South Africa had their champions in both houses of Parliament, and other organizations, such as the British Committee of the Indian National Congress, headed by Sir William Wedderburn, and the East Indian Committee strove mightily on their behalf.

1. Mahatma Gandhi in 1900.

2. Aboobaker Amod, the first "Arab" Indian trader, arrived in Natal in 1874. He opened his shop on West Street, Durban, in about 1876.

3. An Indian hawker and his son circa 1890.

4. An Indian ricksha puller who worked for the Bale family of Durban in 1890.

5. Indian laborers in the sugar-cane fields of Natal.

6. The crowd gathering at the Point when Gandhi returned to Natal from India in 1897.

7. The Indian stretcher bearer corps which served in the Anglo-Boer War. Gandhi is seated fifth from the left in the center row.

8. Indians who had determined to return to their native land preparing to board the "Umlazi" at the expiration of their indentures in 1910.

9. Some members of Gandhi's family. From left to right: Gokaldas (Gandhi's sister's son), Manilal (Gandhi's second son), Kasturbai (Gandhi's wife), Ramdas (Gandhi's third son) and Harilal (Gandhi's eldest son).

10. Gandhi, third from the left, outside his Johannesburg law office in 1908. Thambi Naidoo stands to his left and Leung Quinn is sixth from the left.

11. Gokhale in Durban in 1912. Gokhale and Gandhi are seated in the middle of the front row. Hermann Kallenbach is to Gandhi's right, and H. S. L. Polak is second from the left in the top row.

12. A football team of "passive resisters" in 1913. Gandhi is sixth from the left in the back row.

13. Gandhi with Sonja Schlesin and Hermann Kallenbach during the 1913 strike.

14. The march through Volksrust in 1913.

15. Gandhi being placed under arrest in 1914. He is second from the right with Hermann Kallenbach and Sonja Schlesin on either side.

16. Gandhi and the Hindu Women's Association in 1913.

17. Gandhi and Kasturbai in 1914. In order to identify with the indentured laborers in their fight against the £3 tax, Gandhi for the first time adopted Indian dress.

IV / The Problem Spreads

ALTHOUGH Gandhi's early years in South Africa were spent in Natal, the home of the vast majority of Indian immigrants, his focus was never parochial, and his writings and activities manifested a deep involvement with the whole Indian question, as it pertained not only to Natal but to Cape Colony and the Afrikaner republics of the Orange Free State and the Transvaal. By the early 1880's, both "Arabs" and time-expired indentured laborers were making their appearance in all three areas, and it is vital to understand the course of events in these regions to comprehend the breadth of Gandhi's concern and the complexity of his self-appointed task of winning dignity and respect for his fellow countrymen.

In the Cape, the reaction toward the Indians who seeped across the colony's border was mild in comparison to that in the rest of South Africa; but then the Cape had traditionally been more liberal in racial matters, and very few Indians entered its precincts in any case.[1] In 1892, however, a franchise and ballot act was introduced into the Cape legislature which stipulated that an eligible voter would have to be able to write his name, address and occupation in English. Of greater significance, the bill raised the property qualifications for the franchise from £25 to £75. The governor, Sir Henry Loch, and the Cape cabinet claimed that the measure was

[1] There were some 8,489 Indians in Cape Colony in 1904 and only 7,963 in 1921.

necessary, moderate, and nonracial, and that it had been passed by a large majority in the Cape parliament,[2] but the secretary of state, Lord Ripon, was soon in receipt of petitions of protest from both colored and Indian objectors.[3] Ripon, after studying the measure, came to feel that the "legislation is contrary to the spirit and tendency of public opinion in the present day." [4] Yet he could not properly veto a technically nondiscriminatory bill passed by the legislature of a self-governing colony, especially as it had already received the assent of the governor. The bill consequently was not disallowed by the British Government, despite the personal reservations of the secretary of state.

Three years later, in 1895, the Cape legislature passed an "Act to Amend and Add to the Laws Regulating the Municipal Corporation and Government of East London." This law gave the municipal authorities of East London the power to require the residence of natives and Asiatics in specially designated locations outside the town, and also permitted the passage of municipal ordinances

fixing the hours within which it shall not be lawful for natives and Asiatics to be in the streets, public places or thoroughfares . . . without a written pass or certificate . . . and for fixing such parts of streets and open spaces or pavements of the same on which natives and Asiatics may not walk or be. . . . For regulating and setting apart portions of the rivers and sea where natives and Asiatics may not bathe, and where clothes may or may not be washed.

As one witness remarked to the select committee on the bill appointed by the Cape House of Assembly, there was great fear in East London about the possible influx of Indians, who were considered by many to be inferior even to the natives in their habits, customs and morals. There were not many Indians yet, but the municipality wished to be fore-

[2] CO, 48/521.   [3] CO, 48/521, CO, 48/524.
[4] CO, 48/521, sec. of state to gov., Jan 27, 1893.

armed.[5] Again the British Government did not disallow the act. It was not considered a truly discriminatory measure in a racial sense, as in its final form the law exempted all natives and Asiatics "who are at present or may in future become registered owners of land within the municipality valued for municipal purposes at not less than £75." [6] Perhaps of greater moment in the eyes of the British Government was the feeling expressed by the governor, as spokesman for his ministers, that the Cape would rather secede from the British Empire than brook any interference with what it considered its domestic affairs.[7]

The position of the British Government in regard to the rights of Indians in the two Dutch republics was, of course, more complicated than it was vis-à-vis the British colonies in South Africa. There were but very few Indians in the Orange Free State by 1890—in fact, only nine on annual license.[8] Yet the government of the Free State in that year passed legislation prohibiting Indians from owning land or carrying on trade within the republic.[9] As a consequence, the Indians hired an advocate to act on their behalf. But neither he nor the British authorities in Cape Town could gain any material concessions.

The High Commissioner consulted his Legal Adviser (Schreiner), who advised him that any State could without offense pass laws to exclude undesirable classes, and that from the absence of a treaty only vested *rights* or interests could afford legitimate ground for remonstrance. These persons had been trading under annual licenses, which gave no right to claim one in perpetuity. They had entered the State taking all the risks of the situation, and cannot lawfully complain of an injury if required to retire.[10]

[5] NAI, Jan. 1898, proc. no. 31, report of the select committee of the house of assembly on East London's municipal bill, printed by order of the house of assembly, July 1894, hearings on the bill.

[6] *Ibid.*   [7] CO, 48/521.   [8] CO, 179/202.

[9] Orange Free State Act 29, 1890—"Law to Provide Against the Influx of Asiatics and for the Removal of White Criminals Entering This State from Elsewhere."

[10] CO, 179/202.

As W. P. Schreiner indicated, the Indians were really in the Free State on mere sufferance. Acts in 1876 and 1885 had allowed their presence only with the special permission of the executive, and they had never had any right of permanent residence. The Free State Government was generous in allowing Indians over a year to liquidate their businesses and in providing compensation for losses incurred.[11]

The British Government tried to save the situation despite the lack of a legal basis on which to intervene.[12] The Colonial Office ordered the high commissioner to protest to the Free State Government in the strongest terms. "It is quite certain," the secretary of state contended, "that such a proscription of one section of the settled population of a country, imposed by the Government without any colour of necessity or ground of provocation, would be contrary to the uses of civilised States." [13] The high commissioner, as a result, in a final effort to prevent the expulsion of the Indians, proposed to President Reitz that the Indian question in the Orange Free State be submitted to arbitration. "It would probably be convenient," the high commissioner wrote, "that the arbitrator should be a judge of one of the South African Supreme Courts, but this is a matter that may be left open for further discussion if, as I confidently anticipate, the principle of arbitration be accepted by Your Honour." [14] It was all, however, to no avail. The high commissioner, in a letter to the secretary of state, presented the Free State's position:

It will be observed that the Volksraad [legislature] of the Orange Free State, in the report drawn up by the Committee of that body, take the ground that the action of the Indian Traders was illegal from their first entry into the country; that the Constitution of the State established the distinction between white and coloured races; that in trading in the State the Indians violated

[11] CO, 417/42, 45, 49, 61, 64, 66, 67, 68, 72, 74, 75, 82.   [12] *Ibid.*
[13] CO, 179/202.
[14] CO, 417/82, draft of a letter to be sent by the high commissioner to the president of the Orange Free State, c. Oct. 8, 1892.

this Law; that the subsequent legislation was of a declaratory nature emphasizing and enforcing pre-existing law.[15]

The situation in the Transvaal was considerably more complex than that in the Orange Free State. The British Government had in April 1881, through the Pretoria Convention, conceded the Transvaal "complete self-government subject to the suzerainty of Her Majesty." In 1884, a second agreement, the London Convention, was promulgated in order to increase the Transvaal's jurisdiction over its own affairs. No mention was made in the London Convention of suzerainty, and as the British Government was in future years to base much of its claim to the right to protect Indians in the Transvaal on its position as suzerain, this was a matter of some importance. The Transvaal claimed that British suzerainty no longer obtained from the moment that the London Convention replaced the Pretoria Convention. The British Government, on the other hand, took the position that the London Convention merely amended the Pretoria Convention, and that those articles of the London Convention not specifically altered by the second document were still in effect. To confuse the issue still further, article 14 of the London Convention (which was the same as article 26 of the Pretoria Convention) stipulated that

all persons other than natives, conforming themselves to the laws of the South African Republic

a) will have full liberty, with their families, to enter, travel, or reside in any part of the South African Republic;

b) will be entitled to hire or possess houses, manufactures, warehouses, shops, and premises;

c) may carry on their commerce either in person, or by any agents whom they may think fit to employ;

d) will not be subject in respect to their persons or property, or in respect of their commerce or industry, to any taxes, whether general or local, other than those which are or may be imposed upon citizens of the said Republic.

[15] CO, 417/97, gov. to sec. of state, July 24, 1893.

Indians were by no means the only British subjects in the Transvaal. Indeed, with the booming gold mines, they were only a small minority.[16] Still they were in the most difficult position. The first paragraph of article 14 stated that all persons, to be eligible for the rights stipulated, must conform themselves to the laws of the South African Republic. The republic's basic law, the "Grondwet," clearly proclaimed that colored persons, a designation which included Indians, could not receive the same treatment as white persons and would be subject to special laws. Did the "Grondwet" take precedence over the London Convention, and did the first lines of article 14 thus obviate the guarantees of subsequent paragraphs as far as Indians were concerned? A long and acrimonious correspondence ensued between the British and Transvaal governments,[17] complicated by the suzerainty issue and a general confusion as to what the term suzerainty meant in the first place. Lord Kimberley, in the Colonial Office, was no doubt aware of the difficulties that lay ahead when he wrote to Gladstone on the question of whether the burghers of the Transvaal, being under British suzerainty, were British subjects. His opinion was in the negative, and he based it on the following reasoning:

The Indians were as much under the Queen as the Transvaalers were, (more so in fact) but were never included under the term "British subjects." There are numerous Indian Princes under the suzerainty of the Queen as Empress of India, whose people have never, I apprehend, been considered "British subjects" in the technical sense of the word.[18]

There being so few Indians in the Transvaal in 1881, the framers of the Pretoria Convention were little concerned

[16] The total Indian population of the Transvaal in 1899 was about 17,000. Of this number, approximately 5,500 were merchants or hawkers. TA, Records of the British agent in the Transvaal, agent to the high comm., March 24, 1899.

[17] *Ibid.*, records of the British agent in the Transvaal, 1892–1899.

[18] Gladstone papers, 44, 226. Kimberly to Gladstone, July 6, 1881.

with the Indian question, and evidence in the report of the Asiatic Inquiry Commission of 1921 bears this out.

When the 1881 Convention was concluded, there were no Indians in the Transvaal, and there is little or no doubt that the Asiatic side of the question never presented itself to the authors of that document sitting in Pretoria and a study of the whole of the provisions of that document clearly shows that the white races and the native residents in the Colony alone were contemplated.[19]

The rapid growth of the Indian population in the Transvaal between 1881 and 1884, however, forced the government to take cognizance of a growing anti-Indian feeling in the republic. And the Transvaal state secretary [20] wrote London that the members of the Volksraad "were not unwilling to meet the wishes of the White petitioners, either entirely or partly, for instance, by pointing out to the Orientals thus immigrated locations or wards within certain prescribed limits." [21] What the state secretary wished to ascertain was

whether, according to the opinion of Her Majesty's Government, this government is at liberty, under the Convention now in force . . . to frame such regulations relative to the coloured persons . . . as may appear to them to be in the interests of the inhabitants of this Republic, and if not, whether Her Majesty's government by its consent will empower this government to meet either entirely or partly the wishes of the petitioners of European descent.[22]

The British authorities had always had some sympathy for the republic's desire to protect itself from the "dirty habits"

[19] Iqbal Narain, *The Politics of Racialism* (Ahmedabad, 1957), 158–159. Report of the Asiatic Inquiry Commission (1921), par. 39.

[20] The state secretary of the South African Republic was the chief executive and administrative officer of the Republic under the state president.

[21] C. 7911, papers relating to the grievances of H. M. Indian subjects in the S.A.R., Sept., 1895, 51, state sec. to Derby, Jan. 6, 1885.

[22] *Ibid.*

of so-called lower-class Indians. Consequently, Sir Hercules Robinson, the high commissioner, in forwarding the state secretary's letter to the Colonial Office, advised the British Government to permit the amendment of article 14, so that its provisions would not apply to "Indians or Chinese Coolie immigrants." [23]

As it was doubtless not the intention of Lord Kimberley to prohibit the Transvaal Government from adopting, if necessary, Special legislation for the regulation of Indian or Chinese Coolie immigrants, I should be disposed to recommend that the Government of the South African Republic be informed that Her Majesty's Government will be willing to amend Article 14 of the Convention by inserting the words "African natives or Indian or Chinese Coolie Immigrants." The article would then read as follows:—

"All persons other than African natives or Indian or Chinese Coolie immigrants conforming themselves to the laws of the South African Republic will have full liberty with their families to enter, travel, or reside, etc. etc."

The article so amended would still leave the few Arab traders at present in Pretoria entitled to the liberties secured under the existing article to "all persons other than natives," and I can see no sufficient grounds for their being deprived of these rights.[24]

British officials in South Africa and England were more interested in preserving the vested interests of upper-class Indians than in securing the rights of "coolies" and newly arrived immigrants. But the admission that it was not the intention of article 14 of the London Convention to cover equally all British subjects was destined to cause grave difficulties in the future.

Lord Derby, the secretary of state for the colonies, in general agreed with Robinson's proposals. "I have carefully considered your suggestion as to the amendment of the Convention," the secretary of state wrote,

[23] *Ibid.*, 50, high comm. to sec. of state, Jan. 28, 1885.   [24] *Ibid.*

and, if you are of opinion that it would be preferable and more satisfactory to the Government of the South African Republic to proceed as you propose, Her Majesty's Government will be willing to amend the Convention as suggested. It seems to deserve consideration, however, whether it would not be more correct for the Volksraad to legislate in the proposed sense, having received an assurance that Her Majesty's Government will not desire to insist upon any such construction of the terms of the Convention as would interfere with reasonable legislation in the desired direction.[25]

As a consequence of Derby's attitude, the Transvaal Volksraad passed Law 3 of 1885, the provisions of which were to apply to persons belonging to one of the aboriginal races of Asia, a designation that included "the so-called coolies, Arabs, Malays and Mahommedan subjects of the Turkish Empire." [26] Individuals belonging to the classes listed could not acquire the rights of citizenship in the republic and could not be owners of landed property. Those who settled in the republic to engage in trade or for other purposes, had to register within eight days of their arrival and pay a registration fee of £25. The registration of persons covered by the law who were in the republic before its passage, was to be free of charge, if they reported their presence in Pretoria within eight days of the law coming into effect or within thirty days in other districts. Failure to register was declared a penal offense punishable by a fine of £10 to £100, or, in case of inability to pay, by imprisonment for a term of not less than fourteen days or more than six months. Of greatest importance, the Transvaal government assumed the right to designate certain streets, wards, and locations where persons covered by Law 3 would be forced to reside.[27]

Law 3, in the eyes of the British Government, went well beyond the concessions to which it had agreed. The law permitted the Transvaal authorities to interfere with the rights

[25] *Ibid.*, 52, sec. of state to high comm., March 19, 1885.
[26] *Locale Wetten Der Z.A.R.*, Wet no. 3, 1885.   [27] *Ibid.*

of Indian traders already established in the republic—a group the high commissioner had specifically designated for continued protection. It deprived all Indians of political and property rights and restricted their freedom of movement. The Transvaal Government replied to the British protests by claiming that Law 3 was in keeping with the provisions of Derby's letter of March 19, which gave it the power to legislate in the "proposed sense" and which committed the British Government not to "interfere with reasonable legislation in the desired direction." [28] The Transvaal Government based its position on the assumption that Lord Derby in his dispatch was responding to the letter of January 6 from the South African Republic, rather than to the suggestions contained in the high commissioner's covering note. The British Government, of course, denied the Transvaal's contention and refused to modify its stand. The Earl of Granville, the new secretary of state, demanded that Law 3 "be revised, as it is in direct opposition to the views of Her Majesty's Government, and in its present form is a contravention of the Convention of London." [29]

The state secretary, Dr. Willem Leyds, explained his government's position to the high commissioner.

It was for the sake of public health, having in view that experience acquired in other countries and colonies, and here also already, very desirable and necessary, to take sanitary measures regarding those Eastern strangers who established themselves here in increasing numbers after the conclusion of the Pretoria Convention, and chose their dwelling places everywhere in the midst of the white population.[30]

Leyds's statement showed the way out of an embarrassing predicament to a British Government still more interested in the technicalities of legal construction than in the spirit

[28] C. 7911, 54, state sec. to imperial sec., Cape Town, Dec. 3, 1885.
[29] *Ibid.*, 55, sec. of state to high comm., Feb. 24, 1886.
[30] *Ibid.*, 56, sec. of state to high comm., Sept. 6, 1886.

and true purpose of legislation.[31] The need for preserving adequate standards of sanitation in the cities of the Transvaal must be made the rationale for the establishment of locations. The Transvaal Volksraad consequently amended Law 3 so that the significant sections read as follows:

1. This law shall apply to the persons belonging to one of the native races of Asia, including the so-called Coolies, Arabs, Malays, and Mahommedan subjects of the Turkish Empire.

2. With regard to the persons mentioned in Article 1, the following provisions shall apply:

(a) They cannot obtain the burgher right of the South African Republic.

(b) They cannot be owners of fixed property in the Republic, except only in such streets, wards, and locations as the Government for purposes of sanitation shall assign to them to live in. This provision has no retrospective force.

(c) They shall, as far as those who settle in the Republic with the object of trading, etc., are concerned, be inscribed in a register to be specially kept for that purpose.

(d) The Government shall have the right, for purposes of sanitation, to assign to them certain streets, wards, and locations to live in (*terbewoning*). This provision does not apply to those who live with their employers.[32]

Once the amended law had passed the Transvaal Volksraad, the high commissioner informed the republic's president that,

although the amended law is still a contravention of the 14th Article of the Convention of London, I shall not advise Her Majesty's Government to offer further opposition to it in view of your Honour's opinion that it is necessary for the protection of the public health.[33]

[31] South African Republic Green Book no. 1 of 1894, Asiatic Coloured Persons, 46, high comm. to state president, South African Republic, Sept. 24, 1886.

[32] The amended version of Law 3 also reduced the registration fee from £25 to £3.

[33] South African Republic Green Book no. 1 of 1894, 46, high comm. to state pres., Sept. 24, 1886.

Three months later, the high commissioner again wrote the state president.

I have the honour to enclose, for your Honour's information, a copy of a despatch which I have received from the Secretary of State, directing me to acquaint you that Her Majesty's Government do not see occasion any longer to object to the legislation of the South African Republic in regard to the Asiatics, having regard to the amendments which the Volksraad has introduced into the law of 1885.[34]

Despite the British Government's acquiescence, the republic was dilatory in implementing the new law, and it was not until late 1888 that any active moves were made in this direction. Municipal authorities were the first to act, and it soon became apparent that in the opinion of the Transvaal Government, Law 3 demanded that Indians must both reside and trade in special locations separated from the municipality.

The British Government took immediate issue, for Law 3, according to the Transvaal's interpretation, was aimed at the one group whose position officials in England were determined to defend. The Colonial Office's sense of annoyance and frustration was reflected in a minute of November 26, 1888.

You all see the Transvaal govt. insisted that the law was required for sanitary reasons only, and on that on this ground, altho' we held it to be a clear breach of art: 14 of the Convention of London, we acquiesced in the legislation.—But I imagine this would not have been the case if there had been any idea that it was to be used for the purposes of driving out these Indian traders. Sir H. Robinson seems to me to take the matter too coolly, and in his friendship for the Boers to forget that these people have claims to our protection as British subjects.[35]

[34] C. 7911, 59, acting high comm. to state pres., Pretoria, Dec. 2, 1886.
[35] CO, 417/24.

Shortly after being thus castigated, Robinson was replaced as high commissioner by Sir Henry Loch, who immediately stated it to be his opinion that Law 3 referred only to locations for habitation and that Indians could, consequently, continue to conduct business in the towns as had heretofore been the case.[36] Besides, the high commissioner claimed, Law 3 clearly implied that Indians would be placed in "streets, wards, and locations" within, rather than outside, the municipalities.[37] Lord Knutsford, the secretary of state, expressed himself in similar terms.

The right of residing, trading, etc., under the London Convention appears to be restricted, as regards Asiatics, by the law of 1885, amended in 1886, by requiring residence in certain localities selected for sanitary reasons and by registration, but not otherwise, and if trading licenses are granted to other persons on application, Indian traders have clearly a right to obtain them. Moreover, the law only prescribes locations for "habitation," and there does not appear to be any prohibition as to "trading" in places other than locations.[38]

The Government of India joined the Colonial Office in strongly opposing the Transvaal Government's interpretation of Law 3. But the basis of its resentment was of a quite different nature. The Colonial Office was concerned about Indian traders—"Arabs" with vested interests. The Indian Government, however, was determined to protect the "coolies," whose immigration to South Africa it had originally sponsored. As a spokesman of the India Office advised the Colonial Office, "I am to say that the India Office has no special concern with any Arabs." [39]

To test the legality of the Transvaal Government's interpretation of Law 3, the firm of Ismail Suleiman, in August

[36] TA, records of the British agent in the Transvaal, SAR, no. 50, high comm. to agent, Dec. 18, 1892.

[37] Ibid.   [38] C. 7911, sec. of state to high comm., Nov. 26, 1889.

[39] CO, 417/37, Ind. Off. to Col. Off., Nov. 19, 1899. It is quite possible that the writer confused Arabian Arabs with Indian "Arabs."

1888, applied to the Transvaal high court for an order to compel the town of Middleburg to issue it a license to trade. But the court supported the government's view, and ruled that Law 3 required Indians to maintain their businesses as well as their residences in locations.[40] The Transvaal administration was caught between a British Government it was not too anxious to offend, and the Volksraad which, driven on by the white population of the republic, was determined to force the earliest possible implementation of Law 3. Volksraad resolutions in 1888, 1889, and 1890 urged prompt action on the government,[41] but to little avail. Finally, the legislature lost patience, and on September 8, 1893, it resolved that all persons covered by Law 3 of 1885, as amended in 1886, would have to move to locations on or before January 29, 1894.[42]

By this time, however, the whole situation was so vague and confused that the British and Transvaal governments agreed to submit their interpretations of Law 3 to the arbitration of the chief justice of the Orange Free State, Melius de Villiers.[43] The British case rested on the contention that Law 3 of 1885, as amended in 1886, merely required Indians and other Asiatic traders who were British subjects to reside in certain designated wards and streets, within towns, to which they were assigned for reasons of sanitation, while permitting them to continue to trade in any part of the municipality.[44] The South African Republic, for its part, claimed that its government was fully entitled to make such regula-

[40] Narain, op cit., 167.

[41] Statute Law of the Transvaal, vol. 1, resolutions of July 5, 1888; June 27, 1889; May 17, 1890.

[42] South African Republic Green Book no. 2 of 1894, 79.

[43] Despite the constitutional importance of the case, the British Government was very reluctant to allocate the necessary £500, and a lengthy correspondence on the matter developed—a revealing example of how very tightly the Imperial purse strings were clutched by the treasury, CO, 417/118.

[44] C. 7911, 5–7.

tions concerning coolies, Arabs (Indian traders), Malays, and Mahommedan subjects of the Turkish Empire as it might see fit, and that the British Government had no right to object if the Government of the South African Republic prohibited those persons covered by Law 3 from maintaining business premises in places other than those designated by the government for that purpose.[45]

As the arbitrator pondered the case, the matter of British acquiescence to the passage of Law 3 of 1885, as amended in 1886, became of increasing importance. It was the pivotal issue, and in the end it decided De Villiers in favor of the South African Republic.

As regards the terms upon which Her Majesty's Government gave their assent to Law 3 of 1885 (as subsequently amended), after the law had been passed, it was contended on behalf of the South African Republic that after such assent had been given in the manner in which it was given, Her Majesty's Government could no longer raise the objection that the law was not in conformity with the 14th article of the Convention of London, I concur with this view entirely.[46]

The arbitrator's full decision could now follow only one path, and on April 2, 1895, he handed down his ruling.

(a.) The claims of Her Majesty's Government and of the Government of the South African Republic respectively are disallowed, save and except to the extent and degree following, that is to say:

(b.) The South African Republic is bound and entitled in its treatment of Indian and other Asiatic traders, being British subjects, to give full force and effect to Law No. 3 of 1885, enacted, and in the year 1886 amended, by the Volksraad of the South African Republic, subject (in case of objections being raised by or on behalf of any such persons to any such treatment as not being in accordance with the provisions of the said law as amended) to

[45] *Ibid.,* 8–10.   [46] *Ibid.,* 26.

sole and exclusive interpretation in the ordinary course by the tribunals of the country.[47]

The final settlement of the issue, as De Villiers had indicated, required the testing of Law 3 in the courts of the South African Republic itself, and to make such a case possible, the Volksraad, on October 8, 1895, repealed its resolution of September 1893 and the resulting circular of December 1893.[48] But a considerable delay ensued. The Indians had confidently anticipated that the British Government would sponsor the test case and underwrite the expenses. The Colonial Office, however, felt that it was the duty of the Indian community of the Transvaal to assume full responsibility, although the British Government was willing to engage counsel to observe the proceedings on its behalf.[49] To justify his position, Chamberlain claimed that the Indians would probably receive a fairer judgment if they brought the case themselves. Besides, he contended, if the British Government paid the costs, it would set a precedent that could be followed by all aggrieved British subjects.[50] With no prospect of financial aid from the British Government, the Indian community set about raising the necessary funds from its own resources. Early in 1898, the necessary papers were filed and the trial was set for April of that year. The British agent in the Transvaal [51] was of the opinion that the Indians were bound to lose, as the court was so completely

[47] *Ibid.*, 14. Numerous Indian petitions resulted from the arbitrator's decision. Nearly all were eloquent, and many emphasized the imperial implications of the question.

[48] *Statute Law of the Transvaal,* vol. 1.

[49] TA, Records of the British agent in the Transvaal, Tel. no. 24, sec. of state to high comm., April 24, 1897.

[50] *Ibid.,* SA, conf., sec. of state to high comm., June 17, 1897.

[51] The agent was the British representative in the South African Republic appointed under the London Convention to replace the resident provided for in the Pretoria Convention.

dependent on the government,[52] and the Indians themselves became increasingly pessimistic after it was announced that the case would be heard by Justices Morice, Esser, and Jorissen.[53] The plaintiff was Tayob Hajee Khan Mahomed, and the defendant Dr. Willem Johannes Leyds, the state secretary of the South African Republic.

The substance of the case was similar to that heard by the Chief Justice of the Orange Free State. The plaintiff claimed that he had been illegally deprived of the right to trade on Church Street in Pretoria and had been ordered to move his business to a location and to pay a monthly rent of 7/6 for his new premises. The government again contended that to protect the health of the community it was necessary for Indians to both trade and reside in locations outside the municipalities. Justices Morice and Esser, representing a majority of the court, ruled for the defendant with costs—Justice Esser basing his opinion on the precedence he assigned the Grondwet over the London Convention.[54] Justice Jorissen dissented from the decision, and Justice Morice, it was said, would have ruled for Tayob Hajee, had it not been for the Suleiman case.[55]

The Indians had apparently lost their last hope for success in the struggle to preserve their vested interests in the towns of the Transvaal. Whatever efforts the British Government continued to make on their behalf were complicated by a decision of the crown law officers that British suzerainty over the Transvaal no longer existed, as the term suzerainty was not even mentioned in the London Convention.[56] When the ruling in the arbitration hearing reached him, Chamberlain conceded that the issues raised by Law 3 had now been set-

[52] TA, Records of the British agent in the Transvaal, agent to the high comm., March 10, 1898.

[53] *Ibid.*   [54] *Ibid.*, report of the British Indian test case.

[55] *Ibid.*, Transvaal Indians to the sec. of state for the colonies, Dec. 31, 1898.

[56] *Ibid.*, SAR, 279, high comm. to acting agent, July 13, 1899, encl., law officers to sec. of state for the colonies, July 3, 1899.

tled.[57] The India Office was no less resigned after the conclusion of the test case. "While I cannot consider the present position of this question to be satisfactory," the secretary of state for India wrote,

the Despatches from Her Majesty's High Commissioner in South Africa show that under existing conditions, it is impractical to secure any important concession for the British Indian subjects resident in the Transvaal, since the policy of the Government of the South African Republic appears to be approved by the great majority of Europeans, both English and Dutch, in the various colonies and States. I have therefore, caused Mr. Secretary Chamberlain to be informed that I am unable to offer any objection to his acceptance of the situation.[58]

Nevertheless, the British Government, through its agent in the Transvaal, did not cease working on behalf of the Indians.[59] Peripheral issues, such as the right of Indians to ob-

[57] South African Republic Green Book no. 1 of 1899, 56–58, sec. of state to high comm., Sept. 4, 1895.

[58] NAI, June 1899, proc. 1, no. 57, Pub. (Em.), sec. of state for India to viceroy, May 4, 1899.

[59] Although Gandhi's main sphere of activity before the Boer War was Natal, he still frequently addressed himself to the problems faced by his confreres in the Transvaal. On July 21, 1899, he sent a long letter to the British agent in Pretoria. He urged the agent to insist that only Indians proved to be living in unsanitary circumstances be removed to locations. He pointed out that there were some 125 British Indian shopkeepers in Johannesburg and its suburbs and 4,000 hawkers. The storekeepers, Gandhi claimed, possessed unliquidated assets of about £375,000 and the hawkers of about £400,000. A forced move to locations would place a heavy and unwarranted financial burden on them. As for the planned Johannesburg Indian location, it was over four and a half miles from the middle of the town. There were no proper sanitary facilities and no arrangements for police protection. The site was adjacent to the area where the refuse and night soil of Johannesburg were dumped. The proposed transfer of the Indians to locations, Gandhi concluded, would, if implemented, have the effect of driving most of the Indians out of the Transvaal. *Works*, III, 86–90; Gandhi to British agent, Pretoria, July 21, 1899.

tain town passes, use sidewalks, and travel in first-class train compartments and cabs, were discussed with the Transvaal authorities.[60] Through the agent's efforts, the publication of the order officially demanding that all Indians move to locations, both for purposes of business and habitation, was constantly delayed.[61]

In his attempts to ameliorate the conditions under which Indians lived in the Transvaal, the agent was, however, hampered by white British subjects in the republic who, much as they might despise the Transvaal Government in general, at least agreed with its attitude and actions toward Indians. The Johannesburg chamber of commerce, an almost exclusively British organization, telegraphed the high commissioner that it fully appreciated "the action of the Transvaal Government in enforcing the Law whereby Asiatics must be specially located." [62] The Transvaal Traders Defense Association of Johannesburg informed the high commissioner that it had presented a petition to the Volksraad, signed by

[60] TA, records of the British agent in the Transvaal, agent to high comm., March 19, 1898. Further circumscriptions on the Indians' freedom of action manifested themselves with the passage of the Gold Law (Act 15) of 1898, section 92 of which placed Asians under special restrictions in areas proclaimed to be gold bearing. Only a white man could acquire leasehold right on proclaimed land, and he could not transfer, sublet, or rent his holding to any colored person, nor allow any colored person to occupy his ground. It was further stipulated that in the mining areas of the Witwatersrand, no colored person would be allowed to reside on proclaimed land, except in such bazaars, locations, and mining compounds as might be designated by the mining commissioner. Section 133 of the act prohibited any colored person from holding a license to trade or being in any way connected with the gold diggings, although he could act as a laborer in the service of a white man. The Gold Law of 1898 was the latest in a long series of gold laws which had placed restrictions on Indians.

[61] *Ibid.*, March 24, 1899.

[62] CO, 417/94, chamber of commerce, Johannesburg, to high comm., April 20, 1893.

six thousand British subjects, demanding the immediate establishment of locations for "Arabs" and other Asiatics. Had time permitted, thirty thousand signatures could have been obtained.[63] The Johannesburg *Star,* a British newspaper in the Transvaal, strongly supported the republic's Indian policy.

Apart from the question of his loathesome habits, the coolie is not an immigrant to be encouraged. He lowers the standard of comfort and closes the avenues to prosperity to the European trader. Economically he is of no advantage to the country he visits—for, be it remembered that he does not settle. He accumulates money by virtue of the wretchedness in which he lives—a wretchedness constituting a terrible danger to the rest of the community—and he takes 80 per cent of that money back again to Asia. In Natal we actually have the spectacle of European trade being gradually destroyed by the impossible competition of the coolie. The Asiatic is thus a menace to the European's life, an obstacle to his commercial progress.[64]

On November 15, 1898, the Transvaal authorities finally tried to at least partially implement Law 3. All Indians, not already leasing business premises within the bounds of the municipalities, were ordered to move to locations no later than January 1, 1899. Small traders in towns would have to move after having been given three months' notice, and larger traders after having been given six months' notice. Holders of leases signed before Law 3 came into effect would not have to move until their leases expired.[65]

The promulgation of the Transvaal Government's notice forced Edmund Fraser, the acting agent, into advocating a far-reaching compromise. He proposed that all nonwhites be divided into two categories—colored persons of whatever or-

[63] *Ibid.,* tel. from Transvaal Traders Defense Association, Johannesburg, to high comm., April 20, 1893.

[64] Johannesburg *Star,* March 1, 1899.

[65] *Statute Law of the Transvaal,* vol. 1, govt. notice no. 621, Nov. 19, 1898.

igin and the aboriginal natives of South Africa. All persons in the first category then resident in the Transvaal could continue both to reside and trade in the towns, and their colored employees could live on the premises. Once an existing business terminated, however, whether it was due to the death of the proprietor or to some other reason, it could be sold or transferred only to a white successor. All new Indian immigrants to the Republic would have to confine their activities to the locations, although hawking would continue to be permitted both in the towns and in the country. As a *quid pro quo,* Fraser proposed that the £3 registration fee payable by all Asians entering the Transvaal be raised to £25, as Law 3 had stipulated before its amendment.[66] The initially favorable response of the Transvaal authorities encouraged the agent to refine and liberalize his proposals still further. In his revised scheme, Fraser made the restrictions on Indian businessmen less stringent. The transfer of a business was to be allowed to a deceased owner's brother or to his father's brother, and a full year was to be permitted heirs for the liquidation of a business. Cab owners in the towns were to be allowed to transfer their franchise to others of their own class. A £3 rather than a £25 registration fee would be payable by an Indian entering the Transvaal on an employment pass to work for a white person as a gardener, domestic servant, waiter, or coachman. Should such an Indian quit his employment and choose to remain in the Republic, he would have to pay the balance of the £25. Fraser's second proposal went well beyond the bounds of his original plan in many ways. Any owner or partner in a business located in a town, and his clerks, Fraser suggested, should be able to walk on the sidewalk, and Indians dressed in European manner should be allowed to use first-class train compartments. A certain number of cabs should be licensed to carry those colored persons having business in a town.[67]

[66] TA, records of the British agent in the Transvaal, tel., no. 192, act. agent to act. high comm., Sir W. Butler, Dec. 13, 1898.

[67] *Ibid.,* conf. no. 91, act. agent to act. high comm., Dec. 14, 1898.

J. C. Smuts, at that time the state attorney of the South African Republic, was sufficiently intrigued with Fraser's proposition to delay yet again the implementation of Law 3.[68] Smuts informed the British representative (now Conyngham Greene, the permanent agent and Fraser's superior) that he would have to consult the republic's executive council before proceeding further, but, he pointed out encouragingly, President Kruger was more sympathetic toward the Indians than was the Volksraad, which wanted them all routed out of the Transvaal, root and branch.[69] The progress of events seemed to be leading toward a viable compromise until the reason for the Transvaal's apparent moderation became clear. The republic's government demanded as its price the inclusion of the Cape colored people (who had heretofore not been treated as ordinary colored persons but more as white British subjects) in any new interpretation of Law 3 that might be effected.[70] And to this the British Government would not agree.[71]

All negotiations now came to an end, and the situation deteriorated even further when the Transvaal closed its eastern border to all "coloured persons coming from Asia, Mauritius, Madagascar, and such other countries as shall be further proclaimed," and restricted the freedom of movement of Indians in the Transvaal because of an ostensible danger of bubonic plague.[72] The British Government immediately protested that the proclamation was a violation of article 14, but in the long run it did nothing. The Colonial Office found it more advantageous to use the supposed danger of

[68] Ibid., tel., no. 199, act. agent to high comm., Dec. 22, 1898.

[69] Ibid., agent to high comm., March 24, 1899.

[70] Ibid., state attorney to agent, March 29, 1899.

[71] NAI, June 1889, proc. 1, high comm. to sec. of state, April 24, 1899.

[72] CO, 417/259, proclamation of Feb. 13, 1899. In January 1899, a conference of all the South African governments was held in Pretoria to discuss the danger of bubonic plague gaining a foothold in South Africa.

bubonic plague as an excuse for not actively intervening on behalf of the Indians in the Transvaal. One Colonial Office official put the matter quite succinctly. "We must make the most of the Bubonic Plague as an excuse for not intervening *just now.*" [73]

On March 22, 1899, the executive council of the South African Republic again resolved to implement Law 3 of 1885, as amended in 1886.[74] Coolies and other Asiatic colored persons, except in such cases where special relief had been granted by the government, were to remove themselves and their businesses to a location by June 30, and in future, coolies and other Asiatic colored persons would be able to obtain licenses to trade only in the locations. Peddler's licenses would not be issued beyond June 30, while Indians who lived in the rural districts would be permitted three months to move to a location, but would have to take out a special license for the intervening period.

Despite the firm tone of the first articles of the government notice, sections 7, 8, and 9 seemed to indicate that the Transvaal Government was still reluctant to take the final step. Those Indians who felt that they were in a difficult position were allowed to petition for special treatment, and local officials were granted discretion to recommend extensions when they appeared warranted. Why the Transvaal Government remained unwilling to implement Law 3 despite its strong legal position is not altogether clear.[75] Whether it was because of a certain economic dependence

[73] *Ibid.*, minuting by F. G. (Frederick Graham), March 14, 1899, on high comm. to agent, Feb. 22, 1899.

[74] *Statute Law of the Transvaal*, vol. 1, govt. notice, no. 208, April 25, 1899.

[75] There was at least one Afrikaner delegation from the countryside which journeyed to Pretoria to protest the application of Law 3. The members of this group claimed they could purchase goods more cheaply from Indian merchants. CO, 417/244, agent to high comm., April 30, 1898.

on the Indian merchants or a fear of excessively affronting the British Government cannot be stated with assurance. Certainly, the British authorities were not intending to pursue the matter. Sir Alfred Milner, the high commissioner, left no doubt as to his government's position in a letter to Greene.

If . . . you are satisfied that the Streets, Wards and Locations are selected with a reasonable regard to the interests of the Indians, I think Her Majesty's Government will have done all that they can be expected to do for the Traders, having regard to existing circumstances.[76]

Nevertheless, Greene was able to inform Milner:

At an interview which I had yesterday with the State's Attorney he assured me that the Government had no desire to deal harshly with those Indian Traders who are established and have vested interests in the shape of leases or other legal contracts. Each individual would, he said, be reasonably dealt with, the object of the Government being rather to restrict immigration in future, than to interfere unduly with those who have settled in the towns and put money into their businesses.[77]

That the Transvaal Government was more moderate than the white merchants, both British and Boer, who were exerting their influence in the Volksraad, was eminently clear. In late May, Greene wrote Milner that the Transvaal Government had agreed to set aside twenty-two sites for Indians within the towns,[78] and on July 3, he telegraphed the high commissioner that the state attorney had just advised him that Indians who had acquired property in towns before the passage of Law 3, or who held valid leases, could continue to be issued licenses to trade as long as they maintained their

[76] CO, 417/261, high comm. to agent, May 12, 1899.

[77] *Ibid.,* agent to high comm., April 28, 1899.

[78] TA, records of the British agent in the Transvaal, agent to high comm., May 22, 1899.

existing status.[79] The Transvaal Government had also decreed, Greene reported, that all Indian traders would be eligible to receive three months' license extensions.[80] The Indians were not loathe to take advantage of the Transvaal's equivocations. They violated even the noncontroversial sections of Law 3 with impunity—often with the full knowledge of the Transvaal Government. Thus, Indians frequently acquired property through the medium of white trustees. In 1888, for example, a certain Mahomed Ismail purchased several stands (lots) at a government land sale in Klerksdorp, and the government permitted him to register them in the name of the mining commissioner.[81]

The differences between the British Government and an independent Transvaal on the Indian question were destined never to be settled. Before negotiations could proceed further, the Anglo-Boer War erupted, and the South African Republic was relegated to the pages of history.

[79] *Ibid.*, tel., agent to high comm., July 3, 1899.

[80] *Ibid.*

[81] Narain, *op. cit.*, 181; report of the Asiatic Inquiry Commission (1921), par. 32.

V / Gandhi and the Indians of the Interior, 1902–1906

THE WAR which finally burst upon the South African scene in late 1899 naturally relegated the Indian question in Natal and the Afrikaner republics to the background. Indian refugees streamed into Natal from the South African Republic, and the colony's government relaxed its stringent immigration restrictions to receive them. The Indian population of the British colonies led by Gandhi saw in the conflict an opportunity finally to impress upon the white settlers their loyalty as British subjects and their consequent right to equal treatment under the law. As soon as news of the hostilities became known, Gandhi organized an Indian ambulance corps whose eight hundred free and three hundred indentured members placed their services at the disposal of the Natal Government. The corps performed with great distinction, often evacuating the wounded under heavy fire.[1] General Sir William Olpherts is reported to have said:

While fully sharing the enthusiasm for bravery of our troops fighting in South Africa, I think that sufficient attention has not been called to the devotion of the Indian dhoolie-bearers who do their work of mercy on the battlefields. Under the heaviest fire they seek the wounded, fearing nothing, although without means of defense. These Indian fellow-subjects of ours are doing

[1] At the Battle Spion Kop, in January 1900, for instance.

in Natal a work which requires even more courage than that of a soldier.[2]

The special correspondent of the *Witness* wrote:

One hundred miles in five days may be accounted fairly good walking for a man unburdened with any weight but that of his own carcass and clothes. When the wounded have to be carried on stretchers for nearly half that distance, and the greater portion of the remainder is traversed by men laden with heavy kit, such marching, I think, will be acknowledged as very creditable work. Such is the feat lately performed by the Indian Ambulance Corps, and one that any body of men may be proud of.[3]

Indians performed other duties with valor. Throughout the siege of Ladysmith, Parbu Singh, an indentured laborer, exposed himself continuously to the enemy while spotting the besiegers' artillery. Sir John Robinson, the prime minister of Natal, thanked "Mr. Gandhi, upon his timely, unselfish and most useful action in voluntarily organising a corps of bearers for ambulance work at the front at a moment when their labours were sorely needed in discharging arduous duties which experience showed to be by no means devoid of peril. All engaged in that service deserve the grateful recognition of the community." [4]

In October 1901, Gandhi, still believing that the principles of equality officially espoused in Westminster were the bases of British imperial rule, and convinced that the successful progress of the war and the active part assumed by the Indians in the struggle had at last turned the tide of public sentiment in favor of the South African Indian population, returned to India. Not that he thought the problem was immediately to be solved; for he attended the Calcutta session of the Indian National Congress, where he moved the resolution on South Africa, and he addressed numerous public meetings on the conditions of Indians in South Africa.

[2] *Works*, III, 137.   [3] *Ibid.*, 140.   [4] *Ibid.*, 160

But Gandhi's sojourn in India turned out to be exceptionally brief. He had promised his followers in South Africa that he would return if he were ever needed, and in November 1902 the impending visit to South Africa of the secretary of state for the colonies, Joseph Chamberlain, caused the call to sent out. Thus it was Gandhi who led the Indian delegation that met the secretary of state in Durban and presented him with a long petition recapitulating Indian grievances in Natal.[5] Gandhi could not have realized at the time that he was destined to spend yet another twelve years in South Africa and that it was the Transvaal which was to be his new battleground rather than Natal.

Gandhi's move to the interior did not imply that the war had changed the government's attitude in Natal. Essentially the opposite was true. The colony was determined finally to solve the Indian question in a manner favorable exclusively to the white man. It was, however, to take several more years for Gandhi to become disenchanted with the British Empire and to lose his conviction that the Indians of South Africa needed only to prove their loyalty to the British Empire convincingly to be accepted by the white population. In 1906 he again led a stretcher company during the Bambata Rebellion in Zululand. Even the anti-Indian governor of Natal, Sir Henry McCallum, felt constrained to write a letter of thanks to "Sergeant-Major Gandhi." "I cannot allow demobilization to take place," the governor wrote,

without placing on record on behalf of the Government my appreciation of the patriotic movement made by the Indian community of Natal in providing a bearer company for service in the field during the rebellion.

2. The number of casualties in our forces have been providentially small and the labours of the company have not therefore been so heavy as they would otherwise have been.

3. At the same time mention has been made to me of the good services rendered by those who volunteered for this service and of

[5] *Ibid.*, 265–269; Gandhi *et al.* to Chamberlain, Dec. 27, 1902.

the steadiness displayed by them. I should feel obliged if you will be good enough to convey to all ranks who served under your command my best thanks for the assistance they have given.[6]

Nevertheless, after both occasions when Gandhi led his followers into the field to aid the British forces, the anticipated amelioration of the Indian condition in Natal did not occur.

Gandhi began to perceive Natal's intentions soon after the termination of the war, but the situation in the Transvaal was yet more threatening, and it was consequently to Johannesburg that Gandhi moved immediately after his meeting with Chamberlain. Here, the lessons he had learned in the coastal province were to be put to their severest test. He left as his legacy to Natal the newspaper *Indian Opinion,* which commenced publication in Durban in 1903 and was the following year moved to the hundred-acre communal Phoenix Estate, founded by Gandhi and his friends Albert West and H. S. L. Polak, just fourteen miles from the town. *Indian Opinion,* with Gandhi as its chief contributor, became the voice of the Indian population in South Africa, while Gandhi was to consider Phoenix his official home throughout the decade he was still to remain on the African continent.

The formal hostilities in the territories of the two republics were essentially over by early 1901. Municipal government, under the aegis of British military authority, was re-established in Johannesburg in May and in Pretoria in January 1902. Four months later, the Treaty of Vereeniging officially ended the Anglo-Boer War, and by June the military governments in both the Transvaal and the Orange Free State (until May 1910 the Orange River Colony) were replaced by nominated executive councils, presided over by lieutenant-governors subordinate to Lord Milner, who was appointed high commissioner for South Africa and governor of the Transvaal and the Orange River Colony, with jurisdiction over all conquered territories.

[6] NA, Natal no. 259 of 1906, encl. McCallum to Gandhi, Aug. 7, 1906.

The Indians of the Transvaal, many of whom had fled to Natal or the Cape, and some even as far as India, started streaming back to the province as soon as the danger had subsided. They confidently expected that British victory presaged the end of their troubles. It soon became apparent, however, that little had changed and that the attitude of the British masters of the Transvaal toward the Indians differed little from that of their Boer predecessors. If anything the position of the Indians deteriorated, for, whereas the republic had been inhibited from implementing much of its anti-Indian legislation by protests from London and Cape Town, the newly established colonial governments, rather than initiating fresh policies, proceeded to enforce republican legislation with considerable zeal.[7]

From the first, the Asian question absorbed the energies of the governing community and of the colonists, white and Indian alike. A heated controversy developed which was not to be even partially settled for some thirteen years. The debate that raged indicated how little separated the British and Afrikaner view of the Indian and the degree to which the roots of modern apartheid are sunk in the British as much as in the Afrikaner mentality. Whereas the republican government had indeed ordered the Indians of the Transvaal into locations, it had never actually made them move. The British military governor of Pretoria, on the other hand, forced

[7] An example of increased stringency under the British can be observed in the matter of leases in Indian locations. The South African Republic had offered 99-year terms while the British allowed no comparable privilege. The Indian press was quick to pick up the point. The *Indian Mirror* remarked that "when the pluck and self-sacrifice of the Indian dooli-bearers and others playing a subordinate part in the war in South Africa formed the theme of the world's praise and admiration, it was the custom to refer to Indians as 'Sons of the Empire.' It may be remembered that Lord Lansdowne stated that one of the causes which led to the war was the anti-Indian policy of the Boer Government. Yet under the Boer Government many of the restrictions placed upon Indians remained a dead letter while under the British rule they have begun to be enforced in all their rigour." Reports of the Native Press, Bengal, June 7, 1901.

the city's Indians into locations as early as 1901 [8]—an action in which he was strongly supported by Sir Godfrey Lagden, the commissioner of native affairs in the Transvaal.[9] "It would be intolerable," Lagden thought, "if the comfort and convenience required by and provided for higher civilisation were to be seized and invaded by a lower stratum who have no natural desire to do so but are inspired by philanthropists and professional agitators." Lagden favored the granting of exemptions from liquor and Asiatic restriction laws to upper-class Indians, but, he felt,

the lower castes who form the mass are as a rule filthy in habit and a menace to public health. To admit them freely into the life of civilised thoroughfares would be as detrimental to themselves as it would be exasperating to civilised communities. It may be urged that they could be limited for residence but not for trade. I am however persuaded that permission to open shops anywhere and everywhere would be abused by evasion of regulations binding them to reside for sanitary reasons in places set apart.[10]

W. Wybergh, the commissioner for mines, enunciated a philosophy very similar to apartheid. "What is aimed at," he claimed,

is the avoidance of close personal contact between two races with entirely different ideals and customs and frequently with strong personal antipathies. . . . We do not wish, in the interests of the Indian, to make him a fifth-rate copy of an European, but rather

[8] TA, no. 126, Trans. to Col. Off., June 28, 1901, encl., supervisor of Ind. imm. to pvt. sec. to the Trans. admin.

[9] This was the same Lagden who at the South African Customs Union Conference of March, 1903, had moved: "This Conference is of the opinion that South Africa is essentially a white man's country, and the permanent settlement upon the land of Asiatic races is injurious and should not be permitted." Cd. 1640 (1903)—minutes of proceedings of the South African Customs Union Conference, Bloemfontein, March, 1903.

[10] TA, memo., Lagden to high commissioner, Jan. 4, in disp. no. 177, Trans. to Col. Off., July 26, 1901.

to develop him on his own lines. In short, I believe it is both just, advisable, and practicable to adopt this policy, and to recognise frankly the fundamental differences between European and Coloured races.

Wybergh espoused the division of municipal and mining areas into European and Asiatic zones, but he would allow no Asians into the High Veld. He went on to refine his proposals. "Within the European quarter," he recommended, "no Asiatic should be allowed to reside or carry on business in person and the same should apply to Europeans within the Asiatic quarters. . . . During the night no Asiatic should be permitted within the European quarters and vice versa." Significantly enough, there was to be no restriction on the investment of capital. Wybergh concluded by suggesting that, "public vehicles should be divided into those for Europeans only and for Coloured persons only and the use of these vehicles strictly confined to the two classes respectively." [11]

The recipe offered by the colonial secretary, Patrick Duncan (destined to become a governor-general of the Union of South Africa) is again reminiscent of more recent formulations of South African racial policy. He wrote:

(a) It is of paramount importance for the future of this Colony that as large a white population as possible should be induced to settle in those parts which are fit for settlement by whites.

(b) There are certain parts of the Colony which require for their development a population used to tropical climates, but at a higher level of intelligence than the native tribes.

If it appears that these last-named districts could be economically developed by Indians, it might be worth our while to consider the advisability of setting apart certain districts for Indian or Asiatic immigrants, either for indentured labour (as is done in Natal) or, if possible, as free settlers. But, except in such districts,

[11] TA, no. 126, Trans. to Col. Off., June 28, 1901, encl. memo. by Wybergh.

it seems to me undesirable to allow Asiatics to settle on the land even as labourers, or to acquire land, unless it is quite clear that such settlement will not tend to dispossess or to keep out white settlers. The fact that Indians are subjects of the British Empire cannot justify, and ought not to entail encouragement of the free overflow of the Indian population into the Transvaal, except where the immigration is in the interests of the Colony. These interests demand, insofar as the immigration of Indians tends to retard or discourage, that it would be a bad policy, especially at present, to allow it.[12]

The administrator of the Transvaal urged the secretary of state to support the township scheme. "The bulk of the Indians," he stated,

do not object to separate townships if properly situated; the better class will be on our side because of their privileged position; and European sentiment on the subject will be conciliated. But if we once allow the lower class of Indians to live wherever they please, it will be more difficult afterwards to bring them together.[13]

In the upper reaches of the hierarchy, the opinions expressed essentially echoed those of the more subordinate officials. Sir Arthur Lawley, the lieutenant-governor of the colony, claimed that

under the old Grondwet the line was distinctly drawn between coloured and white; and, though in the eye of the law they are equal, there is not one man in a hundred who would agree to recognise the coloured man as capable of admission to the same social standard as the white. I do not urge that these sentiments are reasonable, but they imbue the mind of every white South African, and find expression in the universal cry of "a white

[12] TA, memo. on position of Indians in the Trans. by P. Duncan, Feb. 14, 1902.

[13] TA, admin. of Trans. to sec. of state, June 20, 1902.

man's country." An attempt to ignore them would be attended, I feel sure, with most deplorable results.[14]

Milner, himself, felt that any "attempt to place coloured people on an equality with whites in South Africa is wholly impracticable, and that moreover, it is in principle wrong. But I hold that when a coloured person possesses a certain high degree of civilisation he ought to obtain what I may call 'white privileges,' irrespective of colour." [15] Milner's concluding words were the most telling: "For the present," he predicted, "there is no prospect whatever of [the above situation] . . . prevailing, certainly as far as Asiatics are concerned. . . . The Asiatics are strangers forcing themselves upon a community reluctant to receive them." [16]

It is, of course, temptingly easy to moralize and voice sanctimonious condemnations *ex cathedra*. Great Britain had poured all of her resources into an embarrassingly difficult war in South Africa. It had finally won, and the prize was at that time perhaps the richest place on earth. But the Transvaal was peopled by a British minority whose views toward the Indians have already been made clear and by a majority of hardy Old Testament folk, the Afrikaners, whose *kragdadigheid* (strength, power, determination) and emphasis on *baasskap* (white dominance) allowed no dilution of a racial philosophy which saw all men of color as the sons of Ham—condemned to a lesser existence.[17] No government, however imposed, the British conquerors contended, could effectively rule and exploit the wealth of the Transvaal without the participation and consent of the governed. The imperial philosophy of equality before the law was all very well, but a

[14] TA, conf., high comm. to sec. of state, April 18, 1904, encl., lt. gov. to high comm.

[15] TA, conf., high comm. to sec. of state, April 18, 1904.   [16] *Ibid.*

[17] The comparatively generous attitude of the South African Republic toward the Indians, as described in chapter IV, should, however, be borne in mind.

few thousand Indians were just not as important as the tranquillity of a significant portion of His Majesty's dominions and the prosperity of many of his white subjects both at home and abroad.

To his credit, the secretary of state was less sure of what course to follow than Milner and his associates. He did, at least, from his vantage point in London, see the problem from an imperial point of view, and he was able to discern that what the Transvaal authorities were essentially proposing was the establishment of the same system formerly espoused by the South African Republic. As he put it: "It would be difficult to defend in Parliament what is . . . practically a continuance of the system of the late Republic." [18] As was so often the case, however, the arguments of "the man on the spot," in this case Lord Milner, wore down the opposition of the Colonial Office. Milner was convinced that until such time as a different policy could be determined, the British authorities had no choice but to administer the laws of the South African Republic, imperfect as they might be. "Had we to deal merely with the Asiatic population, as it existed before the war," the high commissioner wrote,

it might have been possible to remain passive, until a law could have been framed to the satisfaction of His Majesty's Government. But with so many new-comers continually pouring in and applying for licenses to trade,[19] and with the European population protesting with ever increasing vehemence against the indiscriminate granting of such licenses and against the neglect of the Government to enforce the law, which restricts Asiatics to loca-

[18] TA, sec. of state to high comm., Aug. 6, 1902.

[19] Gandhi vigorously denied Milner's implication. He pointed out that there were only 10,000 Indians in the Transvaal at that time, where before the war there had been about 15,000. Those who were returning were bona fide former residents. *Works*, III, 417–419. Gandhi's criticism stung Milner into remarking: "Some clever baboo [Gandhi] makes play with an old despatch of mine." TA, Milner to Lawley, Jan. 21, 1904.

tions especially set apart for their residence, it becomes impossible to persist in the policy of complete inaction.[20]

Milner won his point, and government notice no. 356 of 1903—a repromulgation of Law 3 of 1885 (as amended in 1886)—the very law against which the British Government had fought so hard in the decade before the war—became almost the first major act of a British government, unhampered by an elected legislature. In the notice the executive council agreed to respect the vested interests of Indians who were trading outside locations before the commencement of hostilities. But, more significantly, the government promised to "take immediate steps to have bazaars in every town set apart in which Asiatics alone may reside and trade." [21] The notice continued to stipulate that "no new licenses to trade shall be granted to any Asiatic except to carry on his business in Bazaars set apart for that purpose." Although Indians, who had been permitted by the Boer authorities to trade outside locations, could continue to renew their licenses, no transfers were to be permitted; nor was the number of licenses held by any trader to be increased beyond the total granted by the Republic.

The notice did make one slight concession to the Indian population, over and above the provisions of Law 3:

With regard to the residence of Asiatics which by the Law above mentioned [Law 3] is confined to those streets, wards and locations which may be set apart for the purpose, His Excellency has decided that an exception shall be made in favour of those whose intellectual attainments or social qualities and habits of life appear to entitle them to it and has accordingly resolved that any Asiatic who shall prove to the satisfaction of the Colonial Secretary that he holds any higher educational certificate from the Education Department in this or any other British Colony or Dependency, or that he is able and willing to adopt a mode of

[20] TA, tel., high comm. to sec. of state, May 11, 1903.
[21] The Transvaal administration planned the establishment of locations at 54 places at a cost of £10,000.

living not repugnant to European ideas nor in conflict with sanitary laws, may apply to the Colonial Secretary for a letter of exemption which shall enable him to reside [but not to trade] elsewhere than in a place especially set aside for Asiatics.

It is worthy of note that the £3 residence license fee for which all Indians were liable under the republic was retained by the British administration.

Milner fully realized that the position assumed by his government was not without its embarrassments, and he equivocated and attempted to rationalize his stand. "It is true," he confessed,

that Law No. 3 of 1885 . . . was, at the time of its passing and a number of years subsequently, the object of controversy between the Government of the late Republic and His Majesty's Government. But the late Chief Justice of the Orange Free State, Mr. Melius de Villiers, to whose arbitration the question was referred by the two Governments, came to the conclusion, and declared in his award, that the South African Republic was entitled to give effect to this law. Its provisions had, according to the Arbitrator, received the assent of previous Secretaries of State, and his award was based on that assent. And as the award was accepted by the present Secretary of State, the Government of the Transvaal does not feel justified, at the present juncture, in altering the law, although it intends to interpret it as liberally as possible.[22]

The Indians of the Transvaal, under Gandhi's leadership, rallied against the attacks of those on whom they had hoped to depend as friends. But Gandhi was not totally opposed to the principle of locations, as long as Indians were not *forced* to reside in them. He only demanded that bazaars should be located in the central business section of any town; that those Indians who had traded outside locations before the war should be allowed to continue this practice; and that Indians should be permitted to purchase property in estab-

[22] TA, tel., high comm. to sec. of state, May 11, 1903.

lished bazaars, subject to building and sanitary regulations.[23]

Milner continued on the defensive. He denied that Indians were worse off under the British than they had been under the Republic.[24] He claimed that British policy differed materially from that of Boers. Locations were being selected that were healthy and afforded reasonable opportunities for trade. Indians in business before the war were not to be moved, and "Asiatics of a superior class" were to be exempted from all special legislation. "The policy of the present Government," Milner concluded, "is not directed against colour or against any special race. It is dictated by the necessity of preventing people of a higher degree of civilisation, whatever their race or colour may be, from being degraded by enforced contact with people of lower grade." [25]

Milner's words attempted to hide some ugly, and yet familiar, truths. The white colonists of the Transvaal—Briton and Afrikaner alike—were determined to curtail the business opportunities afforded Indians and to prevent, insofar as possible, their entry into the colony. As early as February 1903 the British Indian Association complained to the lieutenant-governor that new licenses were being refused to Indians who had traded in the Transvaal before the war and that transfers of licenses were being denied even if the proposed new location of a store was in the same district and street. An Indian, it was claimed, was not allowed to transfer a license to another Indian, thus preventing the sale of a business to anyone but a European. Finally, partners in firms which had traded in the Transvaal before the war were denied licenses to trade in their own names, despite the ac-

[23] *Works,* III, 279, Gandhi to col. sec., Pretoria, Feb. 18, 1904.

[24] Gandhi denied the veracity of Milner's statement. He claimed that trading licenses were only being granted to former license holders by the British, while the Afrikaners had allowed traders to conduct their businesses on the basis of applications for licenses which were, in fact, never granted them. This practice, he asserted, was carried on with the full knowledge of the Republic's government.

[25] TA, tel., high comm. to sec. of state, May 11, 1903.

quiescence of the firm and the other partners.[26] As one Asian wrote to Milner:

Last year in 1902 I was trading on stand 52 Georgetown as a General Dealer, and at the end of 1902 I found I could not renew my license. This week I endeavoured to have my license transferred to stand 4893 Hood Street, Johannesburg, also I made two applications to the Receiver of Revenue, Johannesburg, both have been refused without any reason being given.

Consequently, I have on my hands a large amount of stock, and the refusal has prevented me from earning my living. I therefore beg Your Excellency's good office so that I may resume my business.[27]

Milner, although not totally unsympathetic to the plight of the Asians, still inclined more to the position of the white merchants. "It is not altogether a matter of race and colour prejudice," he wrote. "There is behind it a strong feeling that the Asiatic storekeeper—living as he does under conditions involving a much lower level of expenditure than the European—can compete with the smaller white storekeepers at such an advantage as to rapidly drive them from the field." [28]

The conflict as it developed seemed like a problem from the earlier history of Natal. On March 16, 1903, Gandhi described the plight of Hoosen Amod, a merchant of ten years' standing in Wakkerstroom, whose store, the only Indian one in the town, had been forcibly closed and a trading license refused him. The experience of Suliman Ismail in Rustenburg was the same. Throughout the colony transfers and sales to Indians were denied and white landlords were evicting Indian tenants.[29] Gandhi was particularly concerned about the loss engendered by accumulated stock that could not be sold. "In Pietersburg," he wrote on March 30, "some

[26] TA, Brit. Ind. Assoc. to pvt. sec. to lt. gov., Feb. 25, 1903.
[27] TA, Leon Chong to high comm., Feb. 11, 1903.
[28] TA, high comm. to sec. of state, Feb. 1, 1904.
[29] *Works*, III, 283–284.

Indians, who did not reside there before the War, were last year granted licenses to trade in Town. They have imported large stocks. Last December the Magistrate gave them notice that, after March 31st, they would not receive licenses to trade except in location." [30]

At issue also was the question of Indian property ownership in locations. As Gandhi pointed out, Law 3 of 1885 had given Asians unrestricted rights to hold land in the locations that might be established for them. Under British administration locations were being designated in unhealthy areas, far away from towns, and with the most vexatious limitations on freehold and leasehold.[31] In Standerton, for instance, no Indian was to be allowed to occupy a site, even in a location, if he had not previously resided or traded in the town. In Barberton, lots in the bazaar were to be rented on a monthly basis only, and again only to those Asians who were already residing or trading in the town. In Boksburg, tenancy was on a month-to-month basis, and buildings were erected at the builder's own risk.[32] On November 11, 1903, *Indian Opinion* referred to the Klerksdorp district surgeon's statement that the proposed Indian location was thoroughly unsuitable as in the rainy season it would be completely flooded. The town council, in reply, contended that the matter was outside of its jurisdiction as the site had been approved by the government, had been surveyed and declared the Klerksdorp Bazaar.[33]

Throughout 1903 anti-Indian feeling in the Transvaal constantly increased, and the outbreak of plague in Johannesburg in March 1904, ignited already sensitive public feelings. Gandhi blamed the crisis on the Johannesburg municipality, which on September 26 had assumed jurisdiction over the Indian location [34] and had not maintained proper

[30] *Ibid.,* 288.   [31] *Works,* IV, 39–40; *Indian Opinion,* Nov. 12, 1903.
[32] *Works,* IV, 61; *Indian Opinion,* Nov. 26, 1903.   [33] *Ibid.*
[34] Despite the controversy over the mandatory residence of Indians in locations, most did in fact live in them anyway—at least in Johannesburg.

standards of sanitation. More the orthodox Gujerati Vaishya than the ecumenical egalitarian of the future, Gandhi went on to condemn the municipal authorities for having forced Africans into the same location as the Indians. "About this mixing of the Kaffirs with the Indians," he wrote, "I must confess, I feel most strongly. I think it is very unfair to the Indian population, and it is an undue tax even on the proverbial patience of my countrymen." [35] So long as the responsibility lay with the Indians themselves, Gandhi asserted, there had been no problem—a contention that was largely borne out by a local physician, Dr. Porter.[36] Milner took immediate issue. He claimed that the municipality had only taken charge of the location because of the danger of plague; and rather than causing the epidemic it had striven manfully to prevent it for more than a year. "The danger to public health arising from the condition of the Indian location," he wrote, "was brought to the notice of the government as early as 1901 while the war was still in progress and was one of the reasons which led the Town Council to press for power to expropriate the whole area." [37]

Where the truth lay is not certain. Nevertheless, Milner used the plague as the pretext for informing the Colonial Office of his intention to introduce into the legislative coun-

[35] *Works,* III, 245; Gandhi to Dr. Porter, Feb. 15, 1904. It would probably not be unfair to say that Gandhi, at this stage in his career, was only interested in the welfare of the Indians—and mainly upperclass Indians at that. When he met Lord Elgin in November 1908, Gandhi complained that Indians were being included with the general body of Asians under the Transvaal liquor ordinances. It was, he stated, "a wanton insult. . . . We have no connection with anybody else, and we have always endeavoured to show that the British-Indians ought to be treated as British subjects, and ought not to be included with the general body of Asiatics with respect to whom there may be a need for some restrictions which ought not to apply to British-Indians as British subjects." TA, proceedings of the deputation to the Right Honourable Earl of Elgin on behalf of the British Indian subjects in South Africa, Nov. 8, 1906.

[36] *Works,* III, 244–245.

[37] TA, high comm. to sec. of state, July 25, 1904.

cil two ordinances. One was to be an immigration law on the lines of those already in effect in Natal and Cape Colony, which, although it would not mention Indians specifically, would, "in practice have the effect of limiting the influx of Asiatics of the lower class." [38] The other was intended to deal with the status and privileges of Asians already resident in the colony and those who would subsequently arrive—in other words, it would be a measure similar to government notice no. 356 of 1903.[39]

Lawley appeared willing to discuss the situation more forthrightly than Milner. "It is true," he admitted, "that the British Government had laid down the dictum, 'that there shall not be in the eye of the law any distinction or disqualification whatever founded on mere colour, origin, language, or creed.' " But he contended that the history of South Africa had been such as to set an impassable barrier between the European and the colored races. At the beginning of the century, he said,

it was commonly supposed that all races irrespective of race or colour were capable of the same civilisation, and under this idea pledges were then made which the British Government has since struggled in the face of insuperable difficulties to carry out. It was in accordance with this policy that the British Government resisted by every means in its power the imposition by the Transvaal Republic of restrictions upon British Asiatics. The British Government was merely adopting the policy which as a matter of course they would have adopted in any country where the rights of British subjects were being over-ridden, but I do not think that the consequences which must ultimately result from such a policy were realised at that time. To-day, the Government cannot fail to perceive the effects on the social composition of the country which have resulted from the concessions made to British Indians in the past, or to see clearly what will be the consequences of making still further concessions.[40]

[38] TA, conf., high comm. to sec. of state, April 18, 1904.   [39] *Ibid.*

[40] TA, lt. gov. to high comm., April 13, 1904, encl. to conf., high comm. to sec. of state, April 18, 1904.

What the British Government's attitude was to be was made clear in a letter from Lord George Hamilton, the secretary of state for India, to Lord Curzon, the viceroy.

Chamberlain is not unfriendly, but he is greatly impressed with the intense and universal hostility which exists among white traders and working classes against free Asiatic immigration, and he is apprehensive that, if he exercises pressure beyond a certain point, his action will be so resented as to set on foot a movement of secession from the British Empire.[41]

It may seem curious that at the same time as an active program of anti-Indian legislation was being mounted in the Transvaal, the colony had under consideration a proposal to ask the Government of India to supply indentured labor to alleviate the territory's desperate labor shortage (estimated at 129,000 in 1903 with a projected rise to 365,000 in 1908).[42] Early in 1903, Milner telegraphed Chamberlain to formally request 10,000 Indian coolies for work on the railways. He guaranteed their good treatment while in the Transvaal, but stipulated their mandatory repatriation as a precondition to any agreement. "At present," he plaintively concluded, "we are in the absurd position of being flooded by petty Indian traders and [of] not [being] allowed to have Indian labourers, whom we greatly need." [43]

To achieve his purpose, Milner had to enter the lists against one of the more complex and perplexing figures in modern British imperial history. George Nathaniel Curzon was indeed "a most superior person." Haughty, imperious, passionately unloved, he probably worked harder at being viceroy than any of his predecessors or successors, and he would rise to any occasion which would allow him to display

[41] IOL, Curzon paps., F. 111/162, sec. of state to viceroy, May 28, 1903.

[42] Cd. 1896. The labor was needed mainly for railway construction and for the mines.

[43] Cd. 1683, high comm. to sec. of state, May 12, 1903.

himself publicly as the virtuous defender of India. Milner's need allowed Curzon to reopen the whole question of the position of Indians in South Africa. Before news of the high commissioner's dilemma reached him, Curzon had minuted with remarkable moderation:

Two entirely opposite standpoints are occupied by those who regard it [the Indian problem] through Colonial and Imperial glasses respectively. The colonists, to whose Colony has been conceded the right of self-government, argue that the first and most necessary of the rights that he thereby acquires is that of admitting whom he pleases and excluding whom he pleases from his country. Most particularly does he apply this argument to the introduction of labour that is both coloured . . . and cheap. We must concede some reasonableness to this point of view. . . .

The opposite standpoint is that of the Imperialists, who contend that all citizens of the Empire, independent of colour or origin, ought to be at liberty to live and labour in all parts of it on the same footing, unhampered by any racial disabilities or social or economic restrictions. I will only say of this contention that it postulates a development to which the British Empire has not yet attained, or may perhaps never succeed in attaining: and that if logically carried out, it would involve the removal of many differentiations which are not likely to disappear, at least in our time.[44]

Once he had Milner's request in hand, Curzon took a quite different tack. Before even entertaining the proposal, he demanded that Indian languages be included as a test of literacy under any Transvaal immigration legislation; that residence in locations be mandatory only for lower-class Indians; that all established Indian traders, whether they were licensed by the South African Republic or not, be allowed to retain their present places of business; and that all upper-class Indians, including respectable shopkeepers and traders,

[44] NAI, May, 1903, proc. 46, minuting by Curzon, Jan. 27, 1903. It is worthy of note that this statement was written in January 1903, before the receipt of Milner's request.

be exempted from restrictions regarding the use of footpaths, public conveyances, first-class railway carriages, and so on.[45]

London saw the labor question in the Transvaal as a problem of major imperial concern. Consequently, Curzon was placed under heavy pressure to cooperate with Milner and to give up his demands for the amelioration of the position of Indians already resident in South Africa in return. He was threatened with the reversal of any unpopular decision he might make. Sir Arthur Godley, undersecretary in the India Office, informed the viceroy that the cabinet was considerably exercised over Curzon's attitude on the coolie issue, which was

natural enough considering the financial stake that they have in the prosperity of the Transvaal, and it seems to me pretty clear that on this question they will be rather stiff. It really comes to this:—are you, or are you not to use the power that you have of refusing coolie labour to the Transvaal, in order to put on the screw for the better treatment of the natives who are there already? So far as I can make out, the result of the question if answered in the affirmative, will be that the Transvaal will go without coolies, India will lose the very considerable advantage of lucrative employment for 20,000 of her population, and the natives already settled in the Transvaal will be treated no better, but possibly worse, than they are at present.[46]

St. John Brodrick, the secretary of state for India, echoed his colleague's concern. He also informed Curzon that the cabinet was displeased with his attitude, that the prevalent feeling in the India council was that Curzon was stirring up an anti-South African feeling in India not naturally prevalent, and that he was attempting to blackmail the Government of the Transvaal as an act of personal animus [47]—

---

[45] NAI, Nov. 1904, procs. 17–19, tel., viceroy to sec. of state, Jan. 2, 1904.

[46] IOL, Curzon paps., F. 111/162, no. 81, undersec. Ind. Off. to viceroy, Nov. 13, 1903.

[47] *Ibid.*, no. 83, sec. of state to viceroy, Nov. 20, 1903.

surprising allegations to level at a viceroy of India! "Surely," Brodrick contended, "it is too much to ask us to stand aloof, and let all our South African efforts perish because we cannot immediately obtain something for our Indian subjects, which we are resolutely determined to obtain, as soon as circumstances make it possible that it should be granted." [48]

Curzon, now fully engaged, defended his position with courage and considerable eloquence. "If the Empire is what it pretends to be," he asked, "why are Indians excluded from the Transvaal, proscribed in Cape Colony, persecuted in Natal? This attitude has been greatly inflamed by the tendency of the Home Government to sacrifice India to home interests." He would insist upon a juster and more generous recognition of India's aspirations in the designs of the British Government and in the policy of the Empire. "Every effort should be turned to perpetually building bridges over that racial chasm that yawns eternally in our midst, and which, if it becomes wider, and there are no means of getting across it, will one day split the Empire asunder." [49] "For five years," he later wrote, "I have been preaching . . . the doctrine of Imperialism. But they [the Indians] are disposed to regard it as a farce; for in practice it means to India a full share of the battles and burdens of Empire, but uncommon little of the privileges or rights." [50]

Warming to his task, Curzon asked Brodrick to bear in mind that

the name of South Africa stinks in the nostrils of India. The most bitter feeling exists over the treatment meted out to Indians in the Transvaal and Natal. Any attempt to ignore or override this feeling would produce a [great] commotion. . . .

No arrangement that did not provide a good bargain would be tolerated by public opinion here. There are tens of thousands of natives of India in South Africa already. These persons are sub-

---

[48] *Ibid.*, no. 85, sec. of state to viceroy, Nov. 26, 1903.
[49] *Ibid.*, no. 43, Curzon to Salisbury, June 21, 1903.
[50] *Ibid.*, viceroy to sec. of state, Nov. 15, 1903.

ject to invidious, and in some cases odious disabilities. The public wants us to lessen the burden upon them before sending any more.

Curzon was particularly incensed at the threat to override his decision.

I think I am safe in saying that such a step would be without any precedent; while the reception it would meet with here would be such as to make all recent experience pale. . . .

If on any occasion that I feel it to be my duty to stand up for the interests of India, I am suspected of disloyalty to the Government (I know of a Cabinet Minister who said that my refusal to accept the South African scheme was "an act of gross disloyalty to the Ministry")—there will be no getting on.[51]

Milner's initial response to Curzon's demands was not unfavorable. He denied that pass laws and curfew restrictions would or did, in fact, apply to Indians. He was prepared to supply separate but equal transportation facilities for Indians, and he was even willing to allow the use of Indian languages as a test for literacy in any future immigration law. Milner was inclined to allow upper-class Indians to live outside locations. "But, . . . we cannot undertake to allow Indians to trade, except in quarters allotted to them." [52]

If Curzon felt he was under pressure in India, Milner, without doubt, was under heavier pressure in South Africa. On February 1 he reported strong opposition in the legislative council to a proposal that notice no. 356 be amended so that Indians who had traded in the Transvaal without licenses should be allowed to continue to trade outside locations.[53] The exigencies of the situation in the Transvaal forced the high commissioner to modify his stand constantly, until Curzon accused him of having receded from all four of

[51] *Ibid.*

[52] NAI, Nov. 1904, procs. 17–19, tel., high comm. to sec. of state, Jan. 10, 1904.

[53] *Ibid.*, high comm. to sec. of state, Feb. 1, 1904.

the conditions set by the Government of India which he had originally accepted.[54]

In an attempt to breach the impasse, representatives of the India and Colonial offices met in conference on June 29. Alfred Lyttelton, now the secretary of state for the colonies, was willing to urge that concessions be made to the Indians on the matter of mandatory residence and trading in locations. He would allow Indians who had engaged in business before the war, with or without licenses, to continue to hold their existing places of business. He would only require those Indians who were a menace to the public health (i.e., lower-class Indians) to live in the locations. But he would go no further, as the report of the conference indicated:

It was made clear, however, by the Colonial Secretary, that the concessions which it was now proposed to impose on the Transvaal Government would probably cause a geat deal of feeling; they might even greatly accentuate the demand for self-government, and it was in his opinion quite impossible to impose further concessions on the Transvaal with regard to future immigration. To do so would be to enact provisions at variance with the law in Cape Colony and Natal, and uniformity in the legislation of the future was very essential.[55]

The India Office representatives understood that the concessions proposed by Lyttelton were the most that could be expected for the moment. But they also realized that they would not be sufficient to meet the minimum requirements of the Government of India and under the circumstances felt that, "it would be far better to postpone any question of the importation of coolie labour from India." [56] Milner came to the same conclusion. "If, in the opinion of the Government of India," he wrote to the Colonial Office, "it is impossible to allow Coolie immigration into the Transvaal, unless the

[54] *Ibid.*, note by Curzon, May 23, 1904.
[55] *Ibid.*, report of meeting between Ind. Off. and Col. Off., June 29, 1904.
[56] *Ibid.*

laws of the Transvaal with regard to Indians generally are framed in a liberal spirit, then I fear there is nothing for it but for us to renounce, for the time being, the hope of Coolie immigration." [57]

It was now obvious that Indian labor for the Transvaal would never be forthcoming. The answer to the colony's problem still lay in Asia, however. Under the terms of Ordinance no. 17 of 1904, "To regulate the introduction into the Transvaal of Unskilled Non-European Labourers," it was to China that the Transvaal successfully looked for relief rather than to India.[58]

To confuse an increasingly complex situation still further, the supreme court of the Transvaal, in the case of Motan versus the Transvaal Government, heard in May 1904, expressed its consternation that a British government had adopted the position of the South African Republic in requiring that Indians both trade and reside in locations—the very contention it had always denied in its interpretation of Law 3 before the Anglo-Boer War. In discussing the law of

[57] TA, conf., high comm. to sec. of state, April 18, 1904.

[58] The whole question of Asian labor was extremely complicated. It affected all the self-governing members of the empire. In January 1904, Richard Seddon, the prime minister of New Zealand, telegraphed Natal, Canada, Cape Colony and Australia suggesting joint action to prevent the importation of Chinese coolies into Transvaal. NA, G. no. 40/1904, tel., Seddon to prime minister, Natal, Jan. 8, 1904. All three South African colonies protested Seddon's action. Milner was both apprehensive and incensed. "I hope all your influence will be used," he telegraphed the governor of Natal, "to prevent the Government of your colony lending itself to a demonstration so mischievous. Any attempt to interfere with the Transvaal in matter of such vital importance to prosperity of Colonies will certainly be the cause of bitter resentment in the Transvaal and would in all probability lead to a permanent estrangement of the sister colonies between which it has been my constant endeavour to maintain good relations. The utterances of the prime minister of New Zealand make it quite evident that he is in complete ignorance of the state of affairs in the Transvaal." Ibid., minute paper of Jan. 11, 1904, encl. sec., high comm., to gov. Natal, Jan. 11, 1904.

1885, the chief justice, Sir James Rose-Innes, ruled that its provisions only relegated Indians to certain streets, wards, and locations for purposes of residence. He failed to see any basis for the assumption that Law 3 also confined Indian business to locations. "The mischief purported to be aimed at was the insanitary mode of life in the midst of an European population—not an inconvenient competition with European traders." Rose-Innes concluded with a final rebuke to the colonial authorities. "Under the circumstances," he contended, "it does strike one as remarkable that without fresh legislation the officials of the Crown in the Transvaal should put forward a claim which the Government of the Crown in England has always contended was illegal under the Statute and which, in the past, it has strenuously resisted." [59]

Milner, who was not totally surprised by the decision, acted with dispatch to implement it. He informed all officials that the provisions of notice no. 356 as they applied to trading were no longer in effect, and he understood that any future ordinance passed in the colony could not interfere with rights already acquired.[60] But the high commissioner clearly held some reservations about the long-term effects of the decision. "If British Indians who are in the country now," he wrote,

are to enjoy a perpetual right to take out licenses, it will mean that some thousands of British Indians will be able, as of right, to demand a privilege from which, prior to the recent finding of the Supreme Court, they had been excluded and which, in point of fact, they never expected to enjoy when they came here. The British Indian males now registered amount in number to 9,918. The Asiatics holding licenses number 872. A constant increase in the number of Indian traders will be, to the white community, a source of constant irritation.[61]

[59] Johannesburg *Star* (weekly edition), May 14, 1904.
[60] NAI, Nov. 1904, procs. 17–19, tel., high comm. to sec. of state, July 2, 1904.
[61] *Ibid.*, tel., high comm. to sec. of state, July 13, 1904.

The Colonial Office and the British administrators of the Transvaal found themselves in what was by now a famliar position. They were caught between the municipalities, often represented by volunteer organizations, such as the White League and the East Rand Vigilance Association, and the Indians and their adherents.[62] The former demanded an end to Indian immigration and trade competition. The latter insisted on the preservation of the Indians' rights as British subjects. Gandhi's presence was being increasingly felt, and he nettled many government officers. Thoroughly exasperated, the colonial secretary suggested that "a Mr. Ghandi [sic], a lawyer from Natal (who unfavourably impressed me) should not be allowed to pose as the champion of the Asiatics. Their champion is the Protector of Asiatics. They should look to him for defense." [63]

Without doubt it was the municipalities, led by their chambers of commerce, which had the greatest influence with the colonial government. The Pretoria chamber, for instance, moved that "the trading rights of Asiatics already in the country should be restricted to the lines intended to be laid down by Law #3 of 1885, that any trading or other rights obtained prior to the war should be taken into consideration with a view to their expropriation." [64] To emphasize the strong feelings of the colonists respecting the Indians, a National Convention on the Asian Question, attended by representatives from all the Transvaal municipalities, was convened on November 10 in the Pretoria Opera House. R. K. Loveday, one of the organizers, set the tone for the conference in his opening remarks. He referred to "the low scale of civilisation at which the Asiatic is content to live, [which] renders it impossible for any white man to compete

[62] Especially Naoroji and Bhownaggree.

[63] TA, minute by W. E. Davidson, col. sec., no date, probably early 1903.

[64] TA, high comm. to sec. of state, Aug. 29, 1904, encloses resolutions passed by Pretoria Chamber of Commerce, Aug. 28, 1904.

with him." [65] He contended that "the white trader is expected to sink to their mode of life, to abandon civilisation, and to compete if he wishes to live. It is known that all the profits made by the Indian trader are remitted to India." [66] E. F. Bourke, the other organizer, chided the imperial government for its unsympathetic attitude.[67] Louis Botha, the future prime minister of the Transvaal and the Union of South Africa, offered his warm good wishes to the convention. "I am most grateful," he wrote, "to see the movement in connection with the Asiatic question has taken a manly position against a threatening attitude which more and more curtails the rights of the white population." [68]

Milner was the official spokesman and representative of imperial Britain in South Africa, yet it was never hard to discern where his real sympathies lay. In a dispatch to Lyttelton, he saw "little reason to doubt that if no restrictions are imposed to protect the white storekeeper against the competition he will very soon be driven from the field, and one of the chief inducements which lead Europeans to the remote and unsettled parts of the country will be removed." [69] Milner's concern might have been understandable had there been more than the 9,918 Indians he claimed were in the Transvaal at the time (July 1904) and if more than 872 had held licenses to trade.[70]

On the other hand, the Indians were often their own worst enemies. Caste-ridden to some degree even in Africa during the early years, their feelings of communal animus interfered with a successful defense of their position against the assaults of the white colonists. C. M. Pillay, a former official in Indian organizations in Pretoria and Johannesburg, wrote a revealing letter to the *Rand Daily Mail.* "The Bombay Bannias," he claimed,

[65] TA, minutes of the national convention convened at the Pretoria Opera House on Nov. 10, 1904.
[66] *Ibid.*   [67] *Ibid.*   [68] *Ibid.*
[69] TA, high comm. to sec. of state, March 1904.
[70] TA, high comm. to sec. of state, July 13, 1904.

with very few exceptions are the most filthiest class imaginable. The phrase, "living upon the smell of an oiled rag," particularly applies to these people, and they are particularly susceptible to Bubonic Plague. My personal experience has convinced me that it is impossible to impress upon the Bannias those principles of cleanliness and sanitation as comprehended in a purely European community; for they ascribe everything to fate.[71]

In London, the Colonial Office had ponderously accepted the principle of the Transvaal supreme court ruling. "This attitude," it said, "was incumbent upon His Majesty's Government as the trustees of Imperial interests, including those of the Indian subjects of the Crown." [72] But at the same time "the trustees" were implementing a time-tested technique for extricating themselves from an increasingly uncomfortable position. The Colonial Office decided to establish representative government in the Transvaal and thereby greatly reduce its own responsibility. "In debate . . . yesterday," the secretary of state telegraphed Milner,

I stated that His Majesty's Government decided to give representative institutions to Transvaal, substituting for present nominated element in Transvaal Legislative Council an elected element.

With regard to British Indians I said that if Colony chooses to pass a law making it in future difficult for them to come in that though I should regret it I should not resist it.

As for the British Indians already resident in the Transvaal, Lyttelton "was certain that the citizens of the Transvaal who value equally with ourselves the honour of the British name will appreciate that the national honour and dignity is at stake with British Indians resident here." [73]

The secretary of state was dealing in vain hopes. Neither did white citizens seem to share his concern for British

[71] *Rand Daily Mail*, March 28, 1904.
[72] TA, sec. of state to high comm., July 20, 1904.
[73] TA, sec. of state to high comm., July 22, 1904.

honor and dignity, nor was it possible to establish representative government in the Transvaal as rapidly as he had hoped. Milner in a private and confidential telegram of August 11, 1905, urged the Colonial Office to support the Transvaal Government in its efforts to limit the number and location of Indian licenses to trade, in spite of the decision of the supreme court. "The removal of all restrictions upon the granting of licenses to Asiatics already here," he cabled, "is having a more serious effect on the smaller White Traders than you perhaps imagine, and the sympathy of the whole European community is with them."

"I should much prefer to take a high line in the matter," he disingenuously concluded, "but frankly I do not think the game is worth the candle." [74] The high commissioner was the most interested in avoiding the issuance of new licenses and he requested an immediate reaction from the Colonial Office on a proposal to circumscribe the opportunities of Indians not already established in business.[75]

The Colonial Office was promptness itself and its reply manifested what had almost become customary casuistry. "It would be wholly impossible," the secretary of state telegraphed Milner, "to recede from the decision announced in Parliament, unanimously approved by the Cabinet and publicly stated to involve the honor of the country." With the proverbial next breath, however, Lyttelton remarked that he was "sensible of the difficulties with which you have to contend and if you suggest that as in Natal granting of licenses shall be subject to conditions as prescribed by [certain] clauses . . . of Natal Act 18 of 1897, I shall be prepared to consider the proposal favourably." [76] On the surface this seems an incredible suggestion, as the clauses to which the secretary of state was referring were those which vested all power in licensing cases in the municipal boards of Natal with no appeal to the supreme court—a state of affairs

[74] TA, sec. and conf., tel., high comm. to sec. of state, Aug. 11, 1904.
[75] *Ibid.*   [76] TA, tel., sec. of state to high comm., Aug. 11, 1904.

against which successive secretaries of state had fought with considerable vigor. It must be said in Lyttelton's defense, however, that he staunchly defended the rights of Indians already trading in the Transvaal and opposed any suspension of the issuing of new licenses under existing conditions.

Milner was greatly depressed by the Colonial Office's attitude. Clauses 7 and 8 of Natal Act 18 of 1897, he contended, had not prevented white traders from being ousted by Indian competition.[77] "Unless His Majesty's Government can agree to some modification of the views now taken," he ominously warned, "there will be grave trouble here." [78] And indeed he was not far from right. Anti-Indian petitions were received from every town in the Transvaal, and a series of heavily attended protest meetings was held throughout the colony. Milner was "fully alive to the difficulty in which His Majesty's Government is placed by the recent decision of the Court. But I am bound to make one more effort to try and prevent a bad quarrel between the loyal people of this Colony and the Mother-Country." On August 16, 1905, Milner informed the secretary of state that Sir George Farrar, strongly supported by the nonofficial members of the legislative council, had contended that the unrestricted access of Asians to trading licenses was leading to the elimination of the white merchant. He had moved a resolution calling for a commission of enquiry and had requested that "pending the report of such Commission the Secretary of State be respectfully requested to authorize the introduction of legislation suspending the issue of further licenses for Asiatics to trade." [79]

But the secretary of state, to his credit, remained adamant in opposing even a temporary suspension of the issuance of trading licenses to Asians. On September 5, he telegraphed Milner:

[77] TA, high comm. to sec. of state, April 1904.
[78] TA, tel., high comm. to sec. of state, Aug. 4, 1904.
[79] TA, high comm. to sec. of state, Aug. 16, 1904.

If, having regard to the fact that the Legislative Council is not now sitting and that the resolution cannot be replied to, you are convinced that it is absolutely necessary to announce the decision as to licenses, it should be to the effect that you have communicated the resolution to me and that His Majesty's Government desire to point out that any such suspension of licenses as it proposes would entail the temporary denial to British Indian subjects of the rights secured to them by the recent judgment of the Supreme Court.

His Majesty's Government are convinced that the Administration and people of the Transvaal will recognise the impossibility of such a departure from the policy of my despatch of July 20th, in the close adherence to which their honour no less than that of this country is deeply involved.[80]

Faced with such intransigence the colonists and their government temporarily withdrew from combat on the licensing front to regroup their forces.

If Indians, both in South Africa and elsewhere, were incensed by the Transvaal's laws affecting Indians, the ordinances of the old Orange Free State, which like those of the South African Republic were still considered valid, were even more objectionable (see Chapter IV). Essentially Indians had been, and in effect still were, excluded from the territory—a fact which made the Indian question in the Orange Free State far less pressing than it was in the Transvaal and apparently allowed the British administration in the conquered territories to proclaim the imperial philosophy at least once with apparently little clamor. As early as April 1901, Milner had written to the deputy administrator of the Orange River Colony:

It is quite evident that the existing law will have to be modified, and I invite your attention and that of your legal adviser to the matter, with a view to the preparation of a draft ordinance. . . .

It would be impossible for us to prohibit Indian British sub-

[80] TA, tel., sec. of state to high comm., Sept. 5, 1904.

jects as such from farming or carrying on trade in the Orange River Colony.[81]

Despite strong attacks on the situation in the Orange River Colony both by the Transvaal British Indian Association [82] and in the House of Commons,[83] the good intentions of April 1901 were never carried into effect. No doubt the attitude of H. Goold-Adams, the deputy administrator of the colony (later to become the lieutenant governor), had a good deal to do with Milner's failure to force the issue. Goold-Adams claimed to recognize

the necessity for so amending the existing law of this Colony as to allow His Majesty's British Indian subjects free access to this country, and full liberty to pursue whatever trade or calling they may elect, and to grant them the same privileges as are extended to British subjects throughout the Empire.[84]

Having paid the expected lip service to the concept of the equality of all British subjects, Goold-Adams proceeded with the usual arguments against any substantive change in the status of Indians in the Orange River Colony. He did not

consider the present time opportune for a wholesale relaxation of the law as it now stands. Considering the unsettled condition of the Country, which will not improbably continue for some months, it would unquestionably, I think, be most impolitic at present to remove the whole of the restrictions on Asiatic immigration which are enforced by existing law.

Goold-Adams was concerned lest the colony be flooded by Indians, and he used all the familiar clichés to defend the *status quo*. The time was not ripe "for an inrush of impecunious persons, as so many of the present British Indian residents of South Africa are." Only such Asians "as would not

[81] TA, high comm. to dep. admin., Orange River Colony (ORC), April 25, 1901.

[82] TA, Brit. Ind. Assoc. to pvt. sec. of high comm., Jan. 24, 1904.

[83] TA, sec. of state to high comm., July 26, 1901.

[84] TA, dep. admin. ORC to high comm., May 30, 1901.

be a burden to the community" should be admitted. The colony wanted only "those persons who are likely to make good citizens," and any potential "good citizen" had to be thoroughly familiar with English, both spoken and written. Finally, Goold-Adams advised that no Indian should, under any future legislation, be allowed to acquire land in lease-hold, freehold, or otherwise—even if the Indian himself was permitted to reside in the Orange River Colony.[85]

By 1903 Milner had fallen back into line, and, influenced, no doubt, by the state of affairs of the Transvaal, he simply informed the Colonial Office that

pending any general decision as to the policies to be adopted in connection with the immigration of British Indians into South Africa the Government of the Orange River Colony has closely adhered to the law of the late Orange Free State, which embodies the views ordinarily held on the question by the white population of the Colony. Under this law no British Indian can engage in trade or agriculture, and if he desires to reside in the Colony for other purposes, he must obtain permission from the Lieutenant-Governor and Executive Council to do so, and must advertise in the Gazette his intention of doing so.[86]

Apparently amendments of existing laws to the detriment of the Indians did not have to await the determination of a basic policy on the Asian question. In January 1904, the *Government Gazette* of the Orange River Colony published a draft ordinance amending the laws relating to the poll tax on colored persons. Paragraph 1 made all colored (a designation which included Indians) males between eighteen and seventy who were domiciled in the colony subject to an annual poll tax of twenty shillings. Paragraph 13 provided for the involuntary placing into indenture of colored persons

[85] *Ibid.*

[86] TA, ORC no. 17, high comm. to sec. of state, July 25, 1903. Based on H. F. Wilson, act. lt. gov., ORC, to gov., ORC (Milner), July 25, 1903.

who did not pay the levy.[87] When the British Indian Association entered a protest, it is worthy of note that it objected not so much to the draft ordinance, but to the inclusion of Indians in the category of "coloured persons." [88] The high commissioner defended the Orange River Colony's action by again asserting that the draft ordinance "merely reproduces the Old Free State law," and that British Indians were in practice exempt from the strictures of paragraph 13, "since all of those who reside in the Colony are in settled employment and are consequently in a position to pay the tax." [89]

As time went on, the failure of the British Government in South Africa to ameliorate the Indian condition in the Orange River Colony became less and less explicable within the context of the imperial philosophy or by any measure beyond the pure expediency which was expressed as late as July 1905, in a letter from the lieutenant-governor to the high commissioner. "Legislation had not been altered by this Government," the message read,

primarily in consequence of the known antagonism to the removal of such restrictions by every old inhabitant of the Colony. It was considered by the Government that if the said legislation had been repealed it would have only added one more to the list of grievances which the people of the Colony pretended that they have against the British Government.[90]

Goold-Adams admitted that the various municipalities of the Orange River Colony had passed anti-Indian by-laws which required Indians to live only in prescribed locations which they had to reach by 9 P.M., to be in their houses by 11 P.M., and not be back on the streets, even of the location, until 4 or 5 A.M. All Indians had to carry passes, and servants in Bloemfontein were obliged to carry service books. Indians

[87] TA, *Government Gazette* of the ORC, Jan. 16, 1904.

[88] *Vide* n. 73.

[89] TA, G. G. Robinson, pvt. sec. of high comm. to Abdool Gani, chairman, Brit. Ind. Assoc., March 17, 1904.

[90] TA, lt. gov., ORC, to high comm., July 31, 1905.

had to travel third class. They could not of course, enter business, become farmers, or own fixed property.[91]

When the British Indian Association complained about the anti-Indian nature of the Orange River Colony's municipal by-laws,[92] the acting colonial secretary replied: "As there are so few British Indians in the Colony, I think you will agree that the question raised by you is not of great *practical* importance." [93] It was an argument which contained a hard truth. Given the small number of Indians in the Orange River Colony, it was inevitable that their problems would be sacrificed to the greater urgency of the Indian question further north.

In the Transvaal, the failure of the colony's proposals on licensing and locations to receive the sanction of the Colonial Office forced the Transvaal authorities to shift their attack to the question of Indian immigration, on which subject the British Government seemed more tractable.[94] Under existing conditions, the entry of Indians into the Transvaal had, since November 19, 1902, been regulated under the Peace Preservation Ordinance. No Asian was permitted to enter the colony unless he was in possession of a document

[91] *Ibid.* The *Government Gazette* of the Orange River Colony for June 3, 1904, contained amended and new regulations for the town of Winburg. These stipulated that any colored (Indian) person found without a pass from a white master or official could be fined five pounds or indentured for a year to a resident of the district. Any colored person who did not find work as a daily or monthly servant within 24 hours would have to leave the town commonage. No colored person was to be allowed in the streets after 9 P.M. No parties or meetings were to be held in the locations after 10 P.M. without permission. All colored persons over sixteen who had been given permission to reside in the municipality were liable for service and had to register every month at the office of the town clerk. This would entitle them to a residential pass upon payment of sixpence.

[92] TA, Brit. Ind. Assoc. to pvt. sec. of high comm., July 23, 1905.

[93] TA, asst. col. sec., ORC, to chairman, Brit. Ind. Assoc., July 25, 1905.

[94] TA, sec. of state to high comm., tel., July 22, 1904.

signed by the chief officer for permits and the registrar of
Asiatics or one of his staff. Restrictions were constantly made
more stringent by administrative action. Up to August 22,
1903, permits to enter the Transvaal had been issued at the
request of the colonial secretary, who from time to time prepared a list of eligible persons. After August 22, however, jurisdiction had rested entirely with the registrar of Asiatics
who, with the exception of 21 personal servants, granted permission to enter the colony only to those Indians who had
been resident before the war. Even if an Indian were able to
prove former domicile, he had usually to wait for a considerable length of time, as only a few permits were issued each
month.

As a first step in the campaign, Milner, at the urging of
his protégé Lionel Curtis, suggested the registration of all
the Indians resident in the Transvaal. If this were done, he
claimed, it would be impossible for an Indian to smuggle
himself into the colony and then claim to be a legal resident.
Most Indians had, of course, already registered in the days of
the South African Republic, and the proposed new restriction was taken as a serious affront. As the result, however, of
negotiations conducted between Milner and Gandhi, they
agreed to cooperate with the government. "Although the Indians were not bound in law," Gandhi later wrote,

they voluntarily agreed to re-register in the hope that new restrictions might not be imposed upon them, it might be clear to all
concerned that the Indians did not wish to bring in fresh immigrants by unfair means, and the Peace Preservation Ordinance
might no longer be used to harass newcomers. Almost all Indians
thus changed their permits for new ones. This was no small
thing. The community completed like one man with the greatest
promptitude this re-registration, which they were not legally
bound to carry out. This was a proof of their veracity, tact,
large-mindedness, commonsense and humility. It also showed
that the community had no desire to violate in any way any law
in force in the Transvaal. The Indians believed that if they be-

haved towards the Government with such courtesy, it would treat them well, show regard for them and confer fresh rights upon them.[95]

On March 31, 1905, the so-called Lyttelton Constitution, which provided for the establishment in the Transvaal of an elective legislative assembly, was promulgated.[96] Two days later Lord Selborne replaced Milner as high commissioner and resolved to take a fresh approach to the Indian problem. In a long despatch of August 21, 1905, he expressed his views:

I am inclined to think that if the people of the Orange River Colony and the Transvaal are quite assured that there will be no further immigration of Asiatics it would be possible to gradually settle the status of those who are now residing in the country on fairly satisfactory lines. For these men it will be my utmost effort to do full justice, but I may express my strong conviction that there should be no further Asiatic immigration into this country. I am sorry to have to write this in respect of my Indian fellow subjects, but after all *Salus republicae suprema lex,* and what is wanted more than anything else in these two colonies are British subjects, who, if need be, can fight, which is the same thing as saying white British subjects. For in these colonies a white man must always be a fighter, whereas this is the one thing the Asiatic can never be, both owing to the peculiar circumstance of the country and to the fact that the Asiatics who come here are not of any martial race. Owing to the prejudice about the fields of white and black labour which exists in this country, there are only a restricted number of professions open to white British subjects who immigrate here, and of the most important of these is that of trader. It is precisely in his capacity as a trader that the white British subject is hopelessly beaten out of the field by the Asiatic, and it is because we cannot afford to have the white Brit-

[95] M. K. Gandhi, *Satyagraha in South Africa* (Ahmedabad, 1928), 94–95. Hereafter referred to as *Satyagraha.*

[96] Most of the power was, however, retained in the hands of officials responsible to the governor. The assembly was to consist of from six to nine officials and 30 to 35 elected members.

ish trader ousted that I think that any further Asiatic immigration into this country ought to be discouraged. As I have already said, I am sorry thus to discourage the immigration of my Indian fellow subjects, but, in the long run, it would do them no good if this country fell again under Boer domination, owing to the absence of Englishmen, Scotchmen, and Irishmen, ousted by their pressure into other lands.

Selborne was asking the Colonial Office to sanction a policy, "having the practical effect of preventing all future Asiatic immigration in return for a satisfactory assurance of the proper treatment of all Asiatics already in the country." [97]

The Colonial Office essentially accepted Selborne's compromise. It entered the usual caveat, however, that as "His Majesty's Government could not approve the exclusion of Asiatics *eo nomine,* the legislation would be necessarily more or less on the lines of existing acts on the subject in Cape Colony, Natal, and Australasia." [98] In other words, Indians could be excluded from the Transvaal as long as this object was achieved by administrative action, without Indians being specifically discriminated against in the law. The India Office, "while regretting the necessity for a step which entails the practical exclusion of natives of India from a British Colony, agrees with Lord Elgin that the compromise proposed by Lord Selborne is likely to afford the only practicable solution for this difficult question." [99]

Many of the specific proposals for the curtailment of Indian immigration to the Transvaal came from the pen of Lionel Curtis, perhaps the most brilliant member of "Milner's Kindergarten" and the assistant colonial secretary of the Transvaal at the time.[100] He admitted that the proposed exclusion of Indians from the Transvaal was "the most odious

[97] NAI, April 1906, proc. 11, high comm. to sec. of state, Aug. 21, 1905.

[98] *Ibid.,* sec. of state to high comm., Jan. 5, 1906.

[99] TA, India Off. to Col. Off., Jan. 31, 1906.

[100] He later became head of the Asiatic Department.

duty which the British Government could legitimately undertake"; but he thought that the situation was grave enough to warrant even extreme measures. He felt that the Transvaal and the Orange River Colony had to be maintained as white preserves, "with greater firmness than you guard the Native territories as Native reserves, or the Federal Government used in America to protect the Indian reserves in that country." He contended that the Peace Preservation Ordinance, even as amended, had proved inadequate and that new legislation was vitally needed. Curtis wanted to simplify the whole problem by conceding that all Indians, however they might have entered the Transvaal, were legal residents. He would then start *de novo* by requiring the reigistration, once again, of all Indians in the colony. Fingerprints would be required. Curtis was quite willing to countenance some slight abuses of the system and to be liberal on the matter of wives and children. Always the imperialist, he found the £3 fee exacted from all Indians unpalatable and urged its abolition as "a most vexatious and indefensible" affront to British subjects.[101]

The *Times* of May 4, 1907, commented on Curtis' views:

Mr. Curtis refers to the existence of "a theory that all subjects of this imperial rule enjoy equal political rights in every part of the King's dominions." The fact that such a theory "exists and exists 'officially'" constitutes in his opinion a profoundly serious danger to the future of the white communities, and the attempt to carry it to its logical conclusion must mean, if successful, the final submersion by the countless millions of the Indian races.

The *Times* urged the careful consideration of Curtis' position, "for the question is not one which can be settled by arguments of abstract justice, but only by a recognition of the hard logic of facts."

Selborne found "Curtis's paper . . . as usual admirable," [102]

---

[101] TA, Lionel Curtis to col. sec., May 1, 1906.
[102] TA, high comm. to lt. gov., Trans., May 1, 1906.

and he proceeded to present the kernel of the assistant colonial secretary's thoughts to the Colonial Office in a long dispatch of May 21, 1906. With it he enclosed two draft ordinances, one to amend the Peace Preservation Ordinance to allow for the issuing of temporary visitors' permits,[103] and the other to amend Law 3 of 1885 so that all Indians in the Transvaal would be forced to reregister—the abolition of the £3 residence tax being provided to sugar the medicine. The two measures were essentially part of a holding action anticipating the advent of responsible government. As Selborne had explained in a speech at Potchefstroom:

No Indians who were not here before the war will be admitted into the country till you have you own Parliament and by your own representatives you can express your own opinions [Hear, Hear]. I give you that assurance as your Governor and High Commissioner, and, therefore, the future is in your hands when you are in the position, the natural position, of freemen to manage your own affairs by your own representatives.[104]

What the British authorities had the greatest difficulty in rationalizing, however, was how an obligation to British Indian subjects so staunchly proclaimed before 1899 had so fortuitously evaporated after the end of the Anglo-Boer War. Lionel Curtis tried to explain the shift in policy. Before the war, he claimed, the Transvaal was essentially a foreign country whose relations with Britain were regulated under the Pretoria and London conventions. The British Government, at that time, had exerted itself to the utmost on behalf of the Indians, "just as it would have . . . on behalf of any other British subjects in any other foreign country." It had held no responsibility to the white inhabitants of the repub-

[103] An ordinance necessary in view of an interpretation by the attorney-general's office that temporary visitors' permits were not legal under the Peace Preservation Ordinance as it stood, and that consequently all Indians issued these "illegal" permits had, in fact, the right to remain permanently in the Transvaal.

[104] TA, high comm. to sec. of state, May 21, 1906, annexure A.

lic. When the Transvaal was annexed to the British Crown, however,

the Imperial Government undertook, and rightly undertook, to administer the country in accordance with the wishes of the people of the country themselves. . . . The Imperial Government was therefore in this position, that if it used the powers which it wielded under Crown Colony Government, which powers were avowedly of a temporary and provisional nature, to give effect to the policy in respect of Asiatics which it had urged upon the late Republican Government, it would violate obligations, no less sacred, imposed upon it through unforseen circumstances towards the European inhabitants of the Colony.

The only honorable course for the British Government to follow, Curtis contended, was to let the settlement of the Asian question await the advent of responsible government. But such a course was not possible due to the flood of unauthorized Indians into the colony.[105] Consequently it was absolutely essential for the Colonial Office to sanction the two draft ordinances. "If this legislation is passed," Curtis concluded, "I am confident that the European inhabitants of this Country will find that this most difficult of all national questions has not been decided by the Imperial Government while holding their power of attorney, but has been held over in fact and as well as in name to be handled by their own respresentatives." [106]

There is good cause to question the reasoning behind Cur-

[105] The position of both the Transvaal and British governments seemed to be based on a heavy illicit Indian immigration into the Transvaal. Yet in January 1904, the registrar of Asiatics had categorically stated: "There is no reason to believe that Asiatics are entering the Colony without authority." TA, registrar of Asiatics to high comm., Jan. 9, 1904. Figures published on August 3, 1906, showed that in the previous six months there had been 128 convictions for illegal entry and that in the preceding three years there had been only 316. TA, Curtis to Duncan, Aug. 3, 1906.

[106] TA, Curtis to Duncan, Aug. 3, 1906, encl. Curtis to Patrick Russell, Aug. 3, 1906.

tis's and Selborne's contentions. Although Chamberlain had not been able to achieve the elimination of the political color bar in the Transvaal and the Orange Free State at the peace table, he had determined that "we cannot purchase peace by leaving the coloured population in a position in which they were before the war, with not even the ordinary civil rights which the Government of Cape Colony had conceded them." [107] As a consequence, the terms offered the Boers on March 2, 1901, had stipulated: "The legal position of coloured persons will . . . be similar to that which they hold in Cape Colony." [108] There was no mention of colored rights in the version of the treaty drafted in Pretoria on May 20, 1902, and despite Chamberlain's questioning of this fact, the treaty as finally signed at Vereeniging did not restore the excised clause. But despite this negation of its humanitarian and imperial philosophy, there seemed to be no undertaking by the British Government, either actual or implicit, to carry out an Asian policy conceived by the white inhabitants of the two former republics.

It seemed much easier, however, to ignore the actual facts of the matter. On September 21, 1906, Selborne informed the Colonial Office that the two draft ordinances had been replaced by a single one (no. 29 of 1906). It had been passed by the legislative council on the previous day and was a much more comprehensive and far-reaching measure than its two predecessors. No longer were all Asians resident in the Transvaal at the time to be eligible for registration, only those who were "lawfully resident." [109] And even this definition was limited to Asians who were already in the Transvaal or Orange River Colony on May 31, 1902, had been

[107] L. M. Thompson, *The Unification of South Africa* (Oxford, 1960), 11.

[108] *Ibid.*

[109] Women were exempted from the workings of the proposed ordinance.

born there since that date, or had entered the colony under the provisions of the Peace Preservation Ordinance of 1903 or under a permit issued between September 1, 1900,[110] and the passage of the proposed measure. All Asian males would have to register before January 1, 1907, and any who entered the colony after the promulgation of the ordinance and who had not previously registered would have to apply for a permit within eight days. Children under eight on January 1 did not need to register; those between eight and sixteen could be registered by their parents or guardians. Any person covered by the provisions of the law who failed, within the time limit, to register either himself or his children was liable, on conviction, to a £100 fine or, on default, to three months at hard labor. After January 1, any Asian over sixteen who failed to produce upon demand a certificate of registration was liable to arrest without a warrant and to expulsion from the Transvaal by magisterial action. Trading licenses would not be issued to unregistered Indians.[111]

The Colonial Office had not been unsympathetic to Selborne's original proposals of May 21. Lord Elgin, the secretary of state for the colonies, had telegraphed Selborne: "I am prepared to accept legislation on the grounds proposed, as the most that can be obtained on the eve of Responsible Government." [112] At first he had also approved the revised course of action. Sir Frederick Graham, one of the assistant undersecretaries, thought that "the legislation in question, while far from effecting all the improvements in the condition of His Majesty's Indian subjects in the Transvaal which His Majesty's Government would desire, has been approved

[110] The date of the amendment of the Peace Preservation Ordinance.

[111] It would be a mistake to conclude that no action was being taken by the Transvaal authorities pending the ratification of the draft ordinances, as this was clearly not the case.

[112] TA, Ind. Off. to Col. Off., Jan. 31, 1906.

by the Secretary of State as removing some of the hardships to which Asiatics are subject, and goes as far as is possible on the eve of responsible government." [113]

Yet, within one month the secretary of state expressed a quite different view. He explained that the situation had entirely changed since his original approval of the two draft ordinances. He voiced annoyance not only at their replacement by a single new enactment, but at the essential redrafting of many provisions and of alterations that affected not only form but substance.[114] It was the Indian reaction which most strongly influenced Elgin. The Transvaal Indians deluged the governor and the secretary of state with telegrams and memorials, and on September 11 they held a mass meeting at which for the first time the use of *satyagraha* as a political weapon was proposed. Gandhi moved the relevant resolution:

In the event of the Legislative Council, the local Government and the Imperial Authorities rejecting the humble prayer of the British Indian community of the Transvaal in connection with the Draft Asiatic Ordinance, this mass meeting of British Indians here assembled solemnly and regretfully resolves that, rather than submit to the galling, tyrannous and Un-British requirements laid down in the above Draft Ordinance, every British Indian in the Transvaal shall submit himself to imprisonment and shall continue to do so until it shall please His Most Gracious Majesty the King Emperor to grant relief.[115]

When another speaker passionately declared that in the name of God he would never submit to the law, it appeared to Gandhi that the scales had been taken from his eyes, and he wondered how he had not before seen that the pledge to initiate *satyagraha* must be taken in the form of a solemn oath. When Gandhi again obtained the floor he was gripped

[113] TA, sec. of state to officer admin. Govt. of Trans., Sept. 27, 1906, encl. Graham to Naoroji, Sept. 22, 1906.

[114] TA, sec. of state to high comm., Nov. 29, 1906.

[115] *Works*, V, 422–423.

by an enthusiasm which he quickly conveyed to his audience:

I wish to explain to this meeting that there is a vast difference between this resolution and every other resolution we have passed up to date and that there is a wide divergence also in the manner of making it. . . . There were cases in which resolutions passed had not been observed by all concerned. Amendments in resolutions and failure to observe resolutions on the part of persons agreeing thereto are ordinary experiences of public life all over the world. But no one ever imports the name of God into such resolutions. . . . To pledge ourselves or to take an oath in the name of . . . God or with Him as witness is not something to be trifled with. If having taken such an oath we violate our pledge we are guilty before God and man.[116]

Gandhi was, as usual, perfectly honest in explaining to the meeting the implications and responsibilities of *satyagraha*.

Every one of us must think out for himself if he has the will and the ability to pledge himself. Resolutions of this nature cannot be passed by a majority vote. Only those who take the pledge can be bound by it. This pledge must not be taken with a view to produce an effect on outsiders. . . . Everyone must only search his own heart, and if the inner voice assures him that he has the requisite strength to carry him through, then only should he pledge himself and then only would his pledge bear fruit.[117]

Clearly *satyagraha* could not be undertaken lightly. The situation to be fought had to be massively and manifestly wrong, a determination which could only be made after the soul had been leeched of all hate, passion, and prejudice through the practice of nonviolence of the mind. Insight, when combined with the spirit of love, could light the path to the Truth. Once the Truth had been discovered, the *satyagrahi* could boldly assert his opposition to the wrong and refuse to cooperate with those attempting to implement it. The *satyagrahi* might indulge in public acts of dissent and

[116] *Satyagraha,* 103–104.   [117] *Ibid.,* 420–422.

disobedience but he could never act violently, for to do so would cloud his insight and set him on a path as misguided as that of his adversary. If physically assaulted, the *satyagrahi* might never defend himself. He had willingly to go to prison and even to his death. He would win his adversary to his side through love, patience, purity, and humility, would convert him through the eloquence of his own suffering.

Gandhi warned his listeners of all the possible consequences they faced if they pledged themselves.

We might have to go to gaol, where we might be insulted. We might have to go hungry and suffer extreme heat or cold. Hard labour might be imposed on us. We might be flogged by rude warders. We might be fined heavily and our property might be attached and held up to auction. . . . Opulent today, we might be reduced to abject poverty tomorrow. We might be deported. Suffering from starvation and similar hardships in gaol, some of us might fall ill and die. In short, therefore, it is not at all impossible that we might have to endure every hardship that we can imagine, and wisdom lies in pledging ourselves on the understanding that we shall have to suffer all that is worst.[118]

Gandhi emphasized that "going to gaol is a unique step, a sacred step, and only by doing so can the Indian community maintain its honour." [119] Optimistically, he concluded: "I can boldly declare, and with certainty, that as long as there is even a handful of men true to their pledge, there can only be one end to the struggle, and that is victory." [120] With a roar of enthusiasm the Transvaal Indians rose to take the

---

[118] *Ibid.*   [119] *Ibid.*, 461–463.

[120] *Ibid.*, 420–422. The *Rand Daily Mail* of September 12, 1906, paid eloquent testimony to the spirit of the Indians: "The united protest of the British Indian community against the Draft Asiatic Ordinance constituted one of the most remarkable gatherings Johannesburg has seen. The size of the meeting, the enthusiasm of the audience—practically the entire Indian population ceased work for the day—and the depth of feeling displayed, formed a striking testimony to the indignation which the proposed legislation aroused."

pledge as *satyagrahis,* and a new political technique was born.

At the time of the Empire Theater meeting the term *satyagraha* had not even been coined. "Passive resistance" was the first appellation used to explain Gandhi's proposed method of combating the government. But Gandhi found it repugnant, as passivity was hardly what he had in mind, and he consequently offered a prize for a better name. Maganlal Gandhi, a second cousin of Gandhi's, suggested "Sadagraha," meaning firmness in a good cause, which Gandhi altered to "Satyagraha"—"satya," truth implying love, and "agraha," firmness. Hence the whole came to mean truth-force or soul-force. When questioned as to the genesis of *satyagraha,* Gandhi replied:

It was the New Testament which really awakened me to the rightness and value of Passive Resistance. When I read in the "Sermon on the Mount" such passages as "resist not him that is evil, but whosoever smiteth thee on thy right cheek turn to him the other also," and "Love your enemies and pray for them that persecute you, that ye may be sons of your Father which is in heaven," I was simply overjoyed, and found my own opinion confirmed where I least expected it. The *Bhagavad Gita* deepened the impression, and Tolstoy's *The Kingdom of God is Within You* gave it permanent form.[121]

Satyagraha was not to be immediately tested. For the moment, the Indians were satisfied to dispatch a deputation consisting of Gandhi and H. O. Ally, a merchant and chairman of the Hamidia Islamic Society, to convey the views of the Transvaal Indian population to the authorities in London. The two delegates met with Lord Morley, the secretary of state for India, and with various groups of M.P.'s. Most significantly, along with Lord Stanley of Alderley, Sir Lepel Griffin, Sir George Birdwood, Sir Henry Cotton, Dadabhai Naoroji, Sir M. Bhownaggree, and other friends of the South

[121] B. R. Nanda, *Mahatma Gandhi* (London, 1958), 96.

African Indians, they were received by Lord Elgin on November 8.[122]

Gandhi denied that the draft ordinance afforded any relief to the Indians as Elgin had been led to believe. He presented his position incisively and with great conviction. The secretary of state soon found himself on the defensive. But, he declared,

> we have to recognise the fact that all over the world there are difficulties arising on the part of the white communities, and we have to reckon with them. I do not say that they ought always to succeed; they certainly ought not to succeed in points of detail which would, in any way, involve oppression. But the fact of there being that sentiment has to be borne in mind when we do deal with matters of this description.[123]

Gandhi's logic was, however, too much for Elgin, and the secretary of state allowed himself to be swayed from his original course. It was no doubt a genuine, if temporary, change of heart, although it could be interpreted as an essentially empty gesture—one of the type that, in the absence of any real risk (for responsible government in the Transvaal was just around the corner), the Colonial Office was from time to time fond of making.

Be that as it may, Elgin informed Selborne that he had been impressed by the strength of Gandhi's arguments:

> They [the Indians] have protested against the Ordinance, not on the ground that it affords inadequate relief, but on the ground that it actually aggravates the disabilities from which they at present suffer; and they have urged that the retention unamended of Law 3 of 1885 would be preferable to the allowance of the new Ordinance.[124]

[122] The South Africa British Indian Committee, which was to play such an important role in the future history of the Indians in the Transvaal, was formed on December 15, 1906, during the course of Gandhi's visit to London. Lord Ampthill became the organization's president and L. W. Ritch its secretary.

[123] *Works*, VI, 113–126.

[124] TA, sec. of state to high comm., Nov. 29, 1906.

It was the conclusion of Elgin's dispatch that caused the greatest dismay in South Africa. It took the high commissioner completely by surprise. "It is of course possible," the secretary of state wrote,

that the British Indians have formed a mistaken view of their own interests in opposing this Ordinance, but it is not easy for me to urge them to accept as advantageous a measure which they repudiate as detrimental to their interests. . . . Under these circumstances, and in view of the near approach of Responsible Government, I think it expedient to announce at once that it is not proposed in the meantime to proceed further with the measure.[125]

Stunned, Selborne telegraphed in reply:

I am placed in a position of serious difficulty by the decision of His Majesty's Government. I always understood that the policy of His Majesty's Government, as of their predecessors, was to maintain the *status quo* until Responsible Government came into existence in the Transvaal, and more than once I pledged my word publicly to that effect both to Europeans and Indians. When I found that the *status quo* was not being maintained I asked and obtained your leave to introduce the ordinance now under your consideration. Not doubting that His Majesty would be advised by you to assent to the Ordinance, I have influenced the Europeans to forego further agitation against the Indians in every way in my power and have succeeded. It is obvious to everyone that the *status quo* is not being maintained, and public proof of the fact exists. . . . I scarcely see what I shall answer if I am accused of not keeping my word, and I fear that exactly that strong feeling which I have laboured so hard and not unsuccessfully to allay would be excited against the Indians.[126]

Elgin was, however, unwilling to extricate Selborne from his difficulties. He insisted that the draft ordinance affected the *status quo* to the detriment of the Indians. It did not, as Selborne had claimed, ameliorate the position of the Indians in the Transvaal.

[125] *Vide* pp. 165–166 and n. 113.
[126] TA, tel., high comm. to sec. of state, Nov. 29, 1906.

At the heart of the whole controversy lay the question in whose favor the *status quo* was being altered. The high commissioner and his staff claimed that great numbers of illegal Indian immigrants were entering the Transvaal.[127] The Indians, of course, denied the charge. To further enrage the inhabitants of the colony and increase the pressure on Selborne, the supreme court of the Transvaal, in the case of N. H. Moosa vs. Rex, upheld the appeal against the conviction of an eleven-year-old child for having entered the Transvaal without a permit and hence illegally. Selborne telegraphed the Colonial Office: "Effect of this decision will be serious in view of the fact that immigration of Indian boys is assuming large proportions." [128] Without the approval of the draft ordinance it might turn to a flood.[129] On November 17, Selborne forwarded a petition from the chambers of commerce of virtually all the Transvaal municipalities, who desired

to respectfully urge upon His Majesty's Government that it is extremely desirable that the Ordinance dealing with Asiatics which has ˙passed the Transvaal Legislature should be brought into operation at the earliest possible date, and it is earnestly hoped that His Majesty will not be advised to disallow the proposed law.[130]

[127] TA, high comm. to sec. of state, Sept. 29, 1906, encl., report of the registrar of Asiatics, M. Chamney, Sept. 27, 1906.

[128] TA, high comm. to sec. of state, Oct. 16, 1906.

[129] Apparently driven to desperation, the Transvaal authorities at times indulged in rather curious reasoning. On September 26, the colonial secretary commented on a petition by some Parsi residents of Johannesburg who claimed that they had enjoyed privileges under the Republic denied them by the British. "They afford," he wrote, "only another illustration of the readiness of the late Government to allow evasion of its laws when the strict application became inconvenient, or when influence was brought to bear in favour of fortunate individuals." TA, col. sec. (P. Duncan) to act. lt. gov., Sept. 26, 1906.

[130] TA, tel., high comm. to sec. of state, Nov. 17, 1906.

But Elgin stood firm. Perhaps he recalled the words Sir M. Bhownaggree had addressed to a previous secretary of state. "Local autonomy," the Indian member of Parliament had written,

confers upon its possessors under the British flag not the right to undermine the noblest traditions associated with that emblem— otherwise the term "self-government" applied to the overseas possessions of the king would be but a synonym for Imperial anarchy. . . . To gain for the British connection a deeper affection and regard on the part of the Colonies is a great and beneficent task, but its value and significance will be vastly curtailed if the affection of the Indian people for king and empire is undermined by the continuance of the state of affairs in South Africa.[131]

Possibly the secretary of state had even been moved by the passionate (if somewhat awkward) words addressed to him by some Transvaal Indian youths, well aware of the paradox of empire, who were studying at Lincoln's Inn. "It is curious," they had written,

that they who are now being given a liberal education in England are so well aware of freedom, etc., that they will not be allowed to live as freemen in one part of the British Empire which is their home.

Having lived in England, and having breathed its free atmosphere, and having received every consideration in this country, Your Lordship will easily appreciate the anxiety the prospect of the . . . Ordinance engenders. We are here, being nurtured on the teachings of Benson [sic], Austen [sic], and other English writers whose names are a watchword for liberty and independence, and we could hardly believe that anything of the kind referred to [in the ordinance] . . . would possibly apply to us.[132]

[131] TA, tel., Bhownaggree to Lyttelton, Dec. 21, 1905.
[132] TA, Trans. Ind. students at Lincoln's Inn to sec. of state, Nov. 1906.

Unfortunately, subsequent developments cast some doubt on the noble earl's purpose, and even events of the moment indicated a greater concern with form than with substance —an apprehension lest the crisis in the Transvaal shred the veil of decency surrounding the imperial scene. When all the rhetoric is put aside, what the Colonial Office was so desperate to achieve was not the welfare of the Indian population but the avoidance of embarrassment. What happened after the granting of responsible government to the Transvaal was not greatly its concern. For the moment, however, the British Government could not sanction the draft Asiatic ordinance, because, as the secretary of state put it, "for measures passed at this juncture His Majesty's Government cannot disclaim direct responsibility." [133]

[133] TA, sec. of state to high comm., Dec. 10, 1906.

VI / The Battle Joined—
Satyagraha in the
Transvaal, 1907–1910

IT IS impossible fully to understand the Indian problem in the Transvaal and the Orange River Colony without taking into account the political changes that occurred in the two former republics in the years following the Anglo-Boer War. In the first months after the signing of the peace treaty, the Afrikaner leaders held themselves aloof from proffered opportunities in the administration. Botha and Smuts both claimed, in 1903, that the time was not yet ripe for the establishment of representative institutions in the Transvaal, and they consequently refused the seats they were offered in the legislative council and on the labor commission. By 1904, however, Botha had modified his attitude, and in January of the following year he formed the *Het Volk* party, dedicated to reconciliation with the British and to the rapid achievement of self-government. Developments along similar lines occurred in the Orange River Colony.

Although the Afrikaners had now turned their eyes toward self-government, it was the British population that was the most restive. Political uncertainty at home and the high emotions generated by the Chinese labor question, however, convinced Milner and Lyttelton that the moment was not propitious for the greatly increased involvement of the colonists in the conduct of their own affairs. The Lyttelton Constitution delayed the advent of responsible government in the Transvaal, and it was not the intention of its framers that the scheme should be essentially stillborn. But before it could come into operation, the Conservative ministry of Arthur Balfour was replaced by a Liberal regime headed by Henry Campbell-Bannerman. Largely through the influence of Smuts, who was in London at the time, Campbell-Bannerman became convinced of the desirability of immediately granting responsible government to the two conquered territories.[1] Consequently, the British Government issued letters patent instituting responsible government in the Transvaal in December 1906, and in the Orange River Colony in June 1907.

The general election held in the Transvaal on February 20 resulted in the election of the *Het Volk* ministry led by Botha. On March 21, the Transvaal Parliament was formally opened by Lord Selborne and Botha sworn in as the colony's first prime minister. Smuts assumed the post of colonial secretary in the new government and with it the responsibility for the "Asiatic question." Now, at last, the two great protagonists, Smuts and Gandhi, came face to face. On the surface how different they seemed. The two leaders, were, indeed, born within a year of each other. But one was reared in a staunchly Calvinist home on the lush farmlands of the Cape of Good Hope, just a few miles from Cape Town; while the other was part of a Hindu family of the Vaishya caste in the tiny and arid state of Porbander on the west coast of India. Gandhi and Smuts were both, however, products of religious and social orthodoxy—though neither was willing to accept, unquestioningly, the inflexible precepts inherited from his

[1] As early as April 1904, Alfred Lyttelton had predicted to Milner: "When the other side come in, they will be confronted with their dishonest and insincere utterances about Chinese labour by the ignorant and sincere of their fellows [the Liberals had opposed the Chinese labor importation scheme], and I am convinced that they will extricate themselves from a painful dilemma by granting self-government to the new Colonies *sans phrase*." A. P. Thornton, *The Habit of Authority* (Toronto, 1966), 302; Lyttelton to Milner, April 26, 1904.

ancestors. Although each was intimately linked to his ethnic roots, both tended to be philosophical and experimental in outlook and world view.

The confrontation between Smuts, the acknowledged defender of white supremacy in what he deemed to be a white man's country, and Gandhi, the embarrassingly articulate reminder that the British Empire must, above all, stand for the equality of all subjects of the crown, had a telling impact on both their lives. Their encounter was the prologue to two great careers (although Smuts had already been the attorney-general of the South African Republic and styled a general in the Boer Army). At first Gandhi, even more than Smuts, was deeply enamored of the British constitution and the principles he thought stood in back of it. As he himself said, he grafted *Snell on Equity* to the *Bhagavadgita*.[2] Later, of course, it was Smuts who emerged as the great imperial statesman, and Gandhi who proved to be the solvent of the British Empire in India. Too much is often made of the respect in which Smuts and Gandhi held each other and of their mutual affection. In later years they entertained, at least to some degree, these sentiments. But during their eight years of conflict, the sentiments were more latent than real.

At the initial session of the newly constituted legislature, the government introduced an Asiatic law amendment bill which was essentially the same piece of legislation disallowed by the British Government some four months previously. The bill (Act 2 of 1907) was passed with unseemly haste (within twenty-four hours to be exact), and the news of this event was joyously acclaimed throughout the Transvaal. The member from Barberton (Loveday) represented not only his own constituency but all the white colonists when he called the act "the first step to stop what may mean the extinction of the white races in this country by immigration from the

[2] M. K. Gandhi, *The Story of My Experiments with Truth* (Boston, 1957), 265.

East. It has been rightly stated," he continued, "that this measure should appeal to every individual in this country, and it does appeal to every individual." [3]

Where the white colonists were ecstatic, the Indians were distraught; for the Colonial Office seemed totally unperturbed by the measure. Gandhi, in black despair, wrote bitterly of the underhanded subterfuge with which Elgin had misled him and the Indian community. The secretary of state had disguised himself as the Indians' protector, Gandhi contended, at the very same time he was assuring the Transvaal authorities that, despite the negativing of Ordinance 29, a similar enactment passed by the Transvaal legislature after the advent of responsible government would receive his immediate assent. [4] "In Johannesburg," Gandhi later wrote, recalling his return, "the sole topic of conversation was the trick played upon us by Lord Elgin and the Imperial Government. Our disappointment in South Africa was . . . deep." [5]

Gandhi's resentment was not surprising. Defeat had followed too quickly on the heels of apparent triumph. And his accusations against Elgin seem not to be totally devoid of substance. When he compared the Asiatic Law Amendment Act with Ordinance 29, the secretary of state declared: "The Act which is now submitted has behind it a very different weight of authority. It has been introduced by the first responsible Ministry of the Colony, and has been passed unanimously by both Houses of the new Legislature." [6] Recalling his imperial obligations, however, Elgin felt constrained to add:

I consider it my duty to place on record that His Majesty's Government do not consider the position of the Asiatics lawfully resident in the Transvaal, as settled by this Act, to be satisfactory;

[3] Transvaal *Hansard,* March 21, 1907.   [4] *Satyagraha,* 124–126.
[5] *Ibid.*

[6] NAI, papers with acts, India Act XIV of 1914, sec. of state to gov., May 9, 1907.

that they adhere to the opinions which have been expressed by successive Secretaries of State as to the desirability of relaxing the restrictions to which Asiatics are at present subject; and that they commend this view to the Transvaal Government in the hope that it may be carefully considered how far practical effect can be given to it.[7]

His role as enunciator of the imperial philosophy fulfilled, the secretary of state concluded with an almost audible sigh of relief at his recently reduced responsibilities. "They [the British Government] feel," he wrote Selborne, "that they would not be justified in offering resistance to the general will of the Colony clearly expressed by its first elected representatives; and I am accordingly to inform you that His Majesty will not be advised to exercise his power of disallowance with respect to the Act." [8]

Having tasted some measure of success in opposing Ordinance 29 in 1906, the Indians were not about to acquiesce quietly to the promulgation of exactly the same law in a new guise in 1907. On March 29 a mass meeting of protest was held in Johannesburg. The Indians did not so much object to reregistration as they did to the fact that the issuing of new certificates and ten-digit fingerprinting were to be compulsory. On April 7 the British Indian Association telegraphed the secretary of state that the Indian community was willing to cooperate in a program of voluntary registration.[9]

The test of strength between the Indians and the white government of the Transvaal cannot be conceived of only in terms of the Asiatic Law Amendment Act. In the early months of its new life, the colony passed an Immigrants Restriction Act (Act 15 of 1907) which at last repealed the Peace Preservation Ordinance of 1903. In section 2, subsection 1, the now tried and true formula for excluding Indians without specifically mentioning them was established:

[7] *Ibid.*   [8] *Ibid.*

[9] TA, Brit. Ind. Assoc. to Col. Off., April 7, 1907.

Any person who when asked whether within or outside this Colony by a duly authorised officer shall be unable through deficient education to write out (from dictation or otherwise) and sign in the characters of an European language an application for permission to enter this Colony or such other document as such officer may require . . .

would be deemed a prohibited immigrant. The Asiatic Law Amendment Act and the Immigrants Restriction Act were designed to supplement each other. Subsection 4 of section 2 of the latter law implied that all Indians who had not registered under the provisions of the former would be considered prohibited immigrants, and section 8 forbade such persons from acquiring licenses to trade and to own or lease property.

Attacks against the two pieces of legislation were mounted in Westminster by the South Africa British Indian Committee under the leadership of its secretary, L. W. Ritch, but most particularly by the Transvaal Indians themselves. Of every persuasion and walk of life, they combined under Gandhi's leadership to fight the common menace. Their letters to the secretary of state were frequently highly emotional. A group of Punjabis and Pathans, nearly all ex-soldiers, asked,

as men and British Indian soldiers, who are proud to have risked their lives in the cause of the Empire and have braved privations of war, to be spared the degradation of imprisonment or deportation, and further wish that the King-Emperor will command that they be shot by Generals Botha and Smuts on one of the battlefields of South Africa, where they had been under fire while serving their King-Emperor and the British Empire.[10]

Actions were, of course, combined with words. Picketing of registration offices was systematically organized. It was to be peaceful and free from all display of ill-temper or foul language. The registration officers moved from town to town, with little or nothing to do. Less than 5 per cent of

[10] TA, Pathans and Punjabis to sec. of state, Sept. 14, 1908.

the Indian community took out "the bond of slavery," though the time limit for registration was extended again and again. To shame the cowardly and steel the weak, the names of "blacklegs"—the "piano players," as they were also called—were periodically published in *Indian Opinion*. But the appeal was to self-respect, not fear. As time went on, more and more newspapers throughout the empire rallied to the Indian cause.

Gandhi was aware of the transcendental nature of his crusade and its universal meaning. "Indians in the Transvaal," he wrote, "will stagger humanity without shedding a drop of blood." With his faith in the British Empire and its ruling philosophy still unshaken, Gandhi concluded:

It is because I consider myself to be a lover of the Empire for what I have learned to be its beauties that, seeing, rightly or wrongly, in the Asiatic Law Amendment Act seeds of danger to it, I have advised my countrymen at all costs to resist the Act in the most peaceful, and shall I add, Christian manner.[11]

In India, indignation was expressed at public meetings and in the press. *Kesari,* a Marathi weekly, declared that

when any coloured people venture to set their foot in a white man's country the white wolves manage to make their lives unbearable to them. Among these persecuted races, the lot of the Indians is worst for while their own country is freely exploited by the whites, they receive nothing but insults and indignities whenever they go to a white man's country. Our rulers had hitherto succeeded in deluding us into believing in the alleged benefits accruing from the glorious world-wide British Empire, but we are being gradually undeceived and are experiencing the bitter truth of the adage that blood is thicker than water. The Transvaalers had been treating us worse than slaves and all our appeals for protection to the Imperial Government had hitherto proved futile. . . . The present brutal and insulting treatment of the Indians in the British Colonies is sure one day to prove one of the main causes of the downfall of the British Empire.[12]

[11] *Works,* VII, 468; Gandhi to Johannesburg *Star,* Dec. 30, 1907.

[12] NAI, Reports of the Native Press, Bombay, *Kesari,* Feb. 4, 1908.

Although the two acts were so closely related, Indian agitation tended to center, at first, on the Asiatic Law Amendment Act and particularly on the mandatory reregistration clause and the administrative regulation demanding the recording of all ten fingerprints. The agitation on the latter point took the Transvaal authorities by surprise. Selborne reported that his ministers were quite prepared to compromise on the issue but they anticipated that "Indians will raise same objections to five fingerprints as to ten, as their objection is more to the spirit of the law than its details." The Transvaal Government was willing to take the signatures of educated and well-known Indians in place of fingerprints if the Indians would only register.[13] But the fingerprinting and compulsory registration questions were so intertwined that it was impossible to settle the one without the other. Still, it must have been cheering for Selborne to receive the full, if sometimes uneasy, cooperation of London. In 1908, Winston Churchill, then undersecretary in the Colonial Office, telegraphed the governor:

Please tell Botha I am going to support his government most strongly on the Indian question as I thoroughly understand the views of white South Africa.

There will be Parliamentary attacks from our side and from Opposition but the Government majority will be perfectly solid.[14]

The *Times,* in one of its more lucid and eloquent moments, remarked:

As a nation we have little reason to be proud of the treatment now being meted out to our fellow subjects in the Transvaal. . . . If the Republican Government chastised the Indians with whips, since the annexation of the Transvaal they have been chastised by scorpions. . . . .

The wrongs of the Transvaal Indian community will soon be

[13] TA, tel., gov. to sec. of state, Jan. 28, 1908.
[14] TA, draft of tel., undersec., col. off., to high comm., Jan 25, 1908.

known and brooded over by the dumb millions who look to us as all-powerful in India, and, when evil is done, will be used for all they are worth by the agitators against our rule. And the worst of it is that their grievance will be just. Nor can we wash our hands of the business merely by casting the responsibility on the Colonial Government, for Mr. Harold Cox points out with undeniable force that His Majesty's Ministers specially reserved the right of the Imperial Government to deal with questions of this nature.[15]

Others, including Sir Richard Solomon, at that time the Transvaal's agent-general in London, and the Cape's J. X. Merriman, certainly no friend of the Indians, were equally discommoded. The latter felt that rightly or wrongly a certain number of Indians had been admitted into South Africa and that consequently they should not be unnecessarily persecuted. He wrote to Smuts:

If you persist, as you are entitled to do, you will succeed, but I much fear that you will alienate the bulk of liberal opinion in England, you will give the Imperial government a most serious blow in her most vital part—India, and you will above all furnish a pretext for a great deal of mischievous interference in native matters.[16]

Meanwhile the Indians continued their agitation and as the time set for registration expired, many were tried for refusing to obey the "Black Act" and were sent to jail.[17] Exas-

[15] The *Times*, Jan. 7, 1908.

[16] W. K. Hancock, *Smuts*, I, *The Sanguine Years, 1870–1919* (Cambridge, 1962), 332–333.

[17] The whole question of legal representation for Indians undergoing trial was of some importance. On April 25, 1907, Gandhi delineated his position. "If anyone is prosecuted under the new Act, and if the person concerned holds a valid permit or is otherwise entitled to reside in the Transvaal, Mr. Gandhi will defend him in the court free of charge. If the case is to be heard outside Johannesburg, the Association will pay Mr. Gandhi's railway fare; but if the place he is required to visit has made no contribution to the British Indian Association already, the Association will collect the dues. . . . If a person does not

perated, Selborne wrote Smuts: "Mr. Gandhi ardently desires martyrdom, and when a man ardently desires such a thing . . . one's natural instinct is to give it to him." [18] As it turned out, Gandhi was tried on January 10 before a vast crowd, mostly of Indians. He pleaded guilty and asked the court for the maximum sentence of six months hard labor and a £500 fine. The magistrate, however, not altogether sharing Selborne's feelings, saw fit to impose a punishment of two months' imprisonment at hard labor. On January 28, Gandhi, his compatriot Thambi Naidoo, and Leung Quinn,[19] the leader of the Transvaal Chinese and a close collaborator of Gandhi's, addressed a proposal to General Smuts, the colonial secretary in the Transvaal Government, which resulted in a compromise between the two protagonists.

The Indians would indeed register, but they would do so voluntarily and not as a result of compulsion. As for the fingerprints, Gandhi was willing to allow all ten of his to be recorded. "My own view of the matter," he explained to his colleagues, "is that all of us should give digit impressions without the least hesitation. But those who have conscientious objection to giving them or think it to be derogatory to their self-respect, will not be obliged to give those

---

hold a licence and is therefore arrested, he will not be defended free of charge. But a person who has been refused a licence for having failed to take out a new permit will be defended free of charge. Mr. Gandhi will not, with or without fees, defend those who do not desire a gaol sentence." *Works,* VI, 495–496; *Indian Opinion,* April 25, 1907.

[18] W. K. Hancock and J. Van der Poel, *Selections from the Smuts Papers* (Cambridge, 1966) II, 361–366; Selborne to Smuts, Nov. 30, 1907.

[19] The Chinese, some 1,300 of whom fought side by side with the Indians, tended to be even more determined than the Indians, and Gandhi had actually to chide them for their "childish obstinacy" about giving fingerprints. *Works,* VIII, 107; *Indian Opinion,* Feb 29, 1908. On March 28, however, Gandhi admitted: "The Chinese have done something remarkable. They have surpassed us in unity, cleanliness, culture and generosity." *Ibid.,* 162–164.

impressions." [20] On February 3, Selborne reported on the compromise to the Colonial Office. He said that the agreement had resulted from Gandhi's realization that the government would under no circumstances abandon the essential objects for which the Asiatic Law Amendment Act had been passed. The settlement, while securing the government's aims, would enable the Asians to retire without loss of dignity from a position that had become untenable.

The compromise did not, however, please the entire Indian community. To some it seemed a defeat. As Gandhi, whom Smuts had released from jail, explained the nature of the agreement to a meeting of the Indian community in Johannesburg, he was closely questioned and even heckled. A Pathan in the crowd was particularly ugly. He accused Gandhi of having sold the Indians to Smuts for £15,000. "I swear with Allah as my witness," he roared, "that I will kill any man who takes the lead in applying for registration." [21] Gandhi calmly replied: "To die by the hand of a brother, rather than by disease or in such other way, cannot be for me a matter of sorrow." [22] But some of the Pathans were not mollified. On February 10, as Gandhi, accompanied by Essop Mia and Thambi Naidoo, approached the registration office to take out, in accordance with his public promise, the first voluntary registration certificate, he was set upon by Mir Alam, "fully six feet in height and of a large and powerful frame," [23] and several companions. "I took several blows on my left ribs," he recalled a few days later.

Even now I find breathing difficult. My upper lip has a cut on one side. I have a bruise above the left eye and a wound on the forehead. In addition, there are minor injuries on my right hand and left knee. I do not remember the manner of the assault, but people say I fell unconscious with the first blow which was delivered with a stick. Then my assailants struck me with an iron bar and a stick, and they also kicked me. Thinking me dead, they stopped. I only remember having been beaten up. I have an im-

[20] *Satyagraha,* 161.　　[21] *Ibid.,* 162.　　[22] *Ibid.*　　[23] *Ibid.,* 167.

pression that, as the blows started, I uttered the words "He Rama!" [the very words he was to utter some forty years later as he fell mortally wounded]. . . . As I came to, I got up with a smile. In my mind there was not the slightest anger or hatred for the assailants.[24]

Gandhi was severely mauled, and it took him more than ten days to recover sufficient strength to resume his normal activities. It was not to be the last attempt on his life during the months and years of conflict that still lay ahead in South Africa, for he was unpopular both with the whites and some extreme elements in the Indian community.

The apparent settlement of the registration controversy still left a number of unresolved issues. The relevant departments of the British Government, although they did not urge the disallowance of the Immigrants Restriction Act, held their reservations. The India Office was disturbed at the failure of the act to provide for visitors' permits and by its apparent intention of permanently excluding from the Transvaal even the most educated Indians. Lord Morley, the secretary of state for India, also feared that Indians who had established domicile in the colony before 1902 but had temporarily absented themselves might, in future, be forbidden entrance as prohibited immigrants.[25] A few days later, the India Office again addressed the Colonial Office on the same subject. This time the secretary of state focused on the education test." The effect of Section 2(4) in the present bill, as is recognised by Lord Elgin," the India Office pointed out, "will be to exclude perpetually from a portion of His Majesty's Dominions all British Indian subjects, however high their social status or educational attainments, who have not already acquired domiciliary rights." [26]

The Colonial Office, although it agreed with the India Office, was less sharp in its criticism. It "greatly regretted" the

[24] *Works*, VIII, 93–94.
[25] NAI, March 1908, procs. 5–6, Ind. Off. to Col. Off., Oct. 31, 1907.
[26] *Ibid.*, Ind. Off. to Col. Off., Nov. 11, 1907.

language test, but only required the Transvaal to change the bill slightly so as to allow distinguished Indians and high public officials of Asian descent to enter the colony as visitors and to provide magisterial review in the cases of persons expelled from the Transvaal as dangerous to peace, order and good government.[27] With little hesitation the Transvaal Government agreed to the home government's stipulations.[28]

The apparently successful negotiation of the compromise likewise did not mean that the Transvaal Indians were now satisfied with their lot. Not surprisingly, their major dissatisfaction also concerned the Immigrants Restriction Act. On July 27, 1908, the South Africa British Indian Committee forwarded to the Colonial Office a letter from the British Indian Association in which the signatories complained about the designation as prohibited immigrants attached to Indians, whether inside or outside the Transvaal, who held Republican registration certificates for which they had paid either three or twenty-five pounds; and, concomitantly, that Indian refugees who had not yet returned to the Transvaal should in future be considered prohibited immigrants.[29]

Other more minor matters continued to obtrude themselves upon the scene—most significantly, with the introduction of a draft municipal bill, licensing, the curfew, sidewalk restrictions, and limitations on the use of trains and trams. On June 15, 1908, Harold Cox questioned prevailing practices, in the Commons, calling forth the usual minute from Botha. The prime minister pointed out that power to make by-laws "prohibiting the use of the sidewalks of any public street . . . by *coloured persons* who are not respectably dressed and well conducted" was a municipal rather than colonial prerogative. The purpose of such restrictions, he explained, was to guard "against the danger of . . . [European] women and children being jostled off the pavement

27 *Ibid.,* sec. of state to gov., Nov. 27, 1907.
28 *Ibid.,* tel., gov. to sec. of state, Dec. 3, 1907.
29 TA, So. Af. Brit. Ind. Comm. to Col. Off., July 27, 1908.

by unsavory and ill-mannered coloured people." In fact, Botha insisted, these regulations were rarely enforced:

Respectable and well conducted Asiatics and even South African natives can be seen daily walking on the sidewalks of Johannesburg and Pretoria . . . and no one objects. The whole question of the use of sidewalks by coloured persons is one which is in itself unimportant so long as the *status quo* is maintained, but any attempt to legalise the existing practice of tolerance will arouse the bitterest opposition and ferment anti-colour prejudice among the European community to a dangerous extent.[30]

In the town of Vrededorp, an attempt was made by legislation passed in 1906 to deprive Indians of rights in a location they had inhabited since the days of the South African Republic. Considerable agitation accompanied by acrimonious discussion ensued. The Indians won a partial victory when Act 27 of 1907 amended earlier legislation and granted them the right to live in the location for another four years.

Under the definitions clause of Act 35 of 1908—"To Consolidate and Amend the law relating to Prospecting and Mining for Precious Metals and Base Metals and to provide for matters incidental thereto"—Indians were defined as colored persons and were prohibited from dealing in precious metals (section 114). They could not hold or sublet property on proclaimed ground (section 130), nor could they reside on proclaimed ground except in bazaars or locations (section 131)—the only exception being for the bona fide servants of white men (section 130). Once the secretary of state was assured that the rights of colored persons already in the mining areas would be protected and that the governor would have the right to exempt individuals from the workings of the law, he gave the measure his blessing.[31] The Government of India limited itself to protesting the failure of the

[30] TA, minute no. 463, July 29, 1908, encl. in gov. gen. to sec. of state, Aug. 3, 1908.

[31] TA, sec. of state to gov., Dec. 28, 1908.

mining bill to differentiate between the various levels of Indian society. Had the law applied only to so-called lower-class Indians the viceroy and his advisers would have been perfectly satisfied.[32] Transvaal Act 32 of 1908, the Shop Hours Act, was a disguised form of attack on Indian merchants. Debate on the measure indicated that it was directed against peddlers, hawkers, and those in the retail business who, by working long hours, competed too successfully with white merchants.

The compromise seemed, however, to lull all the interested parties to sleep. Only the Government of India remained apprehensive over what Lord Minto, the viceroy, articulately described as the steady and progressive erosion of Indian rights in the Transvaal.[33] The Colonial Office was highly optimistic. "The immediate causes of friction have been removed," it wrote to the India Office. "The settlement seems to be on the lines of the suggestion for the amelioration of the position of Asiatics put forward in the . . . despatch from the Government of India." But, the Colonial Office continued,

Lord Elgin is fully alive to the disabilities unconnected with the Asiatic Law Amendment and Immigrants Restriction Acts, to which Asiatics in the Transvaal are still subjected. In such a matter, however, the governing factor must necessarily be the state of public opinion in the Colony, and in Lord Elgin's judgment it would be useless at the present time to endeavour to secure further concessions for resident Asiatics.[34]

The state of enduring peace which it was thought had been ushered in by the compromise was not, after all, to develop. Rather a crisis, more severe than any heretofore imagined, was destined to erupt in the Transvaal. The first hint of a break came on May 13, when Gandhi asked Smuts to

[32] NAI, July 1908, proc. 1, minuting of July 6, 1908.

[33] NAI, Dept. of Comm. and Ind. (Em.) no. 9, viceroy in council to Ind. Off., Jan. 30, 1908.

[34] TA, Col. Off. to Ind. Off., April 1, 1908.

dispel the rumor that Asians who, at the time of the compromise, were outside the colony were being asked to register under the provisions of the Asiatic Law Amendment Act.[35] It soon became clear that Gandhi had been correctly informed. E. F. C. Lane, the general's private secretary, wrote Gandhi: "General Smuts does not agree with your interpretation of the terms of the settlement. Indians who may come in now must apply for registration [under the law]. General Smuts hopes, therefore, that you will use your influence to persuade fresh Indian entrants to apply for registration accordingly." [36] Thus the stage was set for a renewal of passive resistance (as the technique continued to be known as in South Africa).

Disagreement on the new entrant question led to a confrontation on a much more fundamental issue. The heart of the settlement, the Indians contended, was a promise made by the colonial secretary that the Asiatic Law Amendment Act would be repealed as soon as voluntary registration was implemented. Smuts denied that he had ever made such a commitment. "I could not promise," he argued,

that a certain class of the population here should be in a state outside the law. All I could say was that, pending the meeting of Parliament, there should be this interim state of affairs, and that as soon as Parliament met, it should deal with the situation. It was impossible for me to promise that at a future date Asiatics coming into this country should be left to register as they wished. That was a request with which I could not comply, and which the law of the land would not sanction.[37]

Letters exchanged between Smuts and Gandhi bear out the general's contention. However, what transpired at a meeting held on January 30, when the two protagonists met face to face, is not so clear. Both have been judged honorable men by history, yet they told diametrically opposite stories

---

[35] *Works,* VIII, 230; Gandhi to Smuts, May 13, 1908. [36] *Ibid.,* 248.
[37] TA, gov. to sec. of state, encl. 2, *Transvaal Leader,* Aug. 22, 1908.

concerning what occurred. Smuts resolutely repeated his rejection of the Indian claim: Gandhi countered by rendering his version of the conversation. "I have consulted General Botha," he quoted the colonial secretary as saying, "and I assure you that I will repeal the Asiatic Act as soon as most of you have undergone voluntary registration. . . . I do not wish there should be a recurrence of the trouble and I wish to respect the feelings of your people." [38] Regardless of the truth of the matter, there was no gainsaying the Indians' full cooperation in the program of voluntary registration. Smuts admitted that 9,158 Indians, out of a population of no more than ten to twelve thousand, had voluntarily applied for registration,[39] and that only seventy had refused to allow their fingerprints to be recorded.[40]

Act 36 of 1908, "An Act to Validate Registration of certain Asiatics to comply with the provisions of Act 2 of 1907 and to make further provisions for the Registration of Asiatics," implemented the Transvaal Government's version of the compromise. Several concessions were made to the Indians. The definition of "Asiatic" was amended so as to omit all reference to the definition, odious to the Indians, provided in Law 3 of 1885. Any male Asian, outside the Transvaal at the time the act came into effect, who had been resident in the Transvaal for three years before October 11, 1899, was to be eligible for registration if he applied within one year. Minors were not to be registered separately. They were to be noted on their guardian's certificate and to apply on their own behalf upon reaching the age of sixteen. Asians refused certificates of registration by the registrar of Asiatics could appeal to a magistrate specially appointed for the purpose and ultimately to the supreme court. In obedience to

[38] *Satyagraha*, 156.

[39] Gandhi claimed that the rest would have registered voluntarily if the government had not halted the procedure on May 9. TA, Gandhi and Essop Mia to speaker and members of leg. assem., Aug. 13, 1908.

[40] *Vide* n. 37.

the wishes of the British Government, the right to issue temporary permits to distinguished Asians desiring to visit the Transvaal was vested in the governor in council rather than in the minister as heretofore. Finally, applications for trading licenses could be signed in English, thumb impressions to be required only from those who could not fulfill this requirement. On the negative side, from the Indian point of view, was the new stipulation that Indians entitled to registration, who were outside the colony, would have to apply from that place rather than be given eight days within the Transvaal to conduct their cases as had been allowable under Act 2. Most significantly, the act legalized the voluntary registration that had resulted from the compromise between the Transvaal Government and the Indians, and which was illegal under the terms of Act 2 of 1907. But Act 2 itself was not repealed.

The Indians strongly opposed Act 36 in spite of the various improvements it made in their condition. They contended that the act unfairly deprived Indians outside the Transvaal, who enjoyed domiciliary status, of the right to return. They objected to the classification of holders of old Republican registration certificates who had not reregistered as essentially prohibited immigrants.[41] And, of course, they were deeply aroused by the failure of the Transvaal Government to repeal Act 2 of 1907. As usual, it was largely a matter of principle. Indian registration was already a *fait accompli*. It was the question whether the registration was technically voluntary or compulsory that was at issue. Without the repeal of Act 2, the mailed fist was too apparent behind the velvet glove, and the thin veil of self-respect provided by the concept of a totally voluntary registration was forfeited.

On August 16, the Indians formally commenced their struggle. At a meeting outside the Hamidia Mosque in Jo-

[41] TA, So. Af. Brit. Ind. Comm. to Col. Off., July 27, 1908, encl. Brit. Ind. Assoc. to col. sec., July 26, 1908.

hannesburg, some 3,000 Indians from all over the Transvaal gathered to hear their leaders, who included Essop Ismail Mia, the chairman of the British Indian Association, Leung Quinn, and, of course, Gandhi himself. The *Transvaal Leader* of August 17 described what happened at the close of the session:

A large three-legged pot was filled with the registration certificates, about 1,000 in all, and about 500 trading licenses. Parafin was then poured in, and the certificates set on fire amid a scene of wildest enthusiasm. The crowd hurrahed and shouted themselves hoarse; hats were thrown in the air, and whistles blown. One Indian . . . walked on to the platform and setting alight his certificate held it aloft. The Chinese then mounted the platform and put their certificates in with the others. For a considerable time it was impossible for any leaders on the platform to make themselves heard.

The battle was now fully joined, and it again involved the immigration issue as well as registration—for the two questions were inextricably linked. The Indians immediately appealed to the Colonial and India offices. The former was at first silent, and the latter gave little solace. While he ventured "to point out that the Transvaal Government is entirely responsible for the vexation caused" [42] in regard to Indian immigration, "Lord Morley gladly recognises that [Act 36 of 1908] . . . if adequately represented in the very brief summary which is before him, . . . makes substantial concessions to the Indian community in the Colony." And even on immigration, "Lord Morley does not, of course, wish to reopen this question, which has been definitely settled." [43]

Selborne, for his part, placed constant pressure on the British Government for the rapid approval of Act 36. "It is not easy," he wrote,

to resist the conclusion that Mr. Gandhi and his friends were not very anxious to arrive at a settlement. At present the passive re-

[42] TA, Ind. Off. to Col. Off., Sept. 3, 1908.   [43] *Ibid.*

sistance movement continues, but there are, I am informed, grounds for thinking that the rank and file Asiatic community do not entirely share the views of their leaders, and that, in the absence of reasonable justification for it, the agitation will die a natural death before long.[44]

The governor, however, was indulging in one of his frequent flights of fancy; the Indians were both united and determined, and their struggle was attracting attention throughout the British Empire. The viceroy telegraphed the India Office:

Protests have been received from all parts of India against the treatment to which British Indians are being subjected. Public opinion greatly exercised on the subject. It is most desirable in my opinion that some settlement of the questions in dispute should be arrived at without delay as in present circumstances we regard as a very serious matter the political effect in this country of the measures taken to enforce the law.[45]

Lord Crewe emphasized the unfortunate effect the Indian question in the Transvaal was having in Britain and India; but, he wrote to Selborne,

I am unable to find . . . any sufficient reason for a refusal on the part of the Indians to accept the Act of 1908. I find no promise to repeal the Act of 1907 in the correspondence in which terms of the compromise were set forth. It is not denied that in the subsequent negotiations as to the best method of giving legal sanction to the compromise, the Transvaal Colonial Secretary did consider whether the Act of 1907 might not be repealed. But it is clear that this was only discussed as one of several possible courses, and it seems to me impossible to base a demand for repeal on this fact or to make it the ground for any breach of faith against the Colonial Secretary or the government on whose behalf he was negotiating.[46]

[44] TA, gov. to sec. of state, Sept. 7, 1908.
[45] TA, tel., sec. of state to gov., Oct. 23, 1908, encl. tel., viceroy to Ind. Off.
[46] TA, sec. of state to gov., Dec. 15, 1908.

The merging of the registration and immigration problems into a single issue was inevitable, as failure to register or to produce on demand a registration certificate in effect turned an Indian into a prohibited immigrant and permitted his expulsion from the Transvaal. The Indians had made their case clear on the matter of registration. They now turned to the immigration question. Gandhi had no desire to see the large-scale immigration of Indians and Chinese who could claim no prewar residence.[47] He was, however, determined to secure the *right* of Indians to immigrate to the Transvaal on a basis of equality with other British subjects. What resulted from administrative practice did not so much concern him, for he was pragmatic enough to understand that true parity was impossible. Gandhi consequently conceded that principle would be satisfied if the Transvaal Government admitted six educated Indians a year. As the secretary of state put it when telegraphing Selborne, "British Indians appear now to realise that your government will not concede admission of educated Indians generally and ask as I understand that maximum of six highly educated British Indians shall be admissable as of right in any one year." [48] The suggestion seemed reasonable enough to Crewe and he presumed that "Ministers would not object to give an assurance of this kind with a view to facilitate the final settlement." [49]

Before events could proceed further, however, Gandhi, on October 7, while returning from Natal, refused to produce his registration certificate and was arrested and charged before a magistrate at Volksrust with having violated section nine of the regulations framed under Act 36 of 1908. Gandhi pleaded guilty in his own case and also to having advised others to act similarly. He was consequently convicted and sentenced to a £25 fine or two months' imprisonment with hard labor. He, of course, determined upon the latter alter-

[47] TA, tel., dep. gov. to sec. of state, Oct. 15, 1908.
[48] TA, tel., sec. of state to gov., Oct. 15, 1908.   [49] *Ibid.*

native. Still another, yet more minor, controversy arose over the treatment of Gandhi in jail. The South Africa British Indian Committee claimed he was put to hard labor on the roads. The Transvaal Government insisted he tended a garden.[50] Questions were asked in Parliament,[51] and it was asserted that Gandhi was marched through Johannesburg in prison dress.[52] Stung by the attack, the Transvaal authorities answered:

He was brought from Volksrust as a witness in case being set down for hearing in Johannesburg on 27th October; escort was provided from Johannesburg gaol and he was brought up from Volksrust under orderly conditions in his prison kit; arrived after dark; namely 6:30 p.m. and was conducted from station to fort in prison kit without handcuffs. When in court as a witness he did not appear in prison clothes. As regards work he has never done scavenging but worked on Agricultural Show Grounds digging holes for trees and weeding in municipal plantation and gaol gardens. He never performed hard labour on public streets.[53]

If one of the purposes of *satyagraha* was to focus public attention on a particular situation, it was certainly succeeding.

On November 4, the Transvaal ministers went part way in satisfying the Indians' demands. They were willing to admit a certain number of Indian professional men not eligible to enter the colony or to register in the ordinary way. But they wished to implement this concession through the issuing of temporary permits to be renewed periodically.[54] Had this scheme been accepted, the entire purpose of the Indian demand would have been defeated. But the Indians remained adamant and kept the pressure on the government. They decided to test the immigration law, and Sorabji Shapurji

[50] TA, So. Af. Brit. Ind. Comm. to Col. Off., Dec. 1, 1908.

[51] Lord Ampthill in the lords, for instance. *Hansard,* Lords, March 24, Nov. 16, 1909.

[52] TA, tel., sec. of state to gov., Oct. 29, 1908.

[53] TA, tel., col. sec. to pvt. sec., dep. gov., Nov. 2, 1908.

[54] TA, minute no. 645, Nov. 4, 1908.

Adajamia, a wealthy and educated Parsi from Charlestown, Natal, volunteered to try to enter the Transvaal. The government acted with considerable circumspection. Rather than challenging Sorabji at the border, they allowed him into the colony and later deported him for not registering during the period allowed by law.[55]

The Indians inundated government offices in the Transvaal, Britain, and India with letters, petitions, and memorials. On December 12, Selborne forwarded to Botha, with his comments, a resolution passed by a meeting of Transvaal British Indians some five weeks earlier:

The British Indians demand that the right of free immigration under the general Immigration Act of the Colony be conceded to six highly educated Indians yearly in order to minister to the spiritual and intellectual needs of the people, and unhesitatingly reject the humiliating proposal of the Transvaal government that temporary permits be granted to priests, professional men and teachers.[56]

The secretary of state, concluded Selborne, would be interested in the prime minister's reaction. Neither Crewe nor the governor were to be disappointed. Three days later, Botha addressed a vehement reply to Selborne. "The admission of Indians into the country on the same education qualifications as whites," he wrote, "could not for a moment be entertained as a policy: if they are serious in asking for less, then they should accept the assurance of the government and cease agitation on this point." The prime minister was unable to understand the Indians' objection to the issuing of temporary permits that could be indefinitely extended. The admission of six educated Indians by right, he contended, would not, in view of the intense animosity of the white population, be in the public interest.

[55] During the succeeding months, Sorabji was to offer himself for numerous tests of the Transvaal Asiatic laws.

[56] TA, gov. to prime minister, Dec. 12, 1908.

The difficulties are not so great in themselves, but are very seriously aggravated by the spirit of fanaticism which actuates a portion of the Indian community. The government will continue to do its best to allay this unhappy spirit and hope to be successful in the end. They do not however think the repeal of the Asiatic Act would be a proper solution to the difficulty.[57]

Botha concluded with an interesting confession. "It is quite true," he admitted, "that the Colonial Secretary at one time seriously considered the repeal of Act 2 of 1907 and the introduction of the necessary safeguards into the Immigration Law,[58] it was only when he became convinced that the Indian leaders would undoubtedly continue their crusades against these safeguards, that he gave up the attempt to obtain peace in that way." [59]

[57] TA, prime minister to gov., Dec. 15, 1908.

[58] As early as January 1908, Gandhi had claimed that the Immigrants' Restriction Act was adequate to all the needs of the Transvaal Government. In an interview to the *Transvaal Leader* on January 7, "Mr. Gandhi said the Immigration Restriction Act, which contains the drastic power of deportation under the hand of the Minister, is ample for every purpose. Let the Asiatic Law Amendment Act be slightly amended so that every Asiatic would become a prohibited immigrant. That is to say he would then have to prove that he was entitled to remain in the Colony. If he could produce a certificate issued to him under Law 3 of 1885 he would be given a certificate of domicile. 'This scheme,' Mr. Gandhi contended, 'would give the government all that they reasonably required, viz., would prevent any further immigration of Asiatics, and would ensure complete identification and registration of all Indians and all Asiatics entitled to remain here. Thus the wishes of the government and the people of the Transvaal would be fully met without putting any unnecessary affront on the Indians. Under the amendment suggested by me every Indian would have to prove domicile or his right of residence in the Transvaal in a stipulated time, after which he would be forever estopped. Surely nothing more than this can be required.' " TA, Methuen to Crewe, Oct. 16, 1908.

[59] In a later minute (TA, Feb. 19, 1909), Botha contended: "No promise of repeal was ever made although the matter was discussed, and the government intimated that they were prepared to consider the replacement of the Act by an amendment of Act 15/07—The Immi-

It must have been a disappointment to the Colonial Office that responsible government in the Transvaal had not afforded it the relief so earnestly sought. The secretary of state attempted several stratagems to ameliorate the situation and to assuage the ruffled feelings of Indians on the subcontinent itself. He even proposed the remission of sentences imposed on Indians in the Transvaal to celebrate the fiftieth anniversary of the crown's assumption of the government of India.[60] But the Transvaal would not acquiesce without certain guarantees from the Indian community.[61] On December 15, the secretary of state felt constrained to write another of those ambiguous dispatches that had been so common before January 1908. "It is true," Crewe conceded,

that in 1904 His Majesty's late Government . . . considered that an immigration law on the ordinary lines with the dictation test in a European language would meet the case, though it was realised that under such a law some fresh Asiatics might be expected to enter. When however the first elected Parliament of the Transvaal passed the Asiatic Law Amendment Act and the Immigrants Restriction Act of 1907, His Majesty's Government . . . did not . . . feel that it was possible for them to advise His Majesty to exercise his powers of disallowance in respect to the legislation in question. . . . The later developments appeared to His Majesty's Government to afford additional proof of the . . . intention of the Colonial Government to stop further immigration. . . . It is not in the interests of the Indians themselves that His Majesty's Government should endeavour to press on your Ministers any policy which cannot be expected to find reasonable support among the electors.

grants' Restriction Act—whereby the necessary machinery would be provided for the carrying out of the essential principles of Act 2/07, thus safeguarding the Colony from fresh Asiatic immigration. It was only on the rejection by the Asiatic leaders of this proposal that Act 36/08 was passed and terms of the compromise arrived at in January, 1908."

[60] TA, tel., sec. of state to gov., Oct. 23, 1908.
[61] TA, tel., gov. to sec. of state, Oct. 31, 1908.

Conversely, the secretary of state contended,

> his Majesty's Government cannot remain unaffected by the con-
> tinued movement of Passive Resistance in the Transvaal, arous-
> ing as it does considerable interest in this country and agitation
> in India which shows little sign of abating. They have therefore
> . . . suggested that your Ministers should consider whether a so-
> lution cannot properly be found by giving a promise that when
> registration is complete, the Acts of 1907 and 1908 shall be re-
> pealed, such provisions of them as may be required for identifica-
> tion of Indians being re-enacted, and the entry of new Indian im-
> migrants being regulated under a strict immigration act.[62]

Selborne reported that his ministers were not inclined to
make further concessions. They, "and the whole of public
opinion in the Transvaal, Boers as well as Britons, are solid
in this matter. They are exasperated with the Indians whom
they consider to have tricked them and to be guilty of a
breach of faith." [63] The only inducement that might force
further concessions from the Transvaal Government was an
absolute assurance from both the British and Indian governments that they would fully support the Transvaal against
any renewed pressure aimed at the further dilution of the
corpus of Asian legislation. The governor concluded with
the familiar line that compromise was considered a sign of
weakness by the Indians and did not take sufficient account
of those "who want to keep the pot boiling . . . whatever
concessions are made." [64]

The conscious breaking of the law by a whole community
and the demand by the transgressors that they be allowed to
pay the maximum penalty was so novel and foreign to the
bureaucratic mind that it tended to produce panic. There
were, after all, less than 12,000 Indians in the whole Transvaal, yet they were able to essentially immobilize the colonial government and to hold the attention of an entire em-

[62] TA, sec. of state to gov., Dec. 15, 1908.
[63] TA, gov. to sec. of state, Nov. 7, 1908.   [64] *Ibid.*

pire. The Transvaal ministers tried to delude themselves into believing that the unrest was abating. "The unfortunate situation created by the action of the Asiatic leaders is happily passing away," Botha insisted in a minute of February 19, 1909.[65] "Large numbers of Asiatics previously registered but who have destroyed their certificates are now applying for duplicates."[66] The Transvaal cabinet proclaimed "every confidence that the passive resistance movement is breaking down in all directions, as the great bulk of the Indian population in the Transvaal is submitting to the law."[67]

But it was not so. Throughout the last days of 1908 and in the early weeks of 1909, Indians continued to court arrest, to be tried and sent to prison. January 28 saw the Indian merchants of Johannesburg resolve not to take out licenses and to pay the resulting penalties. The bare recording of some of the subsequent events proves how inaccurate had been Botha's assessment of the situation. On January 30, three prominent Indians, Adam Cachalia, Thambi Naidoo and U. M. Shelat, were sentenced to jail and to pay £50 fines. Four days later, Parsee Rustomjee and several others were arrested for defying a deportation order, while Gandhi's son, Harilal, and some companions were sentenced at Volksrust on February 10. The following day, Parsee Rustomjee and his associates were apprehended for illegally re-entering the Transvaal and were sent to prison for six months. The pattern continued. Reports of arrests and trials were received from such places at Pretoria, Heidelberg, and Germiston. On February 19, six Indians were arrested in Standerton for failure to identify themselves or to produce registration certificates. The Chinese of the Transvaal were again involved. On February 20, their leader, Leung Quinn, was arrested. Finally, on February 25, Gandhi, while returning to Johannesburg from visiting his infirm wife, Kasturba, at Phoenix, was

[65] TA. minute by Botha. Feb. 19, 1909.   [66] *Ibid.*

[67] TA, gov. to sec. of state, March 4, 1909, encl. 2, minute no. 82 by Botha.

stopped at Volksrust. The almost inevitable sequence of events followed. Gandhi was sentenced to three months' imprisonment or the payment of a £50 fine, and, without hesitation, chose to go to jail.

The usual recriminations flew back and forth, the Indians and their adherents claiming Gandhi was being mistreated, the Transvaal authorities denying it. H. S. L. Polak, the European editor of *Indian Opinion* and one of Gandhi's closest associates, described his condition:

In Pretoria, I am informed, he is kept in what might be called solitary confinement. I believe that the work that he is given is not very severe, but that he is subjected to every possible humiliation, with a view to break his spirit.

. . . In all probability Mr. Gandhi is being half-starved, as he was in Johannesburg fort in January of last year, and, in addition, the lack of proper exercise and fresh air is telling upon his constitution.

I am quite sure that Mr. Gandhi himself will make no complaints so long as he is in gaol—you know the spirit of the man —but it is heartbreaking for me, as an Englishman and as a friend, to feel that this highminded gentleman, who has all along conducted a campaign with clean hands and in a lofty spirit, is being tortured in this way.[68]

Once again the manner of Gandhi's progress through the streets became an issue. Polak contended that "Mr. Gandhi was brought from Central Prison to the Magistrate Court as a witness in a certain licensing case, marched through the streets under escort, in full public view, handcuffed." [69] In a minute of April 23, the Transvaal ministers stated in reply: "Prisoner M. K. Gandhi is confined in Pretoria Gaol, where he has been shown special consideration. He was offered ghee [clarified butter] but declined. He has however accepted the sleeping outfit reserved for Europeans and is well supplied with books." [70] Botha admitted that Gandhi had in-

[68] TA, H. S. L. Polak to David Polak, March 27, 1909.   [69] *Ibid.*

[70] TA, minute by ministers no. 169, April 23, 1909.

deed been marched through Pretoria handcuffed. "It is the universal rule," he wrote,

to handcuff prisoners when so marched and they are so marched when the prison van is not available, as happened in the case in point. The rule applies equally to European convicted prisoners and there was no reason therefore for exempting an Indian from its operation. Mr. Gandhi was however allowed to draw his sleeves over his handcuffs and to carry a book, which concealed the fact of his being handcuffed.[71]

If there was some question as to the treatment of Gandhi, there was little doubt that many jailed Indians were both poorly fed and roughly handled. On July 7, the *Rand Daily Mail* printed a statement by one J. Veeramuthoo concerning the case of an Indian named Nagappan. Veeramuthoo claimed that Nagappan had been struck "a fearful blow" by a warder, that subsequently he could not eat for two days, and that when the chief warder had been informed he had replied, "Let him die," and had forced Nagappan to take up a pick and shovel and go to work. Nagappan died shortly after his release. The official causes of death were listed as double pneumonia and heart failure. A Dr. W. Godfrey, however, contended that Nagappan had died as the result of his treatment in prison and that the deceased's body was covered with bruises.

Nyak, a Bengali weekly, expressed the indignation of much of India. Indians in South Africa were oppressed, it contended, because their compatriots, at home, were powerless to render them any assistance. "Are we not the subjects of England," the paper asked,

merely because we happen to be of a dark complexion? Are we not entitled to be protected merely for the reason of our being weak and helpless? Would any Colonial Governors have been able to oppress any white subjects of England in this way? No kingdom in Europe would have remained quiet, if any of its sub-

[71] TA, minute no. 223 by Botha, May 1909.

jects was oppressed even a hundred times less than this. But Asia is not Europe, and Europeans do not care for oppression and injustice meted out to Asiatics. Has Christianity disappeared from Europe? Have Europeans lost their human attributes by losing all the virtues of kindness, justice, and spiritual truthfulness? [72]

As of March 1909, there were 111 Indians in prison for violations of Transvaal Asian legislation. The Indian community through its various organs claimed not only the harsh treatment of its incarcerated fellows, but their illegal deportation from the colony—many of them to India. The South Africa British Indian Committee contended that half of the Indians who were readmitted to the Transvaal at the end of the war upon proof of prewar domicile had been driven out of the province. [73] The Colonial Office denied this charge and claimed that only those Indians who were illegally in the Transvaal and had no domicile elsewhere in South Africa were deported to India, which "seems the most humane course . . . it is possible to take." [74] Questions were again asked in Parliament, [75] and to complicate matters further it turned out that an agreement had been concluded between the Transvaal and the Portuguese authorities in Mozambique to provide for the rapid embarkation from Africa of Indians expelled from the Transvaal. The situation was embarrassing. As Crewe wrote to Selborne:

The position is rendered still more complicated by the fact that Mr. Long [the Transvaal's Agent in Mozambique] is [British] Vice-Consul at Lourenco Marques. Your Ministers will no doubt recognise the anomaly which arises when an officer who in the absence of His Majesty's Consul is charged with the duty of dealing with the grievances of His Majesty's subjects actually assists

[72] Reports of the native press, Bengal, *Nyak,* Jan. 13, 1909.
[73] TA, So. Af. Brit. Ind. Comm. to Col. Off., April 15, 1909.
[74] TA, Col. Off. to So. Af. Brit. Ind. Comm., April 29, 1908.
[75] *I.e., Hansard,* May 6, 1909.

in framing legislation whose chief effect in practice is to impose on a numerous class of these subjects a serious disability.[76]

The Transvaal attempted to minimize the deportation issue. It claimed that as of June 7, 1908, no more than 198 persons had been expelled, of which number only 29 had been sent to India. The remaining 169 had been consigned to the various South African territories of their origin. But, the government claimed, at least 148 of these had already returned to the colony.[77]

In the summer of 1909, both an official delegation from the Transvaal and an unofficial Indian one, consisting of Gandhi and Sheth Haji Habib, proceeded to London in connection with the negotiations to be conducted on the question of uniting the various British colonies in South Africa under a single jurisdiction.[78] Gandhi realized that as long as the Indian problem remained unsettled the chances of achieving union were considerably reduced, and he went immediately to work. From his hotel in Victoria Street, he addressed the Colonial Office in the first of what was to be a continuing stream of letters.[79]

Smuts understood the delicacy of his position, and his determination to resist the Indian demands began to waiver. He essentially conceded the right of six educated Indians to enter the Transvaal, annually, under permanent certificates of registration. He was willing, after some amendment of existing legislation, to repeal Act 2 of 1907. As he wrote to Crewe:

Act 2 of 1907 they [the Indians] have unfortunately come to look upon as derogatory to their national dignity, and besides, they want the introduction under permanent certificates of residence of a limited number of educated Asiatics who are necessary

[76] TA, sec. of state to gov., May 6, 1909.
[77] TA, tel., gov. to sec. of state, June 7, 1909.   [78] See also Chap. VII.
[79] TA, Gandhi to Col. Off., Sept. 10, 1909.

to the spiritual and social needs of their compatriots already largely resident in the Transvaal. If both these contentions are conceded in substance, they should have every reason to be satisfied.

Smuts, however, opposed the establishment of statutory provisions for immigration that would provide for similar treatment for Europeans and Asians and the use of administrative techniques of differentiation to limit the Indian immigrants to six educated Indians per year. "This proposal," he wrote, "is, in my opinion, open to the gravest objection, and would be most strongly resisted by the white people of the Transvaal and of South Africa." Yet, the negation of this seemingly abstruse philosophical point, despite the very real concessions made, denied the heart and substance of the entire Indian case. "We cannot recognise in our legislation," Smuts concluded, "equal rights of all alike to emigrate to South Africa." If the Indian demand were entertained, "the people of South Africa . . . would think, and, I submit, rightly think, that if equality is conceded in principle, the practice would ultimately have to conform to principle, and in the end the Asiatic immigrants would be on the same footing as the Europeans." Using an old strategem, Smuts argued that if it were impossible for the Transvaal Parliament to enact the necessary legislation in its last session, he had every confidence "that the first Union government will show at least the same anxiety to meet His Majesty's Government in this matter as the Transvaal government have done in the past." [80]

On October 10, Crewe telegraphed Selborne. He explained that he had discussed Smuts's proposals with Gandhi and Habib, "who state that as far as practical effect is concerned they would be ready to accept them but it is not possible for them to abandon claim to be equal before the law

[80] TA, Smuts to Crewe, Aug. 29, 1909.

THE BATTLE JOINED / 207

even though equality may be only theoretical and that if claim is not conceded agitation must be continued." [81] Both Crewe and Gandhi felt that it would be advantageous to implement any reforms while the Transvaal still existed as a separate entity.[82] Gandhi again wrote to Crewe on October 20. He said that due to the delicacy of the discussions concerning Union he had not made public the negotiations concerned with the Indian question. If, therefore, Smuts had spoken his final word, he, Gandhi, would have no choice but to expose the entire situation to full public scrutiny.[83]

The battle of thrust and counterthrust was destined to continue for some time. On November 3, the Colonial Office supported Smuts and urged Gandhi to accept, on behalf of the Indians, the concessions the general offered. Three days later Gandhi expressed his regret at Crewe's attitude. After all, the principle of equality before the law of all British subjects "alone, it is respectfully submitted, can justify the holding together of different people of the world under the same sovereignty." Not unaware of the power thrust into his hands by the debate over union, Gandhi repeated the veiled threat that should no further reforms materialize he and his associate could only return to South Africa and place the problem before their constituents.[84]

On November 13, Gandhi and Haji Habib sailed for home aboard the *Kildonan Castle*. Despite the efforts mounted throughout South Africa subsequent to their return, the mission of H. S. L. Polak to India and the campaign of the South Africa British Indian Committee in Britain, the Indians' immediate reward was to be frustration, not victory. The settlement of the Asian question in Natal to the satisfaction of the white colonists and the British and Indian governments assured union without further developments in

[81] TA, tel., sec. of state to gov., Oct. 10, 1909.   [82] *Ibid.*
[83] TA, Gandhi to Col. Off., Oct. 20, 1909.
[84] TA, Gandhi to Col. Off., Nov. 6, 1909.

the Transvaal. Gandhi continued to plead his case,[85] but Smuts and his colleagues were now able to hold their ground.[86] The *Bengalee* of Calcutta perhaps cut to the heart of the matter when it wrote:

The Transvaal policy which is really the policy of the late Boer Government masked in British guise, with the Imperial Government looking on in helpless impotency is one of the saddest facts in modern British history. If ever a single British subject were thus treated by a foreign Government, the entire resources of the Empire would be exerted for the vindication of the status of the British subject. But when a British colony makes it a part of its policy to insult and degrade British subjects, the Government is powerless to afford protection.[87]

The advent of the Union of South Africa on May 31, 1910, did not, therefore, usher in a bright new era for the Transvaal Indians; it merely connoted the continuation of an old struggle in a slightly different context.

[85] TA, gov. to sec. of state, Jan. 24, 1910, encl., Gandhi to Gibson, Jan. 6, 1910.

[86] TA, Smuts in minute of Dec. 20, 1909.

[87] Reports of the native press, Bengal, *Bengalee,* Sept. 25, 1908.

VII / Developments at the Cape
and the Anti-Indian Crusade
in Natal, 1899–1910

AT THE same time as Gandhi and Haji Habib were haunting the corridors of Whitehall on behalf of the Transvaal Indians, a delegation of Indians from Natal was in London on a similar mission. Gandhi had kept in constant touch with the lives of his confreres on the seaboard, for theirs had been the familiar story of governmental harassment and the steady erosion of the never impressive corpus of Indian rights. Likewise, he had remained cognizant of the course of events in the Cape Colony.

With the drive toward union, the Indian question, in Gandhi's mind, was becoming ever less parochial in nature —more a national than a provincial problem. Consequently, to comprehend the Indians' dilemma we must now turn back the clock and trace the course of events in Cape Colony and Natal during the years between the end of the Anglo-Boer War and the London negotiations of 1910.

By 1904 there were 8,489 Indians in the Cape—a figure not greatly different from that for the Transvaal—but because of the traditionally more liberal attitude of the Cape, the problem was less acute there. Nevertheless, in 1902 an immigration restriction act (Assembly Bill 57), admitted by the governor, Sir. W. F. Hely-Hutchinson (formerly the governor of Natal), to be based on the Natal Act, was introduced into the legislature. Although Indians were not specifically mentioned in the law, it was obviously aimed at them. The usual European language test was prescribed, but European illiterates could be excused from its operation. The Colonial Office threatened to disallow the measure, not because of the language test which, after all, was not specifically detrimental to Indians and had also the sanction of precedent—that happy justification for any action, good or bad—but because of the explicit inequity of the exemption for European illiterates only.[1] The governor, thereupon, replied: "Ministers have given the required assurance that they will introduce a Bill next session to amend the existing Bill by omitting the word 'European' from the clause."[2] Based on this promise the Colonial Office approved the act.

The Cape immigration restriction act was much more humane than its equivalent in the other South African colonies. Only Indians desiring permanent residence were affected, and an Asian deemed a prohibited immigrant was not punished but merely sent back to his port of origin at the colony's expense, with £3 in his pocket.[3] It would be a mistake, however, to conclude that the more liberal form of the Cape immigration legislation had been achieved without difficulty. In its original form the bill had been aimed directly at Asians. It was only at the behest of the colonial secretary, Sir P. Faure, reflecting the will of the Colonial Office, that it was stripped of a clause stipulating that "any Asiatic who is not granted a special permit of immigration into the Colony by the Governor on the recommendation of the Min-

[1] NAI, March 1903, procs. 19–20, tel., sec. of state to gov., Dec. 8, 1902. The effectiveness of the act can be attested to by the following figures: In 1903, 1,646 Asians entered Cape Colony; by 1908, the number had fallen to 387. In 1909, the figure was 445, and in 1910–1911 between 400 and 500. Even the reduced numbers, when compared with comparable figures for the other South African colonies, indicate the greater liberality of the Cape measure.

[2] CO, 48/567, tel., gov. to sec. of state, Dec. 12, 1902.

[3] CO, 48/568, laws and regulations applicable to immigrants of Asiatic race, prepared by Mr. Advocate Morgan Evans, Jan. 30, 1903.

ister" was a prohibited immigrant. During the course of the debate, a member of the opposition, the liberal Cape Dutch representative J. W. Sauer, had claimed:

There were 240 millions in India and there were Chinamen who were British subjects who would come into this country to an extent which would swamp it. After all, to them it was a matter of no importance whether a Chinaman was a British subject or not. The point was that they did not want to see Asiatics come here, introducing social, economic, and political trouble in this country, and they would do that whether they were British subjects or not.[4]

It was the approval by the Customs Union Conference at Bloemfontein of the principle of indentured Asian labor for South Africa that particularly aroused the Cape and made the Asian question more emotional than it would ordinarily have been. As reported in the Cape *Hansard,* John X. Merriman, by no means a reactionary, moved the successful resolution in the Cape House of Assembly opposing the conference's action:

Now he thought that the opinion of that House had been expressed many times on the subject of the importation of Asiatics. There had been many discussions, but he had never seen any difference of opinion in that House. It was only last year that they had passed an Act for the special purpose of keeping Asiatic immigrants out of the country, and they passed that almost without a dissenting voice.

Merriman had no faith in any schemes for mandatory repatriation.

He did not think there was any sensible man who sat in that House who could be so blinded as not to see that the protection which was given by that system of government control provided for the indenture, and so forth was absolutely elusive (hear, hear). What had taken place in Natal where they had the same system? Natal had been turned into an Asiatic colony.[5]

[4] Cape *Hansard,* Nov. 12, 1902.   [5] *Ibid.,* July 2, 1903.

When the Colonial Office chided the Cape Government for not having amended the immigration restriction act, the governor replied:

I have received confidential minute from Prime Minister saying that at the time promise was given it was intended fully to carry it out no difficulty being then apparent. Since then however Asiatic immigration has become burning question and the Members of House of Legislature are unanimous in their opposition to it. Immigration Restriction Act of 1902 as it stands affords the means of preventing entry of Asiatics into Cape Colony even if they should be introduced into the Transvaal. But if promised amendment was made it would to a considerable extent lessen that power of prevention; consequently owing to very strong feeling on the subject there would not be slightest chance of carrying amendment through this session. Its introduction would give rise to most heated discussion during which Secretary of State for the Colonies and the High Commissioner would be attacked with violence on the allegation that they were endeavouring to force Asiatic immigration against the wishes of the Legislature of the Colony as expressed in the resolution of both Houses already communicated to Secretary of State for Colonies. Prime Minister therefore recommends that matter stand over for the present as next year agitation against this question then may have subsided and should it appear desirable to amend law as promised Bill may be received and considered by the Legislature in a calm and dispassionate manner.[6]

But the agitation was not to die down for some time. On December 8, 1903, the *South African News* wrote: "He must be a dullard or a pro-Asiatic magnate who could note the solid stately buildings of the Paarl, the spacious gardens, above all the sturdy race which inhabits the district, and not feel the enormity of the treason to South Africa of which the importation party is guilty." It was the fear that ex-indentured Asian laborers from the Transvaal would enter the Cape that shaped the colony's attitude. Should the Chinese

[6] CO, 48/572, tel., gov. to sec. of state, Aug. 3, 1903.

immigration scheme for the Transvaal be sanctioned, the prime minister, J. Gordon Sprigg, proclaimed, "it will be the duty of the government here to submit to the Legislature the measures which they consider necessary to prevent the entry of Asiatics from the neighbouring Colonies into the Cape Colony." [7]

Hely-Hutchinson himself felt that much of the agitation was politically based; for there was no doubt in his mind that the Cape as well as the Transvaal could make good use of Asian labor. Its presence in the Rand mines would certainly allow the Cape to keep much of its own labor force that annually migrated northward. The governor placed the blame at the feet of the *Afrikaner Bond* (the Dutch party in the Cape).

Its objects are to influence the result of the General Election which would otherwise be certain to go against the Bond . . . and to hamper the Administration of the Transvaal by delaying the recovery of its finances: to breed discontent and trouble in the Transvaal, in the hope that the discontent may lead to a demand from the British section of the population for Responsible Government before the Colony has reached such a state of development as would render it safe to grant Responsible Government with due regard for the maintenance of British supremacy. I have no doubt whatever that these are the main objects of the present anti-Asiatic agitation in the Cape Colony.[8]

Despite the passage early in 1904 of a "Bill to Prevent Introduction of [non-British] Chinese into Cape Colony," [9] the governor, upon again being questioned by the Colonial Office in regard to the promised amendment of the immigration act of 1902, could only reply:

In view . . . of the tone of recent discussion that has taken place in the House of Assembly as well as in the Legislative Council on

[7] CO, 48/573, minute by Sprigg, Dec. 9, 1903.
[8] CO, 48/572, tel., gov. to sec. of state, Aug. 3, 1903.
[9] Assembly bill no. 5 of March 7, 1904.

the question of Asiatic immigration Ministers cannot admit that the condition of things is in any way improved. Under the circumstances therefore Ministers regret that they do not feel justified in recommending that steps be taken in the direction desired during the present session of Parliament and would accordingly ask that the matter be allowed to stand over for the present.[10]

When, in 1906, a "Bill to Amend the Law placing Restrictions on Immigration and providing for the Removal from the Colony of Prohibited Immigrants" was finally passed, the exemption for European illiterates from the workings of the law still remained but no similar privilege was accorded Asians. Despite their undertaking to provide parity for Asians in an amendment of the immigration bill of 1902, the Cape ministers were now quite arrogant in their defense of the *status quo*. "To omit the word 'European,'" they claimed,

would be to extend that privilege [the exemption from the language test] to all Nationalities and Races, . . . a course which does not commend itself to Ministers as being in the interests of the Colony; and, as has been explained above, they have found it necessary to adhere in the amending bill to the terms of existing laws so far as it involves the principle now in question.[11]

The governor, for his part, informed the Colonial Office: "I feel quite sure that if Ministers could possibly have met your wishes about the Immigration Bill, without gravely risking the existence of the government, they would have done so."[12]

Not only did the new act (no. 30 of 1906) not ameliorate the existing situation, it actually eroded it further. The old law had stipulated that all persons domiciled in South Africa were not to come under its jurisdiction. The law of 1906 exempted only those "persons born in South Africa" and "persons of European birth domiciled in South Africa." Never-

10 CO, 48/576, gov. to sec. of state, April 12, 1904.
11 CO, 48/585, prime minister to gov., May 31, 1906.
12 NAI, Feb. 1907, procs. 13–15, gov. to sec. of state, June 5, 1906.

theless, Hely-Hutchinson explained that while "it must be admitted that in principle these distinctions are to be regretted . . . in practice they involve little, if any, real hardship." [13] The Colonial Office protested feebly.[14] It tiredly concluded, however, that "H.M.G. is in a weak position. If the Bill is reserved and assent refused, the Cape will fall back on the Act of 1902 which is no less objectionable." [15] H. C. M. Lambert, one of the first-class clerks at the Colonial Office, minuted: "The matter is not of enough importance I think to justify us in trying to force the Cape government to risk its existence." [16] As was so often the case in similar circumstances, the whole question of the amendment of the immigration act of 1902 in the manner promised by the Cape Government died in a whimper. The prime minister [17] informed Hely-Hutchinson that "Ministers have the honour to give the assurance that section 4(g) [the domicile clause] of the said Act will be administered in a liberal and equitable manner, so as to fully safeguard the interests, lawfully acquired by Asiatics residing in the Colony." [18] The Colonial Office accepted this new undertaking, and the India Office, although somewhat more obstinate, agreed that, "in view . . . of the opinion expressed by Lord Elgin, the Secretary of State for India in Council can only . . . trust that section 4(g) will be interpreted in a liberal and equitable manner." [19]

[13] CO, 48/586, gov. to sec. of state, Aug. 21, 1906.

[14] NAI, Feb. 1907, procs. 6–9, minuting on gov. to sec. of state, Aug. 21, 1907.

[15] CO, 48/585, minute paper 22660, June 25, 1906, minuting of July 3, 1906.

[16] *Ibid.*   [17] Now Dr. L. S. Jameson.

[18] NAI, June 1907, proc. 1, prime minister to gov., Feb. 20, 1907.

[19] CO, 45/588, Ind. Off. to Col. Off., Nov. 14, 1906. For many of the colonists the immigration act of 1906 was not sufficiently strong. During debate on the measure in the house of assembly, S. C. Cronwright-Schreiner moved that a clause forbidding the entry of Asians into Cape Colony be inserted into the bill, but the house negatived the motion by a vote of 67 to 23. Cape *Hansard,* Aug. 14, 1906.

It would have been vain to expect the threat to the Indian position in the Cape to be limited to the immigration issue. A proclamation of August 30, 1906, declared that,

> from and after the date hereof, it shall not be lawful for any Arab, Indian or other Asiatic of whatsoever nationality, to enter any of the territories aforesaid (namely, the Transkei, including Gealakaland; Tembuland, including Emigrant Tembuland and Bomnanaland; Pondoland, including East and West Pondoland; Port St. John's; Griqualand East;) without a special permit signed by the Resident Magistrate, or by his order, and approved by the Chief Magistrate of the Transkeian Territories.[20]

As was the case in Natal and the Transvaal, competition by Indian traders aroused the ire of their white counterparts who constantly demanded action from the legislature. Consequently a bill to regulate the trade of general dealers was introduced into the house of assembly. In its initial version the measure very much resembled its Natal counterpart. Appeal to the courts was allowed only when the cancellation of an existing license was the issue. In the case of new licenses the decision of the licensing court was to be final. The law as it emerged from committee and as finally passed in the form of Cape Act 35 of 1906—"To Regulate the Trade of General Dealers and to Amend the Law Relating to Stamp Duties and Licenses"—was obviously not directed toward Indians already in business but at those who would apply for permits to trade in the future. No mention was made of existing licenses. But applicants for new licenses could appeal only to the municipal council, village board, magistrate, or assistant magistrate if their applications were denied by the licensing officer. The question of appeals to higher judicial authority was conveniently ignored.

[20] Cape of Good Hope *Government Gazette*, Aug. 30, 1906, proclamation issued by Maj. Gen. Edmunds Smith Brook, officer administering the colony.

The Indians of Griqualand West immediately addressed the secretary of state. They were convinced that

the proposed bill is merely a disguised attempt to curtail the rights and privileges of British Indian subjects and others who are not Europeans, and that the Bill is aimed solely at British Indians and other non-European persons, and that as such it draws a clear distinction between the European and non-European sections of His Majesty's subjects in this Colony and whilst conferring certain rights and privileges on the former, withholds these self-same rights and privileges from the latter. That such differentiation is a violation of the constitutional rights of your Petitioners as subjects of His Majesty.[21]

The protests from the Cape Indians were, however, few and far between—perhaps because they felt the interests of those already established in the colony were adequately protected by the licensing law.

Gandhi criticized his compatriots for a lack of courage:

We have repeatedly said that there is an urgent need for Indians in the Cape to wake up. We gave an account in the last issue [of *Indian Opinion*] of the efforts being made there to prevent licenses being issued to Indians. In view of this, we ask the Cape Indians once again how long they will remain asleep. Only a little while ago, we were obliged to point out that the Indians must thank their own indifference for the Cape Immigration Act.

Gandhi was particularly incensed at the Cape Indians' failure to object strongly to the lack of appeal to the supreme court in cases involving the issue of new licenses. "On that question," he wrote,

it was necessary for the people of the Cape to take a lesson from the conditions in Natal and put up a strong fight. But it is to be regretted that this was not done. They remained altogether indifferent while the Bill was before Parliament. It needs to be dinned into the minds of the Indians in the South that having

[21] NAI, Jan. 1906, proc. 4, petition from the Indians of Griqualand West to sec. of state, March 28, 1906.

come to this country, they cannot afford to be asleep all the time.[22]

The British Government did not disallow the licensing bill because it could claim that nothing in the measure was specifically detrimental to any particular racial group. Once again reference to debates on the law would have proved embarrassing to the Colonial Office. The Cape *Hansard* of August 16, 1906, reported the words of J. W. Sauer as follows:

The Attorney-General said, when the Bill was introduced, that it was a Bill introduced because certain people could not keep books; and another reason was that it was introduced for sanitary purposes. . . . He would ask the Imperialists who sat opposite, and who talked of British subjects having equal rights wherever they went . . . what they had to say on the point. They had now got the . . . truth. It was to keep out the Asiatics—their fellow-subjects, their brothers—(Opposition laughter).

As it turned out, Gandhi was quite right in being apprehensive about the licensing act. In practice it operated in very much the same way as its Natal model. "At the monthly meeting of the Cape Divisional Council held at Capetown on the 5th inst.," the *Cape Times* reported,

the following applications were considered for permission to apply for licenses to trade as general dealers. Not much time was wasted in refusing the applications or referring them back for further information. . . . The procedure was something as follows: The Secretary read out the Sanitary Inspector's report on the state of the premises, usually to the effect that the ventilation needed looking into, the drains were bad, there was connection between the sleeping apartments and the shops and so on. Before Mr. Sorrie had read a half-dozen lines, Mr. Gibbs would shout out, "Not Granted," and the other Councillors followed suit.

"Indians," said Mr. Gibbs with scorn, "I want . . . none of their nationality. I am not in favour of these Indians coming here at all, and I would like to see as many of them as possible getting out of the country. They work the poor people out of the country, and I really think a good deal of the depression existing at this time is due to them. Why, they live on the smell of an oil-rag, and sleep on the butter, (laughter). I'll do everything possible in my power, whatever Council I'm on, to drive them out.[23]

In August 1908, the house of assembly appointed a select committee to investigate Asian grievances under the immigration and licensing acts. Several Indians testified that, outside of Cape Town, Indians were denied licenses as general dealers or hawkers merely because of their color. The European merchants, on the other hand, demanded legislation of even greater stringency and claimed, as usual, that they were being driven out of business by a people who represented a lower order of civilization. The committee found that there had indeed been some instances of discrimination against Indians but it recommended only a few minor changes in the administration of the two laws. Lending credence to one of the more prevalent folk myths of the time, the committee contended that Indians drove white men out of business, at least in part, because "Indians have as a rule, no domestic establishments to maintain." [24]

The situation in the Cape never achieved the level of complexity or the degree of threat to the Indian population that manifested itself in postwar Natal. There, no sooner had the dust of battle cleared than the government of the colony determined to change the existing terms of Indian immigration and residence in the Natal to its own benefit. All the stratagems, such as the £3 license, that had been employed to force Indians either to return to India or to reindenture having failed, the old dilemma of how to keep a steady supply of Indian laborers flowing to the plantations without at the same time increasing the permanent Indian population of the colony, remained. A raising of the residence license fee

[23] *Cape Times,* Nov. 6, 1907.
[24] Cape Colony, report of the select comm. on Indian grievances, select comm. report no. 19, 1908.

to £10 was suggested,[25] but rejected, as "there is no penalty attached to the non-payment of the license, no means to compel the payment of it, and no method by which Indians can be forced back to India." [26] F. M. Reynolds, a member of the legislative assembly and the Indian Immigration Trust Board, explained the prime defect of the existing system. Indians, he contended, thought the payment of the three-pound license fee made them free men, when all the white colonists of Natal knew that this was not so.[27]

As a first step in its renewed campaign to make life increasingly less comfortable for the colony's free Indians, the Natal legislature passed Act 2 of 1902, which remedied an oversight in the provisions of Act 17 of 1895—the failure to take proper cognizance of the status of Indian minors.[28] In the words of the new law:

Every Indian child to whom this Act applies shall upon attaining the age of majority [thirteen for girls and sixteen for boys] be obliged:

(a) To go to India, or

(b) To remain in Natal under indenture similar to and renewable in the same manner as the re-indenture referred to in Act No. 17, 1895, as amended by subsequent acts, or

(c) To take out year by year, in terms of Section 6 of Act No. 17, 1895, a pass or license to remain in the Colony.[29]

The India Office, supposedly the staunchest guardian of Indian rights, did not object to the new legislation on the grounds that it merely extended the application of a princi-

[25] NA, "Precis of evidence given before Select Committee of the Legislative Assembly appointed to consider the petition (no. 1 of 1902) of the Indian Immigration Trust Board."

[26] *Ibid.*   [27] *Ibid.*

[28] Children brought to Natal after 1895 did not fall under the provisions of Act 17 of 1895 and therefore did not have to choose between entering indentured service and paying the £3 fee, upon achieving their majority, in order to remain in the colony.

[29] Act no. 39 of 1905 increased the penalties on employers who hired unlicensed Indians.

ple which the India Office had already accepted with the passage of Act 17 of 1895.[30]

There was a limit, however, to how far Natal could go without the sanction of the Government of India and the amendment of existing agreements between the two governments. In December 1902, the prime minister of Natal consequently announced that, "a commission appointed by the Government of Natal and consisting of C. D. de Gersigny and H. C. Shepstone, with a secretary, are shortly proceeding to India to enquire into matters affecting immigration into Natal." [31]

The Natal delegates arrived in India early in 1903 and on February 5 met with Sir Denzil Ibbetson, the head of the Department of Revenue and Agriculture (under whose aegis emigration policy fell), in an interview which delineated the issues as seen by the two governments. It soon became apparent that the Government of India, like its counterpart in London, was more concerned with the actual construction of Natal laws than with the spirit behind them. Ibbetson emphasized not that the Indian was the equal of the white man but that he was vastly superior to the African native.

The delegates later wrote to Calcutta:

In the course of the interview . . . you said that there were great grievances regarding the treatment of the Free Indian population in Natal, and that if Natal is to be kept a white man's Colony it should be kept so by legislation, and by measures not open to strong objections; that, in the first place, legislation should not be retrospective, and secondly, that it should not involve personal degradation. You impressed upon us that the Indian is not on a level with the native of Natal; that he is of a far higher order of civilisation.[32]

[30] CO, 179/225, India Off. to Col. Off., Nov. 19, 1902.

[31] NA, prime minister to gov., Dec. 19, 1902. Shepstone was a member of the Indian Immigration Trust Board, de Gersigny a sugar planter.

[32] NA, Govt. House papers, Natal delegation to J. O. Miller, sec. to Govt. of India, Dept. of Rev. and Ag., Calcutta, Feb. 10, 1903.

The delegates reviewed the two major concerns of the Government of India—the lack of an appeal to the colonial courts in licensing cases and the possibility that the word "domiciled" in Act 1 of 1897, the immigration restriction act, might be interpreted to the unfair detriment of Indians returning to Natal from abroad.[33] They declared themselves anxious to assuage the anxieties of the Government of India and agreed that

the refusal of any appeal to the Supreme Court from the decision of the Town Council or Board is a hardship, and we are prepared to represent this hardship to our Government very strongly, and to urge upon it that steps should be taken with as little delay as possible to remedy the matter. We have every reason to believe that our Government will adopt our view and cause legislation on the subject to be introduced into Parliament.[34]

On the second question, the delegates denied that there was any cause for apprehension. But again they were prepared to represent the Government of India's views to their government, "and to urge that something be done to do away with what is feared may be possible under a strict interpretation of the words of the Act." [35]

Of less significance were three additional complaints of the Indian Government: the extension of the pass laws to uncovenanted Indians under the terms of Act 28 of 1897, the application of the curfew or nine o'clock bell to all colored persons, and the defining of all formerly indentured Indians as members of an "uncivilised race" in the definition clause of Act 21 of 1888, the registration of servants law. Although the delegates felt that the Indian Government had been misinformed concerning the administration of the measures referred to and that Indians did not, in fact, suffer under them, they promised, nevertheless, to bring at least the last question to the notice of their government.[36]

[33] *Ibid.*   [34] *Ibid.*   [35] *Ibid.*   [36] *Ibid.*

In a further memorandum, the delegates summarized their government's wishes as follows: (1) the termination of all contracts of indenture in India; (2) certain changes in the procedure for registering prospective emigrants in India; (3) a reduction in the proportion of women in any shipment of immigrants to 40 per cent, as 60 per cent of the Indian population in Natal was at that time female; (4) the removal of restrictions on the emigration of special servants under Indian Act 10 of 1902; and (5) the opening of Bombay Presidency to the recruitment of indentured laborers for Natal.[37] This statement of Natal's desires prompted the Government of India to ask the delegates whether it was the colony's intention to repeal the £3 license fee should the Government of India agree to the compulsory repatriation of indentured laborers.[38] But to this question no immediate answer was forthcoming.

As the negotiations continued, it became clear to the delegates that the Government of India would not be able to countenance the termination of all indentures in India itself. They consequently modified their government's request to forced repatriation after the actual expiration of the indenture, and as a result of considerable discussion this compromise was agreed to by both sides. The Government of India, for its part, saw no reason why the registration method could not be altered providing the presidency government concerned (that of Madras) had no objections. No promise was made in regard to the importation of special servants, but the Government of India intimated that the proportion of women to men in any consignment of laborers might be reduced if there were no legal obstacles and no objections

[37] *Ibid.*, memorandum of points discussed in the interview of Feb. 5, 1903.

[38] *Ibid.*, Miller to Shepstone, Feb. 13, 1903. As in Natal, there had been some talk in the viceroy's council of allowing Natal to raise the license fee to £10. Curzon opposed the idea, largely on the basis of having only just agreed to Act 2 of 1902.

from the relevant provincial governments. There appeared no insuperable difficulty in the way of opening Bombay to the Natal recruiters, in view of the fact that the presidency had been closed in the first instance at the request of the Government of Natal.[39]

Whatever the Government of India was willing to concede, the delegates emphasized in their report to the prime minister, was contingent on certain very material concessions by Natal. These came under six headings: (1) amendment of Act 18 of 1897 to provide an appeal to the supreme court in all licensing cases; (2) the alteration of those clauses in Natal legislation which classed Indians as members of "barbarous or semi-civilised and uncivilised races"; (3) the repeal of the £3 tax ten years after the forced repatriation scheme went into effect; (4) an increase in the pay of indentured laborers during the first five years of indenture and a deferred payment scheme; (5) a revision of pass laws and municipal by-laws insofar as they applied to Indians; and (6) the elimination of all encumbrances to Indians attending government schools.[40]

The Government of India would not press the "domicile" issue, the delegates stated; it had declared itself willing to accept a pledge by the Natal ministry that the immigration restriction act of 1897 would be administered in a fair and reasonable manner. In conclusion, the delegates indicated that the Government of India was more than satisfied with the treatment accorded indentured Indians; although the conditions faced by free Indians, admittedly not Calcutta's prime responsibility, continued to cause concern. The last words of the delegates' report were filed with optimism. They felt that their mission had been a success and that the changes in the immigration procedure, so earnestly sought by Natal, would be effected.[41]

Despite the numerous demands of the Government of

[39] NA, report of the delegates to the prime minister, May, 1903.
[40] *Ibid.*   [41] *Ibid.*

India, it was quite certain that the only one of real importance concerned the right of Indians deprived of their licenses by municipal licensing boards to appeal to the supreme court of Natal. On this issue Calcutta was fully supported by the India Office, which pressed the Colonial Office for action. "As regards the proposed amendment of the dealers' licenses act," a letter of May 13 read,

his Lordship is aware that when the question was dropped, owing to the outbreak of the war in 1899, Mr. Chamberlain was prepared, with the concurrence of this office, to accept in place of the suggested legislation an assurance from the local authorities that they would administer the existing law in an equitable spirit, but I am to repeat the opinion . . . that it would be preferable, if possible, to establish a right of appeal from the decision of these bodies to the Supreme Court.[42]

Once removed from the rhetoric of policy and official correspondence, however, neither the India Office nor the Colonial Office at this time strongly supported the Indians' cause. "The Colonial Office will not, and cannot, press them [Natal] beyond a certain point," the India Office wrote the viceroy, Lord Curzon.

It is vain for us to write strong remonstrances, though we have often done it and are prepared to do it again: and I cannot help feeling that there is a certain amount of unreality and cant about our proceedings, for if the natives of India showed any inclination to immigrate into this country and to supplant and underbid the small British tradesmen or the British working man, we should behave, I believe, exactly as Natal has behaved.[43]

That the apprehensions concerning the licensing issue expressed in South Africa, India, and Britain were not exaggerated was demonstrated by the course of events in postwar Natal. The colonists were not satisfied even with the rigid and uncompromising application of the existing licensing

[42] CO, 179/228, India Off. to Col. Off., May 13, 1903.
[43] IOL, Curzon papers, F. 111/159, Godley to Curzon, July 27, 1900.

law countenanced by their government in violation of ministerial promises to the Colonial Office. Inspired by the essential repromulgation of Law 3 of 1885 (as amended in 1886) by the new British rulers of the Transvaal (Notice 365 of 1903), they prepared to move all the Indians into bazaars or locations. The Greytown local board informed the prime minister's office that it thoroughly approved of the Transvaal's policy, that "it is what the Board have been striving to attain. . . . No fresh Indian license has been granted here since 1897 despite the efforts of the traders, but how to go about to locate the present storekeepers is a matter which now may require the assistance of the Government." [44]

The mayor of Durban, with the full assent of the town council, addressed the prime minister in a similar vein. Despite the immigration restriction and dealers' licenses acts, he complained, the issuing of licenses to Indians had not been sufficiently curtailed:

After giving the matter very careful consideration it appears to me that the time has arrived when this Council should petition Government to introduce legislation, on somewhat similar lines as the Laws in force in the Transvaal, in order to safeguard the health and trade interests not only of Durban, but of the whole Colony, and I would urge that no time be lost.[45]

The opinions of Greytown and Durban were echoed by the other municipalities of Natal, and the whole situation was exacerbated by the untimely arrival of a dispatch from India couched in the disdainful tones which so alienated all those who encountered Lord Curzon throughout his public career. Curzon made it clear that the Government of India would accede to no changes in the existing immigration arrangements unless an appeal to the supreme court were allowed in licensing cases. He condemned the pass laws affecting Indi-

[44] NA, PM 1078/1903, Greytown board to secretary to the prime minister, May 17, 1903.

[45] Ibid., Durban to prime minister, June 6, 1903.

ans, the £3 tax, and the placing of "the Indian in the same category with the Native African, than whom he stands on an immeasurably higher level of civilisation." "It must be distinctly understood," the viceroy concluded, "that . . . [the Government of India] regard the present state of affairs as open to the most serious objection, and that it may not be possible . . . if the terms now offered are rejected to continue existing arrangements upon their present footing." [46] In other words, indentured emigration would be discontinued.

Encouraged by the white public, the Government of Natal was not slow to accept the challenge. Minuting of July 17, 1903, stated: "Ministers are unanimously of opinion that the proposals of the Indian Government should not be accepted." [47] The prime minister, Albert Hime, for his part, felt that "Parliament is, if appealed to, more likely to increase than to mitigate . . . [the licensing] grievance." [48] He contended that the presence of the "Arab" trader posed a mortal danger to Natal which "can never be a matter of indifference to a European population enjoying the rights of Responsible Government." [49] If the removal of all restrictions on Indian traders was the price demanded by the Government of India in return for the repatriation of indentured Indians, it was more than Natal was willing to pay.

Ministers have therefore arrived at the conclusion that the manner in which their negotiations have been met, and the counter-proposals which are made conditions upon which alone the requests of this Government will be granted by the Government of India, render imperative on the Government of this Colony to no longer press for those measures of relief to indentured immigrants which are only to be attained by such concessions to

[46] CO, 179/228, viceroy to gov., conf., April 25, 1903.

[47] NA, G. 450/1903, minute paper, gov. to viceroy, July, 1903.

[48] CO, 179/228, minute by the prime minister of Natal, Aug. 13, 1903.

[49] *Ibid.*

the "Arab" trading population as the people of this Colony will not favour or concede.[50]

The rejection of the Government of India's terms seemed to remove much of the pressure on Natal, especially as the Government of India turned out to be unwilling to implement its threat.[51] The Indian community continued to address memorials to the governor, the prime minister, and the Colonial and India offices, but, with Gandhi in the Transvaal, the attacks were often craven and poorly directed. In June 1903, for instance, the Natal Indian Congress addressed a memorial to the prime minister which admitted a willingness to accept immigration restriction and the general dealers' licenses acts if only locations were not established. Always willing to sacrifice their less fortunate confreres, the members of the Congress claimed that "the poorer classes of Indians are already living in separate localities" [52]

At the cost of desired concessions from the Government of India, Natal had preserved the *status quo* and could now devote its attentions to changing conditions in a manner more to the liking of Pietermaritzburg than of Calcutta. Act 30 of 1903 established the Australian method [53] for keeping free Indians out of the colony. In other words, it was a more subtle and sophisticated version of the immigration act of 1897. Indians were not mentioned in the legislation. Exclusion was to be through administrative interpretation of the law. An immigrant wishing to enter Natal would have to fill out in the characters of some European language an application to enter the colony. He would have to do this "to the satisfaction of the Minister," [54] and the minister was to prove a

[50] *Ibid.*   [51] NA, tel., Govt. of Ind. to Ind. Off., Dec. 19, 1903.

[52] *Ibid.*, prime ministers' corresp., PM-1903, June 29, 1903; Resolution of Natal Indian Congress, June 20, 1903.

[53] The Australian legislation had, of course, received its inspiration from the Natal Act of 1897.

[54] Act no. 30 of 1903, section 5a.

very hard man for an Indian to satisfy. The India Office limited itself to recommending that the language requirement be changed to "English or some European language selected by himself [the immigrant]," [55] but it was not seriously offended when its suggestion was ignored. Natal's action was applauded by the rest of the South African colonies, which, at the South African Customs Conference held at Bloemfontein in March and April 1903, had resolved that "in the opinion of the Conference the permanent settlement in South Africa of Asiatic Races would be injurious and should not be permitted." [56]

Only the Natal Indians were alarmed by the new law. To them the immigration act of 1897 had seemed harsh enough.[57] Yet a comparison of the two measures indicated that the act of 1903 was still more restrictive. The earlier law had asked an immigrant to fill out a simple form in the characters of some European language. Now he would have to write out any application that might be dictated by the immigration officer. The age of majority for minor children was lowered from twenty-one to sixteen years, thus making it more difficult for them to join their parents in Natal. The domicile question was confused still further when it was made clear that five years' indentured service, which in the past could have constituted the establishment of domicile, would no longer do so. Three years' free residence would in future be required to establish domicile instead of two. The

[55] CO, 179/230, Ind. Off. to Col. Off., no date.

[56] Procs. of the So. Af. Customs Conf., March 19, 1903, resolution 11.

[57] *Indian Opinion*, Oct. 8, 1903. The *Natal Government Gazette* on Feb. 27, 1906, published a new schedule of fees connected with the administration of the immigration act which made it still more unpotable to the Indian community: exemption certificate, i.e. special permission to enter the colony—five shillings; certificate of knowledge of language—five shillings; domicile certificate—one pound; temporary visitor's pass—one pound; embarkation pass—one pound; separate pass for wife—five shillings; transit permit—five shillings. *Works*, V, 229; *Indian Opinion*, March 10, 1906.

chairman of the Natal Indian Congress stated at a public meeting:

We thought all our troubles would vanish by a magic wand— that we would breathe free, that we would succeed in waking the colonies up to a sense of their Imperial Duty. But all these hopes seem but a dream. The awful reality is that our struggle for existence has only just commenced. . . . In 1902 alone Mr. Smith excluded 3,907 of our countrymen.[58]

If the Indians still entertained any delusions about the intended order of things after the war, they were now clearly dispelled. The chairman's statement ended with an eloquent plea, in which this time the hand of the absent Gandhi was clearly visible:

They proudly call Natal the most loyal British colony in South Africa. They are members of the British Empire and have sworn allegiance to the old flag. The same flag waves over us. We belong to the same family. We provide seasoned, well-trained soldiers to fight the Empire's battles. Our loyalty is proverbial. Our sobriety, our industry, our law abiding character are acknowledged even in this Colony. We have accepted the principle most dear to them: viz., that they shall have the right to regulate immigration so long as they do not thereby slight a whole race. . . . In the name of humanity, justice, fair play, in the name of the

---

[58] *Natal Mercury,* June 25, 1903. Actual figures on the working of the immigration act of 1897 are as follows: in 1897, 254 Indians (as opposed to eight Britons) were excluded from Natal, and 1,103 Indians allowed to land. Of this last number, all but ten were able to prove former domicile. In 1898, 925 Indians were not permitted to disembark (as opposed to 25 Britons); 400 Indians were allowed to land, of which number 240 proved former domicile. In 1899, 494 Indians were excluded from Natal under the workings of the act; 470 were allowed to land, of which number 306 proved former domicile. In 1900, 364 Indians were excluded and 712 allowed to land; 508 proved former domicile. In 1901, 3,311 Indians were excluded and 1,583 admitted; 1,138 proved former domicile. NA, encl. in report of Natal delegates to Sir Denzil Ibbetson, Feb. 9. 1903.

British Constitution, I ask them to stay their hand, and give us rest, to which we are fairly entitled.[59]

The passage of the immigration act of 1903, by essentially barring the entry of free Indians into Natal, completed one wing of the edifice of anti-Indian legislation that Natal was determined to build. The next attack had logically to be directed upon the rights of those Indians, not indentured, already residing in the colony. Every point at which the Indian came into contact with the European was minutely scrutinized. Even a measure as seemingly innocuous as the shop-closing act of 1905 was passed largely because Europeans had, as one member of the legislative assembly put it, "to compete with the coloured races who have been introduced into this Colony." [60]

The bill, "to amend and consolidate the laws relating to Municipal Corporations," originally passed in 1905, contained a number of articles designed to reduce materially the rights of Indians in Natal. The trouble began as early as the definitions clause. Subsection 6 of section 7 classed all coolies and lascars with Bushmen, Hottentots, and Kaffirs as "coloured persons." While subsection 7 of the same clause stated:

The term "Uncivilised Races" shall include all barbarous and semi-barbarous races, and all Indians introduced into this Colony as indentured labourers, but who shall not at the time be serving under such indenture or a renewal thereof, and their descendants; but shall not include mechanics or artisans, clerks, and other persons of a status above that of labourers or domestic servants.

Subsection c of section 22 attempted to remove the last vestige of Indian political influence in Natal by depriving all persons of the municipal franchise who were disqualified from the parliamentary franchise by Act 8 of 1896 or any

[59] *Natal Mercury,* June 25, 1903.   [60] Natal *Hansard,* July 27, 1905.

like act, unless they were specifically exempted by the governor of the colony.

Of lesser importance were the subsections of section 182, which empowered town councils to regulate the use of pavements, footpaths, and rickshaws by coloured persons; section 200, which authorized town councils "to make By-Laws establishing a system of registration of Natives or persons belonging to uncivilised races, resident and employed by the day or month, or any longer period, or seeking employment within the borough"—largely a repetition of Law 21 of 1888; and section 208, which provided that every colored person found wandering between such hours as the town council might fix and not giving a satisfactory account of himself could be arrested as idle and disorderly—a re-enactment of section 2 of Law 15 of 1869. The attorney-general recommended that the royal assent be given to the bill, but the governor reluctantly reserved it under his instructions, because the measure differentiated between Europeans, natives, colored persons, and members of "uncivilised races."

The first mutterings from the India Office were rather modest. The secretary of state for India hesitated "to express his concurrence in the measure unless it can be made clear that the word 'coolie,' used in the definition of 'coloured persons' in Section 7(5), will not be construed as having a wider application to natives of India than the expression 'uncivilised races' as defined in Section 7(7)." [61] The Colonial Office tended to agree with the India Office's criticism. [62] The Government of India was considerably more outraged. It objected to all the differentiating clauses of the bill but particularly to the extension of the definition of "uncivilised races" in the bill to include the *descendants* of indentured immigrants. [63]

With the protests of the Government of India ringing in

[61] CO, 179/239, Ind. Off. to Col. Off., Nov. 15, 1905.
[62] CO, 179/238, minute paper, Natal no. 40730, Nov. 16, 1905.
[63] *Ibid.*, tel., Govt. of Ind. to Ind. Off., Dec. 27, 1905.

its collective ear, the India Office was forced to take a more forceful stand against the definitions section of the bill. No Indian, Mr. Secretary Morley contended, should be classed as a member of a barbarous, semibarbarous or uncivilized race, and, "he earnestly trusts, if the Government of Natal cannot be prevailed upon altogether to eliminate Indians from the definition of 'coloured persons,' the Royal Assent will not be given to the Bill unless Section 7(5) is so amended as to make it clear that the definition does not embrace any but the lowest classes of Indians." [64]

Under pressure from the India Office, the Colonial Office entered the fray more fully. Again the definitions clauses were the points of issue. The Colonial Office was concerned lest the word "coolie" used in the definition of "coloured persons" should be construed as having a wider application to natives of India than the expression "uncivilised races." The secretary of state observed that "the latter expression as applied to Indians includes only those who, having been introduced into Natal as indentured labourers, and their descendants—not being of status above that of labourer or domestic servants, unless this is the interpretation by the Courts, the word 'coolie" seems to require some further definition." [65]

The Natal Government did its best to counter the criticism, pointing out that most of the sections of the bill objected to were merely repetitions and rephrasings of legislation previously approved. What seems curious in retrospect is that the most significant attack upon the rights of Natal's Indians—their removal from the municipal voters' roll—was not even a point of issue at this stage.[66] It was apparently

[64] *Ibid.*, Ind. Off. to Col. Off., Jan. 31, 1906.

[65] NA, Natal G. no. 1030/1905, no. 104, sec. of state to gov., Dec. 9, 1905.

[66] NA, tel., gov. to sec. of state, Jan. 20, 1906, G. no. 396/1906, minuting by minister of justice, July 23, 1906; minute paper, sec. of state no. 23, April 11, 1906, AG 1448/1906, MJ 2801/1906, PM 489/1906.

not until the Indians of Natal sent a memorial to the secretary of state for the colonies that it was officially realized that the municipal corporations bill, in its existing form, would disenfranchise Indians at the municipal level—their only remaining arena for any kind of political activity. "British Indians resident in Natal," the petition read,

feel that if they are deprived of Municipal franchise, it will be a very serious grievance, and will be a departure from the declaration of the responsible statement of Natal at the time the measure disenfranchising Indians as of the Parliamentary vote was passed. It was recognised that, if India did not possess parliamentary institutions, it certainly enjoyed municipal institutions, and that there were in India thousands of municipal voters.

No legitimate ground has been urged in favour of the contemplated disenfranchisement. Indians do not aspire to any political power in the Colony of Natal but they naturally resent interference with municipal liberty when they pay the same rates as other taxpayers.[67]

When the petition was forwarded to the India Office, Morley rose to its support.[68] The Colonial Office was dismayed and embarrassed by its oversight. One official minuted: "I scarcely think we can press the objection with regard to the Municipal franchise, if Natal holds out, in view of the late stage in the correspondence at which it has been raised by the I.O." [69] But Frederick Graham, now one of the assistant under-secretaries, disagreed. "We can afford to chop logic with Natal," he wrote, "as the Bill is not in operation. I should send a copy of I.O. letter and say that the objection though not taken before is of great force." [70]

The new discussion complicated the picture still further,

[67] NA, G. no. 725/1906, minute paper, sec. of state no. 3, July 25, 1906. Encloses Indian petition to the sec. of state, April 13, 1906.

[68] CO, 179/238, India Off. to Col. Off., Oct. 18, 1906.

[69] *Ibid.*, minuting dated Dec. 12, 1906, Natal minute paper no. 45883, Dec. 13, 1906.

[70] *Ibid.*, minuting by Graham, Dec. 15, 1906.

and it was to be many months before some sort of order emerged from the chaos. Meanwhile the issues raised by the municipal corporations bill became fused with that old problem—Indian trading licenses. Based on reports from all parts of the colony, the South Africa British India Committee, the prime British defender of the South African Indians, addressed a letter to the Colonial Office giving figures as to the beleaguered state of the Indian merchants in Natal. "My Committee feel," L. W. Ritch, the committee's secretary, wrote, that

the facts warrant the conclusion that the Natal Dealers' Licenses Act (Law 18 of 1897) is being deliberately used as an engine of oppression with the object of driving away British Indian trade competition, and [we] respectfully urge His Majesty's Government to take prompt steps to secure relief to those established British Indian traders whose licenses have been arbitrarily refused and to prevent any such future invasion of vested interests.[71]

Several questions were asked in the Commons. Dr. V. H. Rutherford, for instance, on February 18, 1907, asked the under-secretary of state for the colonies,

whether his attention had been called to the position of the British Indian trading communities of Ladysmith, Natal, several of whom are threatened with ruin by reason of the threatened refusal of the Licensing Officer to renew their store licenses under the powers conferred upon him by the Natal Licensing Act of 1897; and whether, seeing that the Licensing Officer is the appointee of the Town Council which is composed of merchants and storekeepers in competition with British Indian traders, he proposes to take any action in the matter.

The secretary of state himself felt that "the incidents, if correctly reported, give rise to grave doubts whether the licens-

[71] NA, G. no. 285/1907, sec. of state to gov., March 23, 1907; encloses So. Af. Brit. Ind. Comm. to Col. Off., March 13, 1907.

ing boards can be trusted to deal with applications in a judicial spirit." [72]

The evidence was indeed damning. At Klip River, eleven Indians were deprived of licenses, not because they did not keep proper books in English, but because they had hired a professional bookkeeper to do the accounting for them. Obviously they were complying with the spirit of the law and had every right to expect the generous treatment promised by the Government of Natal at the time of the passage of the act, without which the royal assent would never have been given. During the course of the appeal against the licensing officer's decision, the licensing board would not permit advocate Kufal, appearing for the defense, to read extracts from speeches made by the prime minister and other government officials at the time of the promulgation of the act; neither would the board allow the bookkeeper to appear as a witness nor the licensing officer's notes to be introduced in evidence. Driven beyond exasperation, Kufal heatedly addressed the board:

I think, Gentlemen, that you are treating this matter with a very light heart indeed, from the jokes you are passing. You are simply persecuting these men. The book-keeper should be heard. . . . Gentlemen, I should be wanting in sincerity if I was to attempt to say that this is not a serious matter. I ask you to give a broad and generous interpretation to the Statute. It was never intended that it should apply to present holders of licenses, but it was passed so as to enable townships to control Asiatic trading in regard to further licenses. Surely it should not be in the power of any individual to refuse a license. It is unjust that these men should be allowed to trade year after year, accumulate stock, and, perhaps liabilities, and then to have their licenses refused. It seems impossible that Parliament could intend that one individual should have power to absolutely ruin a man.

You are the final Court of Appeal and a great responsibility rests upon you. It is only right to ask you to place an extensive

[72] NA, Natal no. 30, sec. of state to gov., March 23, 1907.

interpretation upon the Statute and to admit that a man has a right to a license, provided he has a competent book-keeper. The law provides that the applicant should be able to properly conduct his business. My main point is this: having granted the licenses for so many years, I ask you to seriously consider the matter and renew the licenses.[73]

It took the board but a few moments to turn down the appeals.

In the Lower Umzimkulu Division, Mahomed Saduck Vahed was deprived of his license because he was paying too much interest to his creditors. The licensing officer, upon being questioned by the advocate (Sangmeister) representing Vahed, admitted that the books of the business were well kept and that the sanitary inspector had filed a satisfactory report. "His initial reason for refusal was that the applicant had made a compact with his creditors and was paying 9/- in the £. He thought that the applicant was not a suitable license holder in the civilised and respectable community." [74] Sangmeister presented the licensing board with a petition favoring the granting of a license to the appellant signed by twenty-eight Europeans and concluded his arguments by emphasizing that the deprivation of a license would prevent Vahed from earning a livelihood for himself, his wife and his children. He was an elderly man and served as the priest for the Muslim community.

A certain J. W. Godwin appeared against the granting of the license. He based his objection on the presence of too many stores in the district—eight European and eight "Arab." Besides, the "Arabs" did not compete fairly. "These fellows," he said, "live on practically nothing—on the smell of an oil rag—and we Europeans have to live in a quite different way." [75] J. F. Rethman represented the chamber of commerce. He contended that the "Arab" element was gaining too strong a footing in the community and that it was

[73] *Vide* n. 65.   [74] *Ibid.*   [75] *Ibid.*

the duty of every man to protect the interests of the European against this insidious element in the population. "They had to take the initial steps for getting these people out of the country." [76] The board then retired and after some deliberation read its verdict. "The Board is unanimous," the chairman read, "in its decision that the action of the Licensing Officer should be upheld and the appeal is dismissed without costs." [77]

On March 19, the South Africa British India Committee again addressed the Colonial Office. Besides the eleven licenses withdrawn in the Klip River Division, the committee pointed out that ten applications for renewals had been rejected in Inanda, two in Alexandra, five in Victoria, three in Weenen, and at least six in Pietermaritzburg. The committee admitted that the Government of Natal was itself virtually powerless to act against the municipalities and had even gone so far as to allow Indians to keep their shops open even after the licensing officer and the licensing board had revoked the license. The committee

would however impress upon His Majesty's Government the anomalous character of the law which is liable to give rise to such startling and distressing consequences. As has previously been urged such a law as this, excluding as it does appeal from the decision of the Licensing Boards to the Supreme Court, constitutes altogether too dangerous a weapon to be entrusted to communities frequently most strongly imbued with anti-Asiatic prejudices, and are forced to the conclusion that as long as this law remains unrepealed or at least unmodified a recrudescence of such occurrences as are now complained of is inevitable.[78]

To strengthen its case the committee again enclosed the report of two licensing cases. This time the venue was Ladysmith. Messrs. Goga and Benne, both Indian traders, had appealed to the town council, sitting as a licensing court,

[76] *Ibid.*   [77] *Ibid.*

[78] NA, G. no. 286/1907, Natal no. 31, sec. of state to gov., March 23, 1907; encloses So. Af. Brit. Ind. Comm. to Col. Off., March 19, 1907.

against the decision of the licensing officer depriving them of their licenses. The deliberations were conducted before a large audience of Europeans and Indians. In the case of Goga it was admitted that his books were in perfect order. He was nonetheless deprived of his license because he did not keep the books himself. Advocate Wylie, appearing for the defense, questioned the licensing officer (Lines):

Mr. Wylie: Surely you do not mean to say you interpret the law to mean that a man must keep his own books?

Mr. Lines: Yes, I do.

Mr. Wylie: Will you find it in the law?

Mr. Lines read Section 7 of the Act of 1897 which states that the applicants are required to show to the satisfaction of the Licensing Officer that they are able to fulfil the conditions of Sub. Sec. A, Art. 180 of the Insolvency Law No. 47, 1887.

Mr. Wylie then read Section 180 of the Insolvency Law which requires the applicant to keep such books of accounts in the English language as are usual and proper in the businesses carried on by them and as sufficiently disclose their business transactions, three years preceding insolvency.

Mr. Lines: You will not shake me.

Wylie summed up with great astuteness. He pointed out that Goga had been in business in Ladysmith for seventeen years, that 95 per cent of his business was with Europeans, and that consequently he was a great asset to the burgesses of the town. Swayed by Wylie's arguments, the council returned one of the few reversals of a licensing officer's decision.[79]

Benne's case was similar. He too could not keep books himself but had hired a competent bookkeeper. But where the council had found for Goga, it decided against Benne. Perhaps because his advocate was not so eloquent, or perhaps because the licensing officer had stated that "Benne was a man of the labouring class and he ought to be on a farm not keeping a store." Besides, the licensing officer continued,

[79] *Ibid.*

"the man was not capable, he was getting old and his appearance was not good." [80]

Even the *Times of Natal* could not help being highly critical of licensing practices in Ladysmith:

A more arbitrary and unjust proceeding could not be imagined; and we have no hesitation in saying that had the Boer authorities in the days of the South African Republic, been guilty of such conduct, they would have instantly been brought up with a round turn by the Imperial Government. Here we have a number of reputable Indian storekeepers, who have built up businesses in which a large amount of capital is invested, suddenly and arbitrarily deprived of their trading licenses through alleged non-compliance with the law. They had complied with the law so far as it was in their power to do so, and those who could not write in English had their books made up in English at the end of each week by a competent book-keeper. They have done this for years past, and not a word has been said against the practice until now. We can only describe the decisions of the Ladysmith Licensing Board as a scandalous injustice and illegal as well; and if the applicants had a right of appeal—which, of course under the law they have not—the Board's decisions would immediately be quashed by the Supreme Court.

The newspaper was no friend of the Indians.

We wish to be perfectly clear in this matter. We have no sympathy with Indian traders, and we should be glad to see an end of Indian trading. We would support the most drastic restrictions at the port of entry, and would go so far as to favour no fresh licenses being granted to Indian applicants. But to decline to renew a trading license in the case of Indians who have been allowed to settle in the country, who have been conducting their businesses in a perfectly legitimate manner for years, and who have invested capital in commercial enterprises on the strength of the licenses to trade, is to do something which conflicts with the laws of all civilised nations and with the most elementary notions of justice. We hope that stringent instructions will be issued to all licensing officers in order to prevent a repetition of

[80] *Ibid.*

the Ladysmith scandal, otherwise Natal will gravely embarrass the Imperial Government in its relations with the people of India.[81]

When the Colonial Office telegraphed Natal for an explanation, the governor's reply was similar in tenor to the editorial opinion of the newspaper. "I fully sympathise," he wrote,

with the European storekeepers of the Colony in the almost impossible task which they have of competing against Indian traders and hawkers, but any action taken by the Government or by the local authorities should be directed towards the refusing of new licenses for new traders; those who have carried on business for many years without let or hindrance should not suddenly be deprived of their licenses on the plea only of insufficient bookkeeping.[82]

The governor, Sir Henry McCallum, clearly felt that Indian competition was by its very nature unfair, but as he later pointed out, he had for many years urged access to the supreme court for Indians deprived of their licenses. "They should not be exposed to the vagaries of local boards who are too often subject to local influences." But, he concluded, "my suggestion in this matter was not however adopted." [83]

McCallum enclosed the official transcript of the Vahed case with his dispatch. The full record was even more damning. Rethman's remarks had been slighted in the condensed text. "I am opposed to this license as a matter of principle," he had said.

We have this Arab element getting a footing strongly in our midst and I think it is the duty of every man to protect the interest of the European. I hope the Board will put its foot down and not be guided by technicalities of law. You are to judge whether any further licenses are required and the community have to

81 *Ibid.*
82 NA, Natal conf. no. 1, gov. to sec. of state, May 18, 1908.
83 *Ibid.*

thank the licensing officer for putting his foot down in refusing this license. This is a very serious matter and we have to take the initial steps of getting these people out of the country as the bread will be taken out of the mouths of our children and posterity and we must protect them.[84]

McCallum also enclosed the transcript of the case of one Jan Mahomed of Fort Shepstone who had been deprived of his license despite the fact that the licensing officer admitted the application form was in order and the books properly and neatly kept. "This license is not inimical to the community," he testified, "I simply refused the license because the sentiment was rife at the time against the granting of such licenses. I have no fault to find with the man's books or with him." [85] The licensing board decided in favor of the licensing officer, and the appeal was dismissed without costs.[86]

Faced with such overpowering evidence the Colonial Office chided Natal and reminded the government of previous promises. "I should be glad," the secretary of state wrote, "if you would draw . . . [ministers'] attention to Mr. Chamberlain's confidential despatch of the 20th of November 1897, enclosing a letter from Mr. Escombe, in which he gave it as his opinion that the Act did not require books to be kept by the Indian trader personally." [87]

What caused the Government of Natal the greatest embarrassment, however, was neither memorials from the Indian population nor letters from the Colonial Office, but rather the action of the colony's own supreme court. While the general dealers' licenses act did indeed not permit a direct appeal to the supreme court from a decision of a licensing board, the court could rule on procedural matters concerned with hearings conducted by the boards. In mid-1907 some of the Indian traders of Ladysmith brought such a case before the court. They claimed that despite the numerous protests

[84] Ibid., encl.   [85] Ibid.   [86] Ibid.
[87] NA, G. no. 419/1907, conf., sec. of state to gov., May 25, 1907.

they had been deprived of their licenses without either the licensing officer or his notes being examined at the hearings. The chief justice, with the other two justices sitting on the case concurring, condemned the actions of the licensing board. He only addressed himself to the question whether the licensing board, sitting as a court of appeal, had the right to come to a decision without the complete record of the licensing officer's proceedings being introduced in evidence. Clearly the answer was no. "It was certainly extraordinary," the chief justice thought,

that any Court sitting as a Court of Appeal should decide a question on appeal without having before it all the records that were available. . . . Quite apart from the principle, it seemed to him, having regard to the rules framed under the law, the rules themselves required that the Board should have the report of the Sanitary Officer, the remarks of the Licensing Officer, and also the record of the application, and all the minutes that the Licensing Officer had. . . . The proceedings seemed of the greatest irregularity. . . . The proceedings before the Licensing Board were set aside, the appeal to be recommended de novo.[88]

The court's decision paid eloquent testimony to the need of an appeal to the supreme court in licensing cases and of the court's very limited powers under the law as it stood. The Ladysmith licensing board reheard the cases shortly after the supreme court's decision, and again turned down the appeals against the decision of the licensing officer.[89]

Natal's Indians as they assessed their position became ever more discouraged. The white colonists despised them. The India and Colonial offices cared little for their welfare so long as anti-Indian policies were not explicitly spelled out in

[88] *Ibid.,* encl. *Times of Natal.*

[89] Gandhi, in *Indian Opinion,* Dec. 14, 1907, called attention to new licensing regulations which forced applicants to allow the taking of a thumb print, required them to publish their intent in the newspaper, and to deposit £12-10-0 when making an appeal (the last point was not new). *Works,* VII, 427–428.

law. The Government of India did from time to time intercede on their behalf but its influence was limited. As for the governor, the arm and voice of Imperial Britain, the enunciator of the imperial philosophy in the colony, he nearly always sympathized with the colonists' views. Early in 1907, McCallum scribbled on a minute paper an angry note referring to Gandhi. "The 'Bombay Wallah' has come here knowing the conditions," he wrote, "and he can leave if he does not like them. Because we wanted *indentured labour for agriculture* it is no reason why we should be swamped by black matter in the wrong place—namely storekeepers etc." [90]

That the Natal Indians did not often use the most effective tactics in their own defense cannot be denied. Relatively unimportant enactments were protested strenuously. Upperclass Indians (frequently supported by Gandhi) were too often affronted at being classed with "coolies," and the Indian community as a whole was incensed at being included in the provisions of a law that affected Africans. Act 1 of 1906, the firearms act, which bracketed Indians with natives in regard to the possession of firearms, is a case in point. Dadabhai Naoroji, at the behest of the Natal Indians, objected to the Colonial Office. "I need hardly state," he wrote, "what the moral effect of this is likely to be." [91] The Colonial Office, only too happy to prove its solicitude for the Indians of Natal on an issue not calculated to arouse colonial passions, used a familiar strategem. It did not recommend the disallowance of the measure but rather asked Natal to amend the act at the next session of the legislature so as to allow the governor to exempt Indians from the workings of the law.[92] The Government of Natal did not object to the

[90] NA, minute paper, sec. of state, Dec. 29, 1906; note by McCallum, Jan. 21, 1907.
[91] CO, 179/232, India Off. to Col. Off., encl. Naoroji to St. John Brodrick, June 6, 1905.
[92] *Ibid.*, sec. of state to gov., Oct. 2, 1905.

stipulation, although, in fact, the act was never amended. It was the old problem of sounding the tocsin too frequently. The aid of an embarrassed and unenthusiastic government in London could be mustered only so often.

Despite their basically pusillanimous positions, neither the Colonial Office nor the India Office could afford to ignore the overt challenges of the Indian franchise clause of the municipal corporations act and the ever-increasing persecution of Indian traders under the dealers' licenses act. The Colonial Office discerned the seeds of a solution in a note received from the India Office in August 1907. "If the dealers' licenses act is not amended," Morley had written,

it [is] essential that Indian rate-payers should remain in possession of the municipal franchise, in order that their interests may be adequately represented on the Municipal Boards. He [Morley] therefore trusts that Lord Elgin may be able to agree that, unless the Dealers' Licenses Act be amended, it is impossible to consent to the retention of section 22(c) of the Municipal Corporations Bill.[93]

The secretary of state for the colonies consequently decided that British honor would be vindicated if Natal were given the choice of either disenfranchising Indians at the municipal level or maintaining the *status quo* in the licensing question.[94] It was a rather cynical gamble. Lord Crewe, who had assumed the post of secretary of state for the colonies in Herbert Asquith's liberal government, realized that from his viewpoint the vital issue concerned the issuance of licenses, and he was convinced that Natal would permit appeals to the supreme court rather than allow Indians to retain the municipal franchise.

If Crewe could have been present at a meeting between the Government of Natal and the mayors and chairmen of local boards called in January 1908, he would have recog-

[93] CO, 179/249, Ind. Off. to Col. Off., Aug. 24, 1907.
[94] *Ibid.*, minuting on Natal minute paper, Sept. 2, 1908.

nized the value the colonists placed on the dealers' licenses act as it stood. The minister of justice (Carter) thought it perfectly proper for municipalities to rid themselves of licensing officers who disregarded the communities' wishes and granted licenses to Indians.

They in Maritzburg had not issued one single new license to an Asiatic and if any licenses lapse either through insolvency or death the licenses were in no case renewed. . . . They in Durban had felt something should be done to stop this Asiatic trade, and during the last 4 years they had reduced their licenses by one-third. . . . [Newcastle] granted no transfers and were gradually squeezing them [the Indians] out. Next year they hoped to reduce them [the number of licenses] to about 8 [three years ago there had been 25 Indian licenses and at the present time there were 12]. . . . In Ladysmith they had commenced a crusade against these people and since then they had managed to close 12 Indian stores. . . . At one time they had 45 Indian licenses in Ladysmith, and some of the traders possessed their own stores which were amongst the best in the place. Today by quietly working they had reduced the number to 25, which . . . were 25 too many. . . . Mr. Perkins [Chairman of the local board of Verulam] said his Board were of opinion that from this time forward no new licenses should be issued to Indians nor should there be any transfers. Notice should be given that at the end of say five years all Indian licenses should be terminated. During the last year the Indian licenses in Verulam had been reduced by 5, and these would be further reduced as opportunity offered. . . . Mr. Anderson of Vryheid said he represented a town which had not a single Indian storekeeper. . . . Mr. Dely of Utrecht said they had no Asiatic traders in their district or town and so long as they had the power they would keep them out. . . . A short time ago [Charlestown] was nothing but a coolie town, but things were improving.

As the minister of justice spoke again, he did so with alarming bluntness. His own opinion was that

if there was one law which they should cherish it was the Licensing Law. If the Imperial Government had ever known in what direction the law was going to operate he was certain it would never have obtained the Royal Assent. Already the Imperial Government had asked them to alter this law so that there should be an appeal to the Supreme Court, and that was the one thing the Government would never agree to.

The prime minister, F. R. Moor, concluded the proceedings. "He thought the time had come when they should most seriously consider the advisability of not issuing any more licenses." No doubt aware of the Natal Government's duplicity at the time of the passage of the dealers' licenses act in 1897, he cautioned his listeners not to "blazen the fact abroad, but it was their policy nevertheless." [95]

When Natal reacted to the secretary of state's proposed bargain, its decision ran contrary to Lord Crewe's expectations. The prime minister reported that by promising the municipal association that the government contemplated no amendment of the dealers' licenses act it had gained the association's unanimous consent to changes in the municipal corporations bill.[96] Virtually all the sections of the original bill to which the Colonial and India offices had objected were removed from the version it was intended to introduce into the next session of the legislature. Indians retained the municipal franchise. They were no longer to be considered members of an uncivilized race, and the term "coloured persons" was defined as meaning "any Asiatic labourer or domestic servant (including Asiatic labourers but not including mechanics, artisans, clerks, and other persons of a status above labourer or domestic servant)." [97]

Having altered the municipal corporations bill and having consequently made one of the two choices acceptable to the Colonial Office, Natal confidently awaited a note of approbation from the secretary of state. But Crewe was, of course, on the horns of a dilemma. He had offered Natal a

[95] NA, PM 74/1908, conf., Jan. 23, 1908.

[96] NA, Natal no. 74, gov. to sec. of state, May 7, 1908.

[97] NA, tel., gov. to sec. of state, July 24, 1907.

choice of paths to follow, confident that the colony would amend the dealers' licenses act in preference to allowing Indians to remain on the municipal voters' rolls, and he had been wrong. He now indulged in a series of delaying tactics in order to avoid acceptance of the bargain he had himself proposed. Minor faults were discerned in the revised municipal corporations bill and loud exception was taken to them.[98] The prime minister of Natal quite properly replied that "impediments should not be placed in the way of an otherwise unobjectionable measure because the Association did not go further and repeal existing legislation which has never been questioned by the Imperial Government in the past nor even mentioned prior to the secretary of state's telegram under reply." [99] The prime minister pointed out that the Natal legislative session was already far advanced and unless some indication was soon received from the Colonial Office, it would be too late for the revised bill to pass.[100]

The fulfillment of his bargain not having worked out to his expectations, Crewe determined to abrogate it. The municipal corporations bill might have been satisfactorily altered, but this was after all not enough. In July 1908, the secretary of state, while expressing his pleasure at the proposed amendment of the municipal corporations bill, added:

I feel obliged, however, to express my regret that your Ministers continue to be unwilling to introduce into Parliament a Bill to give to Indians to whom licenses are refused by the local Licensing Authorities a right of appeal to the Supreme Court, for I regard such an appeal as necessary to secure due protection of vested interests, and I am bound to record [my opinion] . . . that traders who have carried on their businesses for many years without let or hindrance should not be suddenly deprived of their licenses on the plea only of insufficient book-keeping.

[98] NA, G. no. 400/1908, tel., sec. of state to gov., June 18, 1908.
[99] *Vide* n. 96. [100] *Ibid.*

Crewe then referred the Government of Natal once more to the promises made prior to the passage of the act.[101] Clearly the right of the Indians deprived of licenses to appeal to the supreme court of Natal was one issue on which even temporizing officials of the Colonial Office found it inexpedient to give way.

Natal's answer to the renewed assault was the introduction of three of the most virulently anti-Indian measures into the legislative assembly. The first bill (Assembly Bill 5 of 1908) was to bring to an end the issue of new trading licenses to Asians. It defined as a new license:

(a) a license to any person who does not hold a license similar in every respect to the license applied for at the date when the application is made for the license.

(b) a license in respect to premises for which a license similar in every respect is not held at a date when application is made for the license.

The transfer of a license was, under the terms of the act, deemed to be the issuance of a new license. The act stipulated that after December 31, 1908, no new license would be issued to an Asian, although rights of inheritance were preserved.

The government and its adherents were at their most eloquent in defending the measure. The colonial secretary in moving the second reading of the bill claimed that Indian traders were driving out those of European extraction. "The object of the Bill," he stated,

was to provide an opening for the European children of the Colony. It might be said that the Bill was un-English, but under the circumstances, when they were driven to look after their own interests, he thought the Bill was justified. . . . If they did not

101 NA, G. no. 54/1901, Natal conf. (2), sec. of state to gov., July 18, 1908.

grasp the nettle, . . . they would earn the contempt of their children, and, further, of the other states of South Africa.[102]

A supporter of the bill (Taylor) regarded Asiatic traders as parasites.

It was unfair to ask white traders to compete against the Asiatics, who lived on practically nothing. It was unfortunate that there were a number of semi-idiots in the Home Parliament who would not take the trouble to understand the position. If the Imperial Government did not sanction the Bill, they would pass it again and again year after year until it was established.[103]

Only a member (Connolly) who claimed to represent the working class seemed in strong opposition to the proposed law. He contended that competition aided the consumer and that the presence of the Indian traders consequently allowed the white laborer to buy at the lowest possible price.[104]

The introduction of the measure allowed the members of the legislative assembly to give voice to a whole spectrum of prejudices. Although most of the colonists were really only worried about competition from the "Arabs," one member (Robinson) had a different point of view. "The Arab is undoubtedly an undesirable resident," he admitted,

but on the question of comparison of degree of danger, do members realise what I have pointed out before, that the sons of Indian immigrants are practising as barristers in this Colony today? That it is a fear—not personal to myself. I disclaim any personal interest in the matter at all. I say that when one views the circumstances that we have practising in Natal the son of an Indian immigrant admitted to the bar [;] as an honourable gentleman says: "Why should he not?" I say he should not. I say that is the question that this House has to decide. There are thousands of these men in the country. Their children are being admitted into all the professions. By a comparison of menace, the Arab is nil. The descendants of the coolie are a very serious menace.[105]

102 Natal *Hansard,* July 15, 1908.   103 *Ibid.*   104 *Ibid.*
105 *Ibid.,* July 23, 1907; statement made in an earlier debate on a similar measure.

Another member (Wylie) "would like to see the provisions of the Bill extended," as there were traders just as undesirable as Indians and Asiatics, such, for instance, as the Polish and other low-class Jews." [106] A third member of the legislative assembly (O'Meara) was even more exotically antisemitic. "[He] wanted the title to the Bill to be extended to include such people as Peruvian Jews, who were the most undesirable class of people he could conceive." [107]

In view of these sentiments, which were by no means atypical, one can imagine with what joy the colonists received Sir Matthew Nathan as their new governor in 1907. First of all, he replaced Sir Henry McCallum, a governor who strongly supported their views; second, he was a Jew, one of the first to achieve a position of eminence in the colonial service; and third, he was much more sympathetic to the Indians' dilemma than any of his predecessors—his greater liberalism no doubt largely due to his own struggle for success in a century when antisemitism in public life was more the rule than the exception. Nathan was critical of the bill "to bring to an end the issue of new trading licenses to Asiatics," [108] and there were those in the assembly who wished to modify the law. All attempted amendments were, however, rejected. The bill was read without a division for the third time on July 28, 1908, and sent to London for ratification by the secretary of state.

The passage of this first of the three pieces of anti-Indian legislation occurred while the assembly was debating the second bill, which would "put an end to further introduction of indentured Indian immigrants." The proposal was, of course, a highly controversial measure. [109] So much so that it

[106] *Ibid.*

[107] *Ibid.* It should be noted that Yiddish was considered a European language under the provisions of the immigration act of 1903.

[108] NA, no. 289, gov. to sec. of state, Dec. 7, 1908.

[109] Opposition to the bill was not limited to the coast planters. Upcountry farmers had been making increasing use of Indian labor in the

was withdrawn to allow appointment of a commission, broadly representative of all shades of colonial opinion, which, under the chairmanship of Walter F. Clayton, was to investigate fully the various facets of the colony's labor situation.

The third bill, the most destructive of the Indian position to date, was passed by the Natal legislature and sent to the governor on August 27, 1908. Its purpose was "to prohibit after a certain time the holding of trading licenses by Asiatics." The act stipulated that after December 31, 1918, "no license shall be issued or transferred to or be capable of being held by or on behalf of an Asiatic." Compensation was to be provided for those still holding licenses at the time the act went into operation, but the scale was singularly niggardly.

The compensation payable as aforesaid shall be a sum equal to three years' purchase of the profits of the business, and shall be calculated upon the average net profits, as nearly as they can be ascertained, for the two years preceding the 31st day of December, 1918, unless, for sufficient reasons appearing to the arbitrators such an average is a manifestly inadequate basis of assessment, in which case the assessment should be made upon the normal yearly profits of the business as nearly as they can be estimated.

In case of difficulty in determining the amount of compensation, article 5 of the law provided for adjudication under the terms of the arbitration act of 1898, or whatever similar act might be in force at the time.

This final bill was so extreme that eleven of the thirty-three members of the assembly opposed it, mainly on the basis of the compensation clause which the colonial secretary stated was more liberal than ordinarily would have been the case and was only included to disarm criticism in London. "They would show that they were prepared to stretch a

---

wattlebark industry, etc., and the railways employed 1,500 indentured and 2,000 free Indians.

point by putting in such a clause as that." [110] The colonial secretary contended that Indians sent two and one-half million pounds out of the country annually, and that "it was their duty to hand down a clear land to their children, and he appealed to members to do their duty." [111] More even than those of the colonial secretary, the statements of Representative Taylor again characterized the attitude of the advocates of the bill. He thought that the provision for a ten-year period during which Indians were permitted to continue in business was excessively generous when a license was issued for only one year at a time. If the licensing officers did not reduce the number of Indian licenses by half before the act went into effect, "he would endeavour to make it hot for them. It would behoove the young men of Natal to get up a Movement and let the rest of the world see that they were not going to allow the thing to go on. He was prepared to take a lead in the matter." [112]

On August 27, Marshall Campbell, the noted sugar planter, rose in the council to oppose the bill in what he knew to be a losing effort. But his words represented the sentiments of the more liberal of Natal's white colonists.

He considered the Bill a most unjust one. The Arabs had been encouraged to come into the Colony to trade by the Government, the Corporations, and individuals. They had built up new houses and businesses, and to get notice that in ten years' time they had to leave everything that was dear to them was cruel. The Council had been especially constituted to protect the two races that were not directly represented. He would again oppose the Bill at the third reading.

Nathan was strongly critical of the measure. He felt that the rationale so often used of passing anti-Indian laws to protect the natives was an obvious sham.[113] But as the governor of a colony possessing the rights of responsible government,

[110] Natal *Hansard,* Aug. 19, 1908. [111] *Ibid.* [112] *Ibid.*
[113] *Vide* n. 108.

he had to be circumspect in his official correspondence. "As in the case of the other Bill," he wrote to the secretary of state, "stress is laid on the present exodus of the Colony's white manhood, an exodus which it may be mentioned has taken place also from the Cape Colony where it has, as far as I am aware, never been attributed to the Asiatic trader." [114] In referring to the compensation clause, Nathan concluded that the stipulated terms were inadequate and designed to force Indians to sell out to Europeans at a loss during the grace period provided by the act. All in all, he was convinced that "the compensation clauses are illusory." [115] And so saying, he reserved the measure for the signification of His Majesty's pleasure.[116]

Yet, Nathan was not totally unsympathetic to the fears of the white population, and he searched his mind for a solution to the problem that the Indians presented. He had no doubt that the three bills, extreme as they were, would never achieve their aims, but the only alternative he could recommend was not really practicable. "Repatriation to India or removal to some Colony which Great Britain governs but does not colonise, for the bulk of the Indians outside of the Tropics in South Africa," he wrote,

is the only solution which would be completely satisfactory to the white races. . . . It might be worthwhile for the United Kingdom to contribute financially and otherwise to the gradual carrying out of the scheme with this view under such conditions of full compensation for injury to vested interests as would prevent it becoming unduly harsh on the persons removed.[117]

When news of the three bills reached the Colonial Office, Lord Crewe reacted with unaccustomed vigor. On July 22 he sent a long dispatch to Natal. He had little to say concerning

[114] NA, no. 290, gov. to sec. of state, Dec. 7, 1908.
[115] NA, Natal conf., gov. to sec. of state, May 8, 1908.
[116] *Vide* n. 114.   [117] *Ibid.*, n. 115.

the bill to halt indentured immigration, but he condemned the other two acts in the strongest terms.

It would be a matter of the greatest difficulty to enumerate any conditions under which it would be possible to justify interdiction of a particular class in a state from engaging in normal legitimate and necessary occupations; it would be still harder to justify dispossessing them from their existing means of livelihood, however liberal might be the terms of compensation. But the imposition of such disabilities on a class which owes its presence in the Colony to the Colony's own necessities and whose numbers have been augmented by the voluntary action, indeed the central policy of successive Colonial Governments, over a period of fifteen years since the advent of self-government, would appear on its merits to constitute a hardship of an especially grievous character.

. . . It is scarcely necessary to point out the disastrous effects of the proposed legislation on feeling in India, already deeply stirred by the Asiatic controversy of the Transvaal; and I do not desire to labour the point because I feel bound to inform you that the inherent defects to which I have referred will make it impossible for me to advise His Majesty to assent to these Bills.[118]

The course of events in Natal, and the Colonial Office's decision of September 1908 finally to approve the municipal corporations bill, convinced the Government of India that indentured Indian emigration to Natal would have to come to a halt. The viceroy consequently addressed the secretary of state for India in order to gain the necessary permission to pass the enabling legislation.[119] As the viceroy pointed out to the presidencies and the United Provinces, he did not have the power to halt indentured emigration to Natal under existing legislation:

Section 9 of the Emigration Act enables the Governor General in Council to suspend emigration to a country where proper treat-

[118] NA, G. no. 555/1908, no. 125, sec. of state to gov., July 22, 1908.
[119] CO, 179/255, viceroy in council, dept. of comm. and ind., no. 104, to sec. of state, Dec. 24, 1908.

ment cannot be secured for the indentured labourers. No question has been raised as to the fulfillment by employers of the terms of indenture; the point at issue is a wider one, which is not covered by the section of the Act, and power will have to be taken by amendment of the Act to withdraw Natal from the list of countries to which emigration is lawful.[120]

The announcement of the Government of India's intentions caused an immediate reaction in Natal and London. The negotiations which were to culminate in the creation of the Union of South Africa were already under way in London, and the Colonial Office, beleaguered by the visiting delegations of Natal and Transvaal Indians, lived in fear of their imminent collapse. Natal was similarly concerned, and Nathan, in a handwritten note, indicated to the Colonial Office that the proposed policy of the Indian Government, if implemented, would endanger the prospects of the colony entering the Union.[121] The negotiations would have been exceedingly complicated under the best of circumstances, but the Indian question made them still more complex.

Both Indian delegations pressed their concerns upon the Colonial and India offices. The Natal delegates emphasized the inability of Indians to enter the public service, the inadequate provisions for Indian education,[122] the definition of land cultivated by Indians as being not beneficially occupied

[120] *Ibid.*, Govt. of Ind. to Bombay, Madras, U.P., Dec. 18, 1908.

[121] CO, 179/255, MSS note, Nathan to Just, April 25, 1909.

[122] Indian teachers were not covered by colonial pension schemes but European ones were. NAI, Oct. 1910, procs. 1 and 2, notes. The prime minister of Natal, when preparing a reply to Curzon on the education question, had said: "It is hopeless to ask Parliament to remove such caste distinctions as to colour. No Government dare throw the doors of their schools open without distinction of colour to all children, and any attempt to advocate the . . . practice will in all probability lead to stringent legislation on the subject. If the question is mooted it will not be left to the boys of white parents to make the presence of boys of coloured parents impossible in the schools." CO, 179/228, minute by the prime minister, Aug. 15, 1903.

and subject to a special tax under the land assessment act (no. 33) of 1908,[123] and, of course, the continuing complaints connected with the £3 license,[124] immigration restrictions, and the licensing laws. The stock reply of the Colonial Office was to claim that conditions would be better under union, but this seemed unlikely. In the main, the South Africa Act preserved to the various provinces control of their own racial policies; although, at the insistence of the British Government, article 17 vested the administration of "matters specially or differentially affecting Asiatics" in the governor-general in council.

The Government of India was meanwhile impatiently awaiting a reply from the India Office and becoming progressively more incensed as the mountain of evidence against Natal grew. The colony had, in order to gain uniformity in licensing decisions, appointed a single licensing officer for the whole of Natal, and the testimony he gave before the Clayton Commission must have been of interest to the Indian authorities. He feared "the imminent risk of moral contamination which our children incur through daily contact with inferior, coloured races" and the commercial competition of the "Arab," whom he accused of having absorbed half of the trade of the Colony through fraudulent business practices and of having sent the proceeds to India.[125] The licen-

[123] Passed for the purpose of forcing Indians off the land and onto the labor market. CO, 179/225, Ind. Off. to Col. Off., Nov. 9, 1909.

[124] The agreement between India and Natal stipulated that criminal procedure was not to be used against Indians for failure to pay the £3 license tax. As it turned out, Indians were imprisoned under the provisions of the small debts act, which, as the Government of India put it, meant that "our stipulation is respected in the letter but not in the spirit." NAI, Oct. 1910, procs. 1 and 2, notes. The Indians had since the inception of the £3 license fee been incensed at its collection from women. They had long urged the end of this practice. Natal Act 19 of 1910 gave magistrates discretion in the matter, leaving the Indians with a somewhat improved situation but one still far short of what they considered just.

[125] NA, CSO 2783, Clayton Commission evidence.

sing officer, E. Wynne Cole, concluded his testimony with a damaging confession. "Since my appointment as Licensing Officer for the Colony," he admitted,

the Arab trader has generally come to understand that he will not get any more licenses issued to him in the future. . . . The reduction of the Arab and Indian licenses will mean prosperity to the Colony, and the settlement of Europeans in our midst in their places. I think this is already apparent from the fact that during the months of November and December, 1908 and in January, February and March 1909, I have refused 32 Arab licenses, many of whom have been trading for years, and during the same period I have issued about 32 new licenses to Europeans in different parts of the Colony.[126]

That the danger of Indians taking over much of the trade of Natal was exaggerated was evidenced by figures Nathan sent to Crewe. In 1895, Indians had held 393 licenses, Europeans 356. In 1908 there were 1,008 Indian and 2,034 European license-holders.[127]

The Indian Government had assumed, at least since the Boer War, that the indentured Indians in Natal, its chief responsibility, were well treated. It was surprised to discover that this was not always true. For instance, John P. Armatage, a plantation owner, cut off the ear lobe of one of his laborers, stating that as it was permissible so to mark sheep it should also be a legal method of identifying Indians.[128] An indentured laborer named Ramsamy was whipped by the planter to whom he was indentured. He fled and was sent to jail for seven days while his employer was only fined ten shillings for assault.[129]

Despite the Government of India's hostility, the India Office promised not to permit the amendment of the Indian emigration laws until after June 10, when the colonists of Natal were to decide on union in a referendum.[130] After the

---

[126] *Ibid.*   [127] NA, Natal conf., gov. to sec. of state, July 9, 1908.

[128] NA, no. 300, gov. to sec. of state, Dec. 28, 1908.

[129] NA, no. 96, sec. of state to gov., May 8, 1909.

[130] CO, 179/255, sec. of state to gov., June 2, 1909.

voters of Natal duly approved union, the Colonial Office asked for a further delay so that discussions could be held with the Natal delegates in London.[131] But the India Office demanded a *quid pro quo*—the amendment of the dealers' licenses act to allow for an appeal to the supreme court.[132]

What the officials of Whitehall and Fort William did not realize at the time was that circumstances in Natal were conspiring toward the achievement of their long-sought goal. The colonial government was in a state of acute tension and nervousness. The Transvaal was demanding the tightening of immigration restrictions. Smuts spoke of the day when the rest of South Africa would have to speak firmly to Natal and say:

You are given to dangerous practices. In the Transvaal we have been at great trouble and expense in trying to stamp out a danger which it has been almost impossible to overcome, whereas you in Natal are still continuing this policy of importing Asiatics from India. . . . If the Government of Natal did not put a stop to this practice and say: "We shall allow no further importation from Asia," they would find that Natal would become a festering sore and danger, which would spread infection through the whole of South Africa and the country will suffer. . . . The sooner . . . they got rid of the Asiatic the better.[133]

Louis Botha, the prime minister of the Transvaal, wrote to his counterpart in Natal that "the great number of Indians in Natal constitutes a serious menace to the realisation of our "White Country" dream and every additional coolie who is allowed to settle in Natal will make the situation worse and the whole question more difficult to be dealt with afterwards." [134]

On the other hand, the Clayton Commission had found that the importation of Indian labor was vital to Natal's

[131] *Ibid.*, Col. Off. to Ind. Off., June 25, 1909.

[132] *Ibid.*, paraphrase of tel., sec. of state to gov., Oct. 1, 1909.

[133] *Rand Daily Mail,* Jan. 29, 1908.

[134] NA, prime ministers' private papers, Botha to Moor, Nov. 20, 1909.

plantations, coal fields, and general prosperity, and its opinion carried more weight than the recriminations of the Transvaal. Act 22 of 1909, passed as the separate existence of Natal as a British colony was coming to an end, at last permitted shopkeepers deprived of licenses to appeal to the supreme court, which could either order the issuing of a license or remit the case for rehearing. As a consequence, the India Office assured the Colonial Office that Indian indentured immigration would not be stopped until the Union Government had come into existence and had had an opportunity to demonstrate its intentions toward the Indian population of South Africa. The period of grace would not, however, exceed one year.[135]

Lord Crewe was delighted; he informed the Natal Indian delegation that the amendment of the dealers' licenses act of 1897 was the single most important reform that Natal could have implemented. He contended that questions of education and immigration restriction could await the advent of union when he was sure a more generous spirit would prevail.[136] In Natal itself the change was surprisingly widely applauded. The *Mercury,* on November 26, 1909, under the headline "Gross Injustice Removed," wondered how the law in its original form had ever been allowed to pass,

as it violated one of the most vital principles of the British Constitution, and was without precedent in any part of the Empire. To deprive any man of the right of appeal to the Courts of the Land was simply a monstrous piece of injustice.

An appeal to a Town Council against the decision of one of its servants was a hollow farce, and in practice proved simply to be the means of upholding the grossest forms of injustice. Men have been absolutely ruined because of the trade jealousy and vindictiveness of individuals vested with certain authority, and there was no redress. As Colonel Greene remarked, the condition of things in the past has become a scandal. There have been shock-

[135] CO, 179/255, Ind. Off. to Col. Off., J. and P. 4140, Dec. 2, 1909.
[136] *Ibid.,* Col. Off. draft to M. Anglia, Dec. 24, 1909.

ing cases of men being deprived of their livelihood, and Licensing Officers and Licensing Boards have shielded themselves behind the iniquitous Law, and have refused to give any reasons for their action.

If the Colonial Office and Natal now basked in the warmth of consciences at last clear, the Indians, though they welcomed the amendment, were less enthusiastic. They emphasized the limited nature of the change, for granting of new licenses and the transfer of existing ones was still left, without appeal, to the discretion of the licensing officer and the licensing boards.[137] The Government of India was even more displeased. "Our position has always been," the viceroy telegraphed London, "that appeal to the Supreme Court should lie against all decisions of licensing boards, and we are not prepared to accept as sufficient a proposal to allow appeal against withdrawal of licenses only." [138] When the secretary of state for India asked the Indian Government to guarantee that "your enabling bill to prohibit emigration will not be used against Natal before South African Union comes into force," [139] the viceroy replied, "We object strongly to pledge desired unless right of appeal is permitted from all decisions of local committees." [140] But the secretary of state chose to overrule the viceroy and informed him:

Right of appeal as to fresh licenses in my judgment is of much less importance than proposed right of appeal in regard to existing licenses. The latter will become in Natal of increasing importance in the future. I propose therefore to give assurance that until Union Government has come into existence and decided on future policy (which it is expected will not take more than a year) immigration of indentured Indians will not be stopped.[141]

[137] *Ibid.*, Anglia to Col. Off., Dec. 7, 1909.

[138] NAI, March 1910, procs. 14–43, viceroy to sec. of state, Oct. 27, 1909.

[139] *Ibid.*, sec. of state to viceroy, Oct. 22, 1909.   [140] *Vide* n. 138.

[141] NAI, March 1910, procs. 14–43, sec. of state to viceroy; postponement limited to one year as per Ind. Off. guarantee to Col. Off.

The secretary of state did not, however, prevent the passage of enabling legislation [142] in the form of the Indian emigration act of 1910.[143]

As for the Colonial Office, it did not dispute the validity of the points made by the Natal Indian delegation and the Government of India, but Sir Frederick Graham concluded that "it is useless to go to Natal again now and I have drafted the various letters now required on that assumption." [144] H. C. M. (now Sir Henry) Lambert perhaps most accurately reflected the Colonial Office's view when he minuted:

The Natal people of course are determined to reduce the number of Indian traders and no doubt feel that if licenses are to be freely transferred the number will never be reduced. This is no doubt from our point of view a blemish, but the amendment does clearly secure that a man trading is not himself thrown out of business by the jealousy of European rivals on the Town Council. The Indian can still transfer his business to a European if he wants to go.[145]

The last major obstacle to the establishment of the Union of South Africa was removed by Natal's amendment of the dealers' licenses act of 1897, and the consequent decision by the India Office to postpone any action on the future of indentured immigration to that colony. The British Government thus saw the fulfillment of its long-time dream for South Africa, while the Natal Indians, although they gained the partial amelioration of their single greatest grievance, had no more reason than their cousins in the interior to look

142 *Ibid.*, tel., sec. of state to viceroy, Sept. 22, 1909.

143 *Ibid.*, tel, viceroy to sec. of state, Feb. 2, 1910. Indentured immigration was actually halted as of July 1, 1911.

144 CO, 179/255, minuting on Natal minute paper no. 39775, Dec. 8, 1909.

145 *Ibid.*, Dec. 9, 1909.

forward to life in the new constitutional creation with any degree of confidence.[146]

[146] Natal population figures at the end of 1909 indicated an Indian population of 103,836, of which number 62,905 were free, 28,548 indentured, and 12,383 reindentured. In 1902 the total Indian population had been 78,004.

VIII / Grim Struggle and Apparent Victory—Gandhi versus Smuts, 1910–1914

WHAT THE establishment of the Union, with Botha and his newly formed South African National Party at its head, achieved was to concentrate the Indian problem, as it had existed in four separate colonies, into a single arena. For the moment, however, the conflict continued to be centered in the Transvaal,[1] and the basic issues remained unaltered. The Indians claimed the government was violating even its own laws by deporting Asians illegally and by constantly increasing the stringency of administrative and judicial practice and interpretation.[2] Lord Gladstone, the governor-gen-

[1] CO, 551/2, minute 570 by Botha, Oct. 3, 1910. There were 4,918 Asians in Johannesburg in 1898 and 5,000 in 1899, plus 2,000 in other parts of the Transvaal. The total as of October 1910 is hard to determine, although Botha contended that it was known that there were 8,600 Asians in Johannesburg and 1,200 in Pretoria, or 2,600 more than resided in these towns before the Anglo-Boer War. The number of Asians registered totaled 8,921—8,581 under Milner's registration of 1903, 630 under the provisions of Act 2 of 1903, 6,449 under the voluntary registration scheme, and 1,842 under the provisions of Act 38 of 1908.

[2] *Ibid.* In 1906–1910 the number of Indians imprisoned for noncompliance with the registration laws was 751; for trading and hawking without a license, 1,373. The sentences for the period Jan. 1, 1906–Jan. 30, 1910, were: simple imprisonment, 320; imprisonment with hard labor for less than three months, 166.

Deportations were as follows: to Natal, 139; to the Cape, 21; to the

eral of the new entity, denied the former point, claiming that only thirty-nine Asians were deported in May 1910, eleven in June, and four in July.[3] But the latter contention tended to be borne out by a decision of the Transvaal division of the supreme court in the case of Chotabhai *vs.* the Minister of Justice. Chotabhai was an Indian whose son had been declared a prohibited immigrant on his sixteenth birthday, although he had entered the Transvaal with his father, who had been legally admitted some years earlier. The court, in upholding a previous judgment, ruled that an Asian minor upon reaching the age of sixteen had no right to receive a certificate of registration and was liable to deportation, unless he was born in the Transvaal or was resident there before Transvaal Act 36 of 1908 became effective. According to Mr. Justice Wessels, who wrote the majority decision, Act 36 had by implication superseded the provisions of Act 2 of 1907 which concerned themselves with the registration of minors.[4] It was a curious but seriously disturbing technicality. The Transvaal Immigration Restriction Act of 1907 allowed any person, not a prohibited immigrant, to bring his wife and minor children under the age of sixteen into the colony. As soon as he was sixteen, Chotabhai's son applied for a registration certificate as an Asian entitled to live in the Transvaal according to Act 36 of 1908. On his sixteenth birthday, however, he became liable to the provisions of section 7 of the act, which required him to produce, on demand, a certificate of registration, and as he had none, and was not, according to the registrar of Asiatics, entitled to one, his application was refused.

It was an absurd situation which unnecessarily aroused the

Orange Free State, 2; to Bechuanaland, 1 (total within British South Africa, 163); to Portuguese territory and then to India, 257; to Portuguese territory and then Mauritius, 3 (total outside British South Africa, 260).

[3] CO, 551/1, gov.-gen. to sec. of state, July 23, 1910.

[4] CO, 551/2, SA no. 187, gov.-gen. to sec. of state, Sept. 23, 1910.

Indians still further and embarrassed the government in an area where they had no quarrel with Gandhi and the passive resisters. Fortunately, on January 25, 1910, the appellate division of the supreme court of South Africa ruled that, although Act 36 of 1908 provided only for the registration of minors resident in the Transvaal at the commencement of the act or born within its boundaries, it did not follow that minors entering lawfully after that date were to be excluded from the registration provided for under the earlier Act 2 of 1907. It seemed improbable to the court that the legislature would permit Asian minors free entry into the Transvaal but allow the registrar no discretion to permit them to remain in the country upon attaining their majority.[5]

The Chotabhai case was no more than a tributary leading from the mainstream of the Indian question in South Africa. From the first, the larger issue preoccupied the Union's recently established legislature. On December 13, 1910, Dr. H. C. Hagger, a Natal representative, spoke in terms not unfamiliar to his home province. "We allowed Asiatics to come here and own property," he cried.

Were they allowed to do that in Australia? In Australia there was a poll tax of £100 on Asiatics. (hear, hear) The restrictions in Australia were much more severe than they were here. With regard to the harsh treatment of these people, he contended that the Government had to obey the laws of the country. He asked the Honourable Members to talk to some of the commercial travelers about it, and they would say that these traders were the curse of the country. These traders had ruined the trade of Natal, and they were ruining the trade in the Cape. . . . There were no people so capable of gross exaggeration. The immigration officers had a hard task, and he marvelled that they were able to perform their duty so well. They [the Indians] were most cunning, and betrayed the quintessence of deceit, they were born in it and bred upon it. . . . If the Minister acted with oriental despotism, these people would find some means of eluding

[5] *Works,* X, 402–405.

him. Let them think of what these Indians had to endure in India, and then they would realise that the country was a Heaven to them.[6]

The following day, the government announced its intention of reopening the whole immigration issue.

A curious circumstance now occurred. The Indian Government had, under heavy pressure from London, agreed to the at least temporary continuation of indentured immigration to Natal after the formation of the Union. In the minds of the viceroy and his officials, their ability to influence affairs in South Africa was essentially finished. By the end of 1910, however, the Government of India, much to its surprise, once more found itself in a strong position to vigorously protest the treatment of Indians in South Africa—not because it was able to wield the threat of an immediate end to indentured emigration as a weapon, but rather because it could allow its continuance! "Refusal [of the Indian Government to halt indentured emigration] . . . will prevent Union Government from going forward with reforms even if reforms introduced," Gladstone commented. "Continued British Indian outflow from Natal would invariably lead to fresh struggle in the Transvaal. Natal by no means unanimous against stoppage. Ethnological and social difficulties in Natal grow in proportion to Asiatic population." [7]

The Union's problem was twofold, as both the Indian Government and the Natal planters had to be cajoled into cooperating. "Real difficulty exists in the Union," Colonial Office minuting of November 1910 read. "They think they cannot really bring their troubles under control until Indian immigration comes to a halt, and yet they are fully aware that the Natal representatives entered Union with the understanding that indentured immigration would not halt for at least a year." [8] If only the Government of India could be

[6] Union *Hansard,* Dec. 13, 1910.

[7] CO, 551/3, tel., gov.-gen. to sec. of state, Nov. 22, 1910.

[8] *Ibid.,* minute paper, no. 33917.

induced to immediately prohibit further indentured emigration unilaterally, the Botha ministry would achieve its end without offending Natal. Botha and Smuts were inclined to enter liberal immigration legislation into parliament, Gladstone informed the Colonial Office,

but they assure me that Indian difficulties cannot be permanently laid to rest until the Indian Government prohibit emigration to Natal. Ministers do not want to take it upon themselves to press you to forbid further immigration because to do so will (a) embarrass somewhat a section of the community in Natal and (b) smack of a bargain, namely such prohibition in return for amending legislation. It seems to me that the Indian Government have plenty of justification of their own policy in minutes and reports to justify an announcement that no more indentured labour will be given to Natal and that this can be done without any formal appeal from here.[9]

In general, the Colonial Office agreed with Gladstone, but minuting reflected a due awareness of the sensitivity of the situation. "There is no difficulty," one of the minuting officials wrote,

in discovering adequate reasons to be given publicly by the Indian Government for bringing into effect prohibition of emigration to Natal. This cannot however be done until some time in December in view of the telegram of 3 March 1910.[10] No specific time in December is stated. The Union Government must produce their amending legislation first and it may be thought that prohibition is illogical because it will be known that the legislation is what H. M. Government have themselves advocated. But that corner also can be turned by a statement that the legislation is good as far as it goes but that the Indian Government prohibit on more general grounds of policy. The object is accordingly to get that government to prohibit on a date in December or later, after the Union legislation is introduced: there is no reason why

[9] *Ibid.*, tel., gov.-gen. to sec. of state, Nov. 4, 1910.

[10] A delay of at least a year was agreed to by the Government of India in Dec. 1909. *Vide,* Chap. VII.

the promise to prohibit later should not be given now or at any time.[11]

Botha hoped for immediate compliance with his wishes. "Such a step without waiting for any action by Government Union of South Africa," he telegraphed, "will be very well received South Africa and would strengthen hand government in removing difficulties connected with Transvaal Indian laws." [12] Lambert, in the Colonial Office, however, was not willing to urge the Government of India to cooperate, "without being quite sure that we got something solid in return." Sir Henry unequivocally proclaimed the imperial view of the matter:

The essential thing that we want and either must have, or must be able to show that we have not simply because it was impossible of attainment, is the abolition of the invidious differentiation against Indians as Indians. This differentiation is the heart of the grievance and is from the point of view of the policy of the Empire and our rule in India quite indefensible. . . . We accepted the differentiation in the T. V. because it was a legacy of the Dutch Republic and we could not help ourselves, but we are I think bound to make a serious attempt to get the grievance righted now that we have a new authority with which to deal. If the Union Government on getting our despatch will give the pledge to renounce differentiation we might then perhaps stop immigration to Natal. But even that would not be quite easy, for we have promised that emigration will not be stopped till the Union Government has decided on its future policy and it will not be easy to say why we stop it of our own accord.[13]

[11] CO, 551/3, tel., gov.-gen. to sec. of state, Nov. 4, 1910. Minuting on CO minute paper 35810 by A. R., 20-11-1910, addressed to Lambert. A. R. was probably W. A. Robinson, a first-class clerk in the dominions division of the Colonial Office.

[12] CO, 551/4, tel., prime min. to gov.-gen., Sept. 20, 1910.

[13] Ibid., minuting by Lambert on Union of South Africa minute paper 29213 re. tel., prime min. to gov. gen., Sept. 20, 1910.

The secretary of state for the colonies directed his action along two main avenues. He tried to convince the India Office and the Government of India to halt indentured emigration to Natal forthwith, and he used the issue as a lever to pry concessions from the Union Government. He pointed out that:

the controversy has led to the imprisonment of many Asiatics who are normally respectable and law-abiding British subjects and to the deportation of a considerable number, and it has been and is a source of very grave embarrassment to His Majesty's Government in their relations with the Indian Empire.[14]

Crewe saw in the three proposals made by Gandhi—(a) the repeal of Act 2 of 1907, (b) the removal from the text of the immigration act of any differential bar to the entrance of Asiatics as such, (c) the exclusion of all Asiatics, with the exception of a small number to be specially exempted, by administrative action alone—the key to a solution that would satisfy both the desires of South Africa and those qualities of style and form demanded by the imperial philosophy. Enamored of the "Australian [really the Natal] solution," he pressed it on Botha and his ministers.

Your Ministers will see that this legislation proposes no hindrance to the entrance of coloured persons as such. In this important respect it conforms to the traditional policy of the Empire, which numbering as it does many millions of coloured men among its subjects, has scrupulously avoided drawing distinctions before the law merely on the grounds of race and colour. Yet the entrance into Australia of coloured persons to whose admission Australian opinion is strongly opposed is effectually checked under the law by the action of the immigration officers.

I need hardly repeat in this connexion that His Majesty's Government while strongly urging that the proscription by act of Parliament of the inhabitants of one part of the Empire by another is open to the gravest objection both from their own point of view and from that of the sufferers, fully recognise the right of

[14] CO, 551/4, sec. of state to gov.-gen., Oct. 7, 1910.

a self-governing community such as the Union to choose the elements of which it shall be constituted, and it is in no way their desire to press your government to admit immigrants whom the people of South Africa are resolved to exclude. They only ask that the exclusion of such immigrants shall not be provided for in a manner which subjects them to unnecessary humiliation.[15]

The India Office on the whole tended to support the Colonial Office. Lord Morley, the secretary of state, was as intrigued with the wonders of the "Australian solution" as his colleague in the Colonial Office. He seemed particularly attracted by the administrative powers at the disposal of immigration officers. "These might require such persons to write a number of words in some European language such as Swedish or modern Greek, with which they are not acquainted."[16] The India Office followed the Colonial Office's lead in urging the Government of India to end indentured immigration to Natal immediately. The secretary of state asked the viceroy whether, in view of the probable nature of the Union immigration bill,

it will not be better to exercise the power of terminating indentured emigration on the 14th of the year of grace without waiting for legislation, the actual date of stoppage being fixed so as to avoid inconvenience to intending emigrants. I apprehend that when details of the proposed Immigration Act become known in India, it will become obvious that the true interests of India will not be served by continuance of emigration to any part of South Africa. This being so, there is no reason why you should refrain from immediately exercising your power to prohibit emigration to Natal.[17]

The Union Government not only wished to halt Indian indentured immigration under the guise of a purely Indian fiat; it also wished to be assured that the reasons for cessation

[15] Ibid.

[16] NAI, Oct. 1910, procs. 41–42, tel., sec. of state to viceroy, Sept. 26, 1910.

[17] Ibid., Jan. 1911, procs. 8–19, tel., Ind. Off. to Govt. of Ind., Dec. 3, 1910.

given by the viceroy were not too damaging. "Colonial Office now inform me," the secretary of state for India telegraphed the viceroy,

that for reasons affecting South Africa only, they consider it most undesirable to base suspension of Natal emigration on failure of Union Government to announce policy. They think it most important for these South African reasons that stoppage should be based on general principle, viz., that in absence of any guarantee that Indians will be accepted as permanent citizens of Union after expiry of indentures, the Government of India cannot allow present unsatisfactory situation to be perpetuated.[18]

The Government of India was not blind to the role the Union's political strategists had assigned to it. "What has occurred," minuted J. L. Jenkins, a member of the viceroy's council,

is probably something like this. The Transvaal has always wished to stop emigration of Indians into Natal, once they threatened the invasion of the Transvaal itself. So the Transvaal is saying, we will not consider the giving of better terms to Indians until emigration is stopped. This is the reason of "domestic policy." When emigration has been stopped, the Transvaal may relax their restrictions, but I do not believe they will ever do so to any great extent. So, in the result, Indians will have lost the very profitable field of emigration to Natal, and will get in return nothing, but a slight relaxation of restrictions elsewhere. That would be a very bad bargain.

If this interpretation is correct we shall simply be playing the game of the Transvaal if we now prohibit emigration. I think we should insist on knowing how matters stand before we take any further steps.[19]

Nevertheless, to the satisfaction of the British and South African authorities, the viceroy on January 2, 1911, telegraphed the secretary of state that on April 1 a notification

[18] *Ibid.*, draft of tel., Ind. Off. to Govt. of Ind., no date.
[19] NAI, Jan. 1911, procs. 8–19, minuting on tel., sec. of state to viceroy, Dec. 3, 1910, by J. L. Jenkins, 7-12-1910.

would be published prohibiting indentured emigration to Natal as of July 1, 1911. "It will be announced," the viceroy declared, "that this decision has been taken in view of the unsatisfactory position created by the divergence between the Indians' and Colonists' standpoints, and by the absence of any guarantee that Indians will be accepted as permanent citizens of the Union after the expiration of their indentures." [20] The secretary of state replied: "The manner in which the decision of the Indian Government has been received here is very satisfactory." [21]

Why had the Government of India so suddenly acquiesced to the wishes of Pretoria and London? Perhaps it was because those who ruled in India, Britain, and to some degree in South Africa were all products of the same environment, members of a class which understood what the imperial philosophy meant pragmatically. As the *Times* expressed it:

The principles by which we must be guided are clear. In the past we have conceived of British citizenship as conferring, in the same way as Roman citizenship of old, an equal *status* in all parts of the King-Emperor's Dominions. It is, in fact, a necessary principle of national self-government that a young and swiftly-expanding people should build up their population from what materials they choose. We cannot dispute on behalf of our Indian fellow-subjects a principle which we admit against ourselves. We have only to acknowledge that, while white men are often excluded as individuals, Indians, in general, will be excluded from many parts of the Empire as a race. The principle is the same in either case, and we must strive to make our Indian fellow-subjects realise that the inequality inevitable in its application is not due to inferior *status* but to facts of race which many of them recognise as strongly on their side.[22]

[20] *Ibid.,* tel., viceroy to sec. of state, Jan. 2, 1911.
[21] *Ibid.,* tel., sec. of state to viceroy, Jan. 16, 1911.
[22] The *Times,* Sept. 12, 1910. On June 11, 1914, R. W. Gillam of the Department of Commerce and Industry in the Government of India wrote to Sir James DuBoulay, the viceroy's secretary, that the espousal by the Government of India of freedom of movement within the em-

With indentured immigration finally halted, the Union Government could turn its full attention to the immigration bill. One of the major problems was how to rationalize the racial policies of the four former colonies, all of whom had approached the question of racial relations differently. Initially, Botha and his colleagues had decided to allow for divergent provincial attitudes within the bill. "Ministers beg to state," Botha had written, "that it is, in their opinion not possible to ignore Provincial boundaries in the administration of the Asiatic or Immigration Act." [23] By February 1911, the Union Government had changed its position. Although each province would pursue its own racial doctrine, as guaranteed by the Act of Union, there would be a single immigration policy, with the "Australian system" as its base, for the entire Union. "Ministers have accepted the suggestion of British Government," Gladstone informed the Colonial Office,

... to have a uniform law with differential administration under which even Asiatics who can pass the education test can be barred from entering except as regards a certain number in any one year.

This policy would have to be carried out under the new law

---

pire was futile, as the other colonies could never accept it. He felt that a frank recognition of this fact by India would greatly improve relations with other parts of the empire. Hardinge papers, v. 61. Hardinge appeared to agree. *Ibid.*, v. 87, Hardinge to Chirol, no. 178, June 30, 1914. Crewe remarked on the matter in a letter to Hardinge: "I shall look out with keen interest for your colonial immigration proposals. When I was at the Colonial Office, I often used to think that though the racial problem in its imperial aspects is in one sense insoluble; yet something might be done on reciprocity even though they could not claim to be inherently fair as between different people. Indian sentiment seems to be curiously open to formal recognition of this sort, and it might be possible to devise some *modus* which would not have the opposite effect of rubbing up colonial vanity, which in its way is not less thorny." *Ibid.*, v. 87, no. 37, Crewe to Hardinge, July 30, 1914.

[23] CO, 551/6, minute, Dec. 20, 1910.

all over the Union irrespective of what policy of late colonies had been.

Ministers have undertaken in their minute deliberation to deal with Asiatic applicants on their merits and do not wish the number twelve to be an absolute limit as it may be possible for them to admit more in any one year. It must be clearly understood the policy as above expressed would have to apply to the whole Union.[24]

At this juncture, there was hope on all sides that an amicable solution to the Indian question would at last be achieved. The Indian community, the Government of India, and the Colonial Office all awaited details of the "Bill to Consolidate and Amend the Laws in force in various Provinces of the Union relating to Restriction upon Immigration thereto, to provide for the Establishment of an Union Immigration Department and to regulate Immigration into the Union or any Province thereof," which the South African Government introduced into parliament in February 1911. When the draft measure was published its salient features were as follows: section 4(1)(a) excluded from the Union "any person who, when an immigration officer dictates to him not less than fifty words in the language selected by such an officer, fails to write out these words in that language to the satisfaction of that officer"—in other words, the Australian formula.[25] Section 6 established punishments for the contravention of the law, and section 7 cumbersomely preserved the rights of the provinces. "The provisions of the last preceding section," it read,

shall apply *mutatis mutandis* in respect of every person who, though domiciled in any Province, enters or is found in any other Province, in which according to the provisions of any law in force at or immediately prior to the commencement of this Act, he has unlawfully entered, or has been found to be residing

[24] CO, 551/9, gov.-gen. to sec. of state, Feb. 17, 1911.
[25] Almost identical to section 3(a) of the Australian Immigration Act (no. 17) of 1901.

unlawfully, and any such person shall in respect of the said other Province, be liable to be dealt with as in the last preceding section as described, and removed to the Province wherein he is domiciled. For the purpose of this Act every such person shall be a prohibited immigrant in respect of the said other Province.

Section 8(1) stipulated:

No prohibited immigrant shall be entitled to obtain a license to carry on any trade or calling in the Union or (as the case may be) in any Province wherein his residence is unlawful, or to acquire therein any interest in land, whether leasehold or freehold.

Section 25 empowered the minister to issue temporary permits to prohibited immigrants to enter and reside in the Union or any particular province thereof. He could also allow a person legally resident in the Union at the commencement of the act temporarily to absent himself from South Africa, thus protecting him from the danger of being classed as a prohibited immigrant upon his return.

Immediately upon the introduction of the bill, difficulties, both foreign and domestic, began to arise. First to enter the fray were the combined forces of the India Office and the Government of India. "There does not appear," the India Office wrote to the Colonial Office,

to be any safeguard for vested rights of provincial domicile except in the cases (covered by the new clause 25) of persons who are allowed to leave the country on temporary pass. Thus, so far as the text of the bill goes, it would seem possible that a domiciled Asiatic if arrested on suspicion of being a prohibited immigrant, might be deported on the ground of being unable to pass the Education Test.[26]

The Union Government answered that "repeated attempts have been made in drafting the bill to include specifically in the exemption clause persons domiciled or resident but it was found impossible to do so without the provision being

[26] CO, 551/20, Ind. Off. to Col. Off., Feb. 15, 1911.

differential in terms," and consequently all reference to domicile and residence was omitted.[27]

The India Office also noted that the bill did not clarify the position of Asian minors left doubtful by the terms of Transvaal Act 36 of 1908, which was retained in force, and that extensive powers to arrest without a warrant were conferred on the police by section 9(1) of the bill.[28] Lord Crewe, who in 1910 had moved to the India Office, was particularly concerned over the Union cabinet's stated policy of admitting only six Asians yearly into the Cape and Natal. "While His Lordship is fully aware of the general desire in South Africa to prevent further Asiatic immigration," the India Office announced to the Colonial Office,

> he must point out that if this determination to admit only about 12 persons into the whole Union is maintained, the effect of the Union of the Colonies, as regards Indian immigration, will be that the Transvaal policy will be extended to the whole Union, whereas it had been hoped that the policy of the Union would be based upon the more generous spirit of the Cape Colony system.[29]

The viceroy supported his colleague in Whitehall. He regarded the admission of twelve Asians into the Union annually as quite insufficient, "and, if the question is raised—as it is certain to be—we shall not hesitate to say so publicly." [30] Those British officials concerned with India, of course, knew that they stood no chance of influencing immigration legislation in a self-governing member of the empire. As Lambert wrote to his counterpart, Seton, in the India Office: "It is, I think, in view of longstanding admissions that Colonies may check immigration though they must not treat residents badly, very difficult to protest any measure directed

[27] U. (Union Government Official Document), 1911, minute 185, Feb. 21, 1911.

[28] CO, 551/20, Ind. Off. to Col. Off., Feb. 15, 1911.   [29] *Ibid.*

[30] *Ibid.*, sec. of state to gov.-gen., Feb. 15, 1910, encl. paraphrase of tel., viceroy to sec. of state for India.

against new immigrants providing it is not differential." [31]

As for the Indians of South Africa, their differences with the government over the draft immigration bill were as usual more in the area of principle than of practice. The first controversy concerned the registration of those educated Indians admitted to the Union under the special exemption. On March 4, Smuts, as minister of the interior in the Union Government, informed Gandhi that these immigrants would be free to enter the Union and to reside in any province without registering. Their signatures at the time of admission would be sufficient.[32] When Gandhi pointed out that this assurance was not reflected in the text of the bill,[33] Smuts promised to move an amendment exempting future immigrants from registration under Transvaal Act 36 of 1908 only.[34] The implication that racial bars existed for the other provinces led to the second and more significant argument. The Indians had throughout their campaign insisted that the *sine qua non* for their acceptance of any immigration bill was the absence of all racial and ethnic differentiation in the actual wording of the law. Gandhi in cabling Smuts demanded that Indians who entered the Union would have the *right* to reside permanently in any province. "They do not now ask for [the] entry [of] educated or other Asiatics [into the] Free State. . . . [35] Indians only protest against Union Parliament ratifying in Bill Free State Policy and thus saying to the world no Indian even though a Potentate can legally enter and reside in a province of the Union." [36] Smuts replied that Gandhi was opening a new issue which had never been a subject for discussion before.[37] But Gan-

[31] *Ibid.*, Lambert to Seton, Feb. 10, 1911.   [32] *Works*, XI, 100.

[33] *Ibid.*, 425–426, Gandhi to E. F. C. Lane, March 4, 1911.

[34] *Ibid.*, X, 466–467, 530–531.

[35] The existing structure of Free State laws made it highly unlikely that any Indian would have wished to enter the province or that he would have been allowed to remain there if he had.

[36] *Works*, X, 482–483.

[37] *Ibid.*, 531; Lane to Gandhi, March 24, 1911.

dhi, undeterred, cited statements by both Botha and Smuts in which they had stated that the specially exempted Indians admitted into the Union would have the right to make their homes in any province.[38] Gandhi was not, however, blind to the difficulties being faced by Smuts, who was under heavy pressure from the Free State members of parliament to insure the sanctity of their borders against any Indian with sufficient temerity to desire entrance to their bastion of white civilization.[39] He was consequently willing to see the Union legislation dropped and only the Transvaal legislation suitably amended.[40] But Smuts had gone too far to accept this means of escape.[41]

For a time it appeared that all problems would be solved by speedy alteration of the bill during its passage through parliament. Amendments were entered to allow the minor children [42] and wives of legal immigrants to enter the

[38] *Ibid.*, 494–496; Gandhi's report of an interview with Smuts on March 27.

[39] The Natal delegation, of course, supported the Free State members, and more liberal voices from the Cape, such as that of the former prime minister, J. X. Merriman, were few and far between. "The whole subject was fraught with the greatest responsibility and difficulty," Merriman exclaimed in Parliament, "but all he asked was that honourable members should not blow the coals up too much, because they might be doing harm in a direction of which they had little idea. They should remain true to the principles of Liberalism which they professed. They knew what it was to be trampled by their Imperialist friends. Do not let them follow their example and do not let them trample on the weak. He did not love the Asiatics, and did not want to see them in South Africa, but if they came, let us give them fair and honest treatment. (cheers)." Union *Hansard*, Feb. 28, 1911.

[40] *Ibid.*

[41] NAI, July 1911, proc. 1, July 1, 1911, pvt. and pers., gov.-gen. to sec. of state, April 12, 1911.

[42] This was to be accomplished through the repeal of Act 2 of 1907, "except as far as it is applicable to the registration of minors resident in the Transvaal." CO, 551/20, paraphrase of tel., sec. of state to viceroy, March 30, 1911.

Union,[43] and to exempt Indians admitted by administrative instructions from registration. The government was willing to move additions to section 5 so that the domiciliary rights of all persons born in the Union and of their wives and children would be protected,[44] and the governor-general gave firm assurance that section 25 would be generously administered.[45] To further assuage the fears of the Indian community and the Government of India, the Union, in defiance, it claimed, of public opinion, stated that "twelve will not be arbitrarily regarded as the limit of the number of permanent admissions, but cases will be considered on their merits." [46] On the vital Free State issue no progress could be made. "With regard to the Orange Free State," Smuts wrote, ". . . I do not think it possible to get adopted by Parliament any amendment the effect of which will be the free entry, without permission of the Governor-General, of these Indians into that Province, and on that point I therefore propose to leave the Bill unaltered." [47] Lord Crewe, at the India Office, was delighted with the changes inaugurated by the Union Government.[48] Gandhi, however, was far from satisfied. "As passive resisters have all along fought against racial bar," Gandhi telegraphed the South Africa British Indian Committee, "struggle must continue if Government go back upon . . . thrice repeated assurance and introduce racial bar. Resisters fight in purely national honour and defending British Constitution." [49]

It must have been sad for Gandhi to see the prospects for a settlement so tantalizingly close and yet still out of reach. *Satyagraha* was the equivalent of a state of war for the Indi-

[43] CO, 551/10, gov.-gen. to sec. of state, March 23, 1911.

[44] CO, 551/20, paraphrase of tel., sec. of state to viceroy, March 30, 1911.

[45] *Ibid.*   [46] *Ibid.*

[47] CO, 551/10, statement by Smuts, March 15, 1911.

[48] CO, 551/20, Ind. Off. to Col. Off., March 31, 1911.

[49] CO, 551/21, tel., Gandhi to So. Af. Brit. Ind. Comm., March 24, 1911.

ans. The current campaign had already lasted more than four years, and many had fallen by the wayside under the strain of battle. A few stalwarts still courted arrest, however, and their families were to some degree supported by the Satyagraha Association. But the funds of the organization were drying up. Since 1906, Gandhi's preoccupation with politics had brought his once lucrative legal practice to a standstill, and he was no longer able to supply financial backing. Money was needed to run the movement's offices in Johannesburg and London and, for that matter, to keep *Indian Opinion* on its feet. It was a war of attrition, and time was on the side of the government. Sporadic gifts, such as that of Sir Ratan Tata, the Indian industrialist who, in 1910, donated Rs. 25,000,[50] delayed the inevitable end. Gandhi came to the conclusion that if the struggle was to be continued, expenditures would have to be drastically cut. If only the families of all the passive resisters in prison could be gathered together on a cooperative farm. But the Phoenix settlement was near Durban, some thirty hours by train from Johannesburg, and in a different province.

It was Hermann Kallenbach, a German architect and a supporter of Gandhi, who came to the rescue. He purchased an 1,100-acre farm twenty-one miles from Johannesburg and offered it to Gandhi, rent free, for the use of the *satyagrahis*. The estate, which Gandhi named the "Tolstoy Farm" in honor of Alexei Tolstoy, whose philosophy he greatly admired, included a small house and about a thousand fruit trees. Gandhi planned to turn it into the sort of communal settlement of which he was so fond. Between them, Gandhi and Kallenbach erected a small cluster of corrugated buildings, and the colonists, who usually numbered between fifty and seventy-five, and who were variously Hindu, Muslim, Parsi, and Christian, moved in. All the residents—men, women, and children—were expected to do their share in

[50] The Indian National Congress, the All-India Muslim League, and the Nizam of Hyderabad also made donations.

running the establishment. There was a common vegetarian kitchen, and Kallenbach, who had learned the art of shoe-making from some German monks, imparted his skill to his fellow residents.[51] As Gandhi put it: "The work before us was to make the Farm a busy hive of industry, thus to save money and in the end to make the families self-supporting. If we achieved this goal, we could battle with the Transvaal Government for an indefinite period." [52] Gandhi, always the experimentalist, was able to pursue his theories on health, education, and the virtuous life. He even tried, in conjunction with Kallenbach, to work out the implications of *ahimsa* (nonviolence) as they applied to snakes! [53] Later Gandhi concluded:

Tolstoy Farm proved to be a centre of spiritual purification and penance for the final campaign. I have serious doubts as to whether the struggle could have been prosecuted for eight years, whether we could have secured larger funds, and whether the thousands of men who participated in the last phase of the struggle would have borne their share in it, if there had been no Tolstoy Farm.[54]

On April 19, Gandhi met with Smuts in an interview of which the former kept notes. The general was his most ingratiating and friendly self. "You belong to a civilisation," he told Gandhi,

that is thousands of years old. Ours, as you say, is but an experiment. Who knows but that the wh[ole] damned thing will perish before long. But you see why we do not want Asia here. But as I say the Natal difficulty being out of the way, I shall cope with the problem here. But I want time. I shall yet beat the Free Staters. But you should not be aggressive. The whole question as you know will be discussed before the Imperial Conference.[55]

[51] It was no doubt from Kallenbach that Gandhi learned to make the famous sandals he later presented to Smuts.

[52] *Satyagraha*, 240.

[53] B. R. Nanda, *Mahatma Gandhi* (London, 1958), 109.

[54] *Satyagraha*, 258.   [55] Scheduled for later in the year.

You should therefore wait. Now just think it over and let me know.[56]

If Gandhi took Smuts's advice, he certainly did not change his basic stance, and Smuts, caught between Indian intransigence and the adamant refusal of the Orange Free State members to modify their position, was forced to an inevitable decision. Gladstone telegraphed L. V. Harcourt, who had replaced Crewe in the Colonial Office, that passage of the bill was highly improbable. "The Jews are hostile. A section of the Unionists . . . do not like it because they fear ulterior use of it by Dutch Ministers against the British. Australian method of excluding is generally unpopular. More serious is the fact that repeal of the Cape Colony Immigration Act would allow entrance into Cape of Good Hope of Natal Indians." [57]

The criticism of the Government of India had weakened the position of the bill but it was the implacable opposition of the Free State members that made progress impossible.

In these circumstances J. C. Smuts thinks best course is to drop the Bill and endeavour to bring in a more acceptable measure next year. He thinks passive resistance is almost at the end, and that he could arrange a truce with Gandhi till a fresh bill was introduced. At the same time he feels bound to proceed if you insist, but he thinks Indian Government dislike Bill so much that they are not likely to object to the course which he proposes.[58]

The secretary of state did not insist, and with a wan and rather desperate optimism, assumed that,

J. C. Smuts is . . . satisfied that he can prevent a renewal of agitation by Gandhi, and there is no likelihood of his action in dropping the Bill in deference to Gandhi's opposition leading to greater trouble in the future by enhancing Gandhi's prestige

[56] *Works*, XI, 32–33.

[57] CO, 551/10, paraphrase of tel., gov.-gen. to sec. of state, April 14, 1911.

[58] *Vide* n. 41.

and his belief that he can dictate terms to the Union Government. . . .[59]

In minute no. 499 from the prime minister's office, dated April 25,[60] Botha announced the dropping of the first attempt under the Union to settle the immigration question to the satisfaction of the Indians and the various segments of the white population in South Africa.

Concurrent with the withdrawal of the immigration bill, Smuts and Gandhi sat down to serious negotiations. On April 22, Gandhi, in a letter to E. F. C. Lane, Smuts's private secretary, outlined his terms for a settlement. Act 2 of 1907 should be repealed, subject to the rights of minors as outlined by the Chotabhai decision. Legal equality of Asians under the immigration law must be guaranteed, and any new legislation, if it removed the racial bar for the Transvaal, should do so for the entire Union. Passive resisters who, but for their political activities, would have been entitled to register, should now be permitted to do so, anything to the contrary in Act 36 of 1908 notwithstanding. Educated passive resisters currently in the Transvaal, who were not legally registerable under the Asiatic act, should be allowed to remain in the province in anticipation of the new law, providing their number did not exceed six.[61] On the very same day, Smuts agreed to Gandhi's proposals in a cautious reply again issued through the fiat of his private secretary, Lane. The minister agreed to Gandhi's last two points without hesitation, but, more important, he undertook to introduce into the new bill "provisions giving legal equality for all immigrants, with, however, differential treatment of an administrative as distinct from a statutory character." [62]

At a public meeting held in Johannesburg on April 28, the Indian community ratified the compact, and for a time at least the struggle was over. On June 1, the Indian prison-

[59] CO 551/10, sec. of state to gov.-gen., April 12, 1911.

[60] CO, 551/10.   [61] Works, XI, 38–39.

[62] CO, 510/10, Lane to Gandhi, April 22, 1911.

ers were released; and on June 5, as a symptom of the new, lighter mood, a soccer match was played between the Pretoria passive resisters and those from Johannesburg. That only an armistice prevailed was reflected by the Indians' attitude to the accession of George V to the throne. They professed their loyalty to the crown, but would not join the official celebrations of the coronation. Gandhi took the opportunity, however, to pronounce once more his adherence to the precepts of the British constitution and the imperial philosophy. "It may seem somewhat anomalous to a stranger," he wrote in *Indian Opinion,*

why and how British Indians of South Africa should tender their loyalty to the Throne and rejoice over the crowning of the sovereign in whose dominions they do not enjoy the ordinary civil rights of ordinary men. British sovereigns represent, in theory, purity and equality of justice. . . . British statesmen make an honest attempt to realise the ideals. That they often fail miserably in doing so is too true but irrelevant to the issue before us. . . . The genius of the British constitution requires that every subject of the Crown should be free as any other, and, if he is not, it is his duty to demand and fight for his freedom so long as he does so without injuring anyone else.[63]

With the cessation of hostilities, Indian political activity returned to more conventional channels. There were still more than enough grievances to occupy the zealous. In a petition of May 1, addressed to the secretary of state, the British Indian Association concentrated their fire on those familiar targets, Law 3 of 1885 and the Gold Law and Townships Act of 1908. Under the provisions of the last measure, the petition pointed out, the position of Indians in Krugersdorp, Klerksdorp, Germiston, Roodeport, and other towns was being increasingly threatened. Furthermore, many of the new locations that were being established were very poorly situated, and although Indians were permitted to

[63] *Works,* XI, 111–112; *Indian Opinion,* June 24, 1911.

own property in the locations, the government, in effect, only allowed them twenty-one-year leases. In the Johannesburg location, Indians existed on a month-to-month basis where, before the war, in the old location, they had been granted ninety-nine-year leases.[64] The Indians of Natal [65] and the Cape [66] called attention to the continued abuse of the licensing authority vested in local boards; for, ministerial denials to the contrary, the situation appeared to be deteriorating even further. The case of Sheikh Abdool Latif was the most recent *cause célèbre*. He had been denied a license near a predominantly Indian part of Durban, and the only reason the licensing officer would give was that he did not think an Indian license should be granted in that area. Latif appealed, and the licensing officer's decision was upheld by the city council without even the benefit of discussion.[67] "This is a hard case," Lambert minuted,

but the action of the authorities was within the law and as it is an application for a new license there is no appeal. It seems however against the principle, which we are always contending for, that though the South Africans may keep out Indians they are not entitled to treat badly those who are in the country. . . .

Although it is perfectly useless to press for reconsideration, I think we ought not to pass over the case without notice. . . . The the facts are correctly stated it would appear that the application was rejected without any consideration of the merits. . . . The

[64] CO, 551/11, petition by A. M. Cachalia, chairman, Brit. Ind. Assoc., to sec. of state, May 1, 1911. The whole question of Indian locations continued to be a running sore. Peremptory and often illegal orders for Indians to abandon stands both inside and outside locations were common. The proposed new location in Germiston had been a dumping ground for night soil and was considered unsafe by a local European physician, Dr. McNab.

[65] *Works*, XI, 70–74; Natal Ind. Cong. to sec. of state, May 15, 1911.

[66] CO, 551/22, petition by Cape Indians to sec. of state, May 3, 1911.

[67] CO, 551/22.

good people of Natal are evidently aiming at effective elimination of the Indian trader.[68]

Had it not been for the unanimity of public opinion, the Union ministers would probably have preferred the judiciary to play a greater role in licensing cases. On the other hand, there was no denying that when they had jurisdiction, the courts of South Africa often acted to the acute embarrassment of the government. In the summer of 1911 two important decisions were issued—one of which was to be of lasting significance. In the Transvaal, Bai Rasul, the wife of a certain Adamjee, was refused permission to join her husband in the Transvaal. "But what is of greater importance," *Indian Opinion* of July 8 wrote,

is the Judge's *obiter dictum* that an Indian may not bring more than one wife. Hitherto those who had more than one wife have been allowed to bring them in without let or hindrance. If the Judge's dictum is sound law, all we can say is that it will have to be altered. In British Dominions, wherein all religions are respected, it is not possible to have laws insulting to any recognised religion flourishing under it.[69]

It was the opening shot on a new front, and more was to be heard on the marriage question later.

The second case, that of Tamblin *vs.* Rex, also concerned the Transvaal. In its ruling the Transvaal provincial division of the supreme court determined that wherever the right to lease stands in mining areas outside of townships to Asiatics had existed before the passage of the Gold Law and Townships Amendment Act of 1908 (no. 35), that right still existed. Smuts was aghast. He considered the decision bad law and was convinced that "the result would be that a large

[68] The same points were made with more formality and couched in imperial terms by Harcourt in a letter to Gladstone, *ibid.*, no. 64, Nov. 21, 1911.

[69] *Works,* XI, 120.

number of Asiatic stores would spring up all over the reef, the white trader would be crowded out, and that a considerable impetus would be given to illicit traffic in gold and liquor in which Asiatics were prone to indulge." [70]

In a minute of September 2, ministers announced their awareness that "the extent to which Asiatics are displacing white traders is rousing considerable feeling, and they are convinced that the Union Parliament will be moved to take some action. . . . Owing to the expansion of Asiatic trading the white traders are gradually being ousted from centres where they have been long established." [71] For the moment they proposed to draft a local government ordinance for the Transvaal which would maintain virtually all existing restrictions on Indians and also establish the Natal licensing system in a province where Indians had heretofore encountered relatively little difficulty in acquiring licenses to trade. The Colonial Office claimed that it could do little as most of the intended restrictions were already recognized in the law. "But the refusal of an appeal to any Court or Magistrate for persons whose applications for Hawkers' Licenses are rejected," one official minuted,

stands on a somewhat different basis, for it is the introduction of that very system of licensing by trade competitors which has given so much trouble in Natal. It is of course fundamentally unjust that a man should be refused the means of getting a livelihood not because he is unfit to have a license, but because (as a Licensing Officer of Durban laid down) they will not have more Indians trading. The Indians' trading competitors on the Council would of course be of opinion that the grant of a license would be "contrary to the public interest," and the Indian without a vote either for town, Province or Union, is absolutely unprotected, if he cannot go to the Courts. On the other hand provisions are not on the face differential. [72]

[70] CO, 551/14.   [71] CO, 551/13, minute 1028, Sept. 2, 1911.
[72] *Ibid.*, minute paper 30262.

The £3 tax on Indians in Natal continued to be a dull irritant. The government contended that "particular cases have been carefully watched and all complaints which have arisen have been enquired into and they are convinced that there has been no undue harshness in the administration of this law by the various Magistrates in the Province of Natal." [73] Yet, there was no denying that abuses were not infrequent. Although the payment of the £3 fee by women was left to the discretion of the magistrate by Natal Act 19 of 1910, *Indian Opinion* of July 8 cited the case of a poor woman with many small children who sold fruit in Stanger. She was arrested for being without a license and was sentenced to pay £9 for the three years she was in arrears.

The relative tranquillity of the summer of 1911 allowed Botha to attend the Imperial Conference in London. Lord Crewe addressed the assembled prime ministers and repeated the usual platitudes about India being the most precious jewel in the imperial crown, and of the need of treating with consideration and respect all the subjects of an empire that recognized men of all races as equal under the law. The prime ministers clucked approvingly but insisted on their right to pass the sort of restrictive immigration legislation that was already in effect in most dominions. Sir Wilfrid Laurier, the prime minister of Canada, reflected the prevailing opinion. He reminded his listeners that "the moment Asiatic labourers were allowed to come into competition with white labour, there was a disturbance of economic conditions, which if allowed to go on might seriously jeopardize the harmony of the British Empire. It is not on account of colour prejudice but because Asiatics have a different civilisation and standard of living." [74]

In October, Botha's government presented a second version of the immigration bill to the Union parliament, but

[73] *Ibid.*, minute paper 1032, Aug. 22, 1911.
[74] Cd. 5741, precis of the proceedings of the Imperial Conference of 1911, June 1911.

with no great hopes for success. There were several significant differences between the old and the new acts. Under section 2 a new clause was inserted to clarify the domicile issue. By stipulating that any domiciled person who left the Union for a continuous period of three years lost his domiciliary status, the new addition only worked to the detriment of the Indians. Subsection 3 of section 3 left it in the discretion of the governor-general to appoint immigration boards at port cities to advise the minister as to whether allegedly prohibited immigrants should be allowed to enter the Union. Subsection g of section 5 provided for the entrance into the Union of the wives and minor children of domiciled Indians, and subsection h exempted certain types of white laborers from the dictation test.[75] Section 7 attempted to settle the delicate relationship between the provinces and the Union. "Notwithstanding that a person is domiciled and entitled to reside in any particular Province either at the commencement of this Act or thereafter," the clause read,

nothing in this Act contained shall be construed as authorising him to enter or reside in any other Province wherein he has not become entitled to reside unless he is able to pass the dictation test prescribed in paragraph (a) of section four and such text may at any time be put to him.

For the purposes of this Act every such person shall unless he has passed the dictation test be a prohibited immigrant in respect of the said other Province and the provisions of the last preceding section shall apply mutatis mutandis to him.

As the main impediment to the passage of the first immigration bill had been the Free State issue and the Indians' determined opposition to section 7 of the original measure, the wording of the revised clause seemed to indicate that the Indians had won their point and that Smuts had convinced

[75] Agricultural or domestic servants, skilled artisans, mechanics, workmen, or miners who had entered the Union due to a shortage of their type of labor under an agreement approved by the governor-general.

the Free State members to give way. But section 28, the final clause of the bill, completely destroyed this impression by reintroducing all the stipulations that the Indians had found so objectionable. Subsection 1 merely kept Smuts's promise that any immigrant who passed the dictation test would not have to register under Transvaal Act 36 of 1908. Subsection 2, however, stated:

Any person being a person as is described in Chapter xxxiii of the Orange Free State Law Book, who, by passing the said dictation test, has been permitted to enter the Union or, by passing the dictation test in accordance with section *seven* of this Act, has been permitted to enter the Orange Free State from any other Province, shall be subject in all respects to the provisions of articles *seven* and *eight* of the said Chapter.

Why Smuts and his colleagues persisted in attempting such a shoddy and transparent piece of chicanery is not altogether clear. Gladstone thought it a last desperate attempt to save a doomed bill,[76] but as he accurately predicted, "subclause 28 is likely to be distasteful to Mr. Gandhi and his adherents." On the other hand, he realized that "the acquiescence of the Orange Free State in the proposed legislation will not be obtainable unless by some means or other the present restrictions in that Province are fully preserved." It seemed to be a maze without either an entrance or an exit. The governor-general concluded with as much optimism as he could muster:

On the whole the Bill seems an improvement on its predecessor, although of course the alternatives are not of a very far-reaching character. I do not anticipate that its reception in Parliament will be cordial, and I have no doubt that attempts will be made to amend it in many particulars. His Majesty's Government will appreciate the difficulties with which my Ministers have to contend, and I venture to express the hope that they will approach in a sympathetic spirit the consideration of a measure which in

[76] CO, 551/14, S.A. conf. 20, gov.-gen. to sec. of state, Oct. 23, 1911.

its principal features is intended to give effect to the proposals put forward by Lord Crewe in his Despatch No. 226 of the 7th. October 1910.[77]

There was no hiding the fact that, as Lambert noted in minuting, "the Bill which is now resuscitated is an infant with somewhat feeble health, or at least one with plenty of enemies." [78]

These enemies gathered soon enough. Criticism was leveled at the bill's failure to provide for the registration of passive resisters, as Smuts had promised Gandhi. It seemed curious that domicile was not defined, but that how this nebulous state could be lost was made painfully clear. The dictation test could, according to section 7, "at any time be put to [an immigrant]," which was not the case in the original bill.[79] Section 7 also, to all intents and purposes, closed the Cape to Natal Indians, a situation which had not maintained under the first immigration bill. Section 5 (h) was an undisguised attempt to implement the provision of the Cape Act of 1902, which the Colonial Office had so vociferously and unsuccessfully fought. The bill did nothing, its opponents pointed out, about the thorny question of polygamous marriage; it left too much power in the hands of the immigration officers and immigration boards; and it did not provide for an appeal to the courts for persons declared prohibited immigrants. As for its anticipated administration, the stated number of twelve Indians to be exempted annually from the dictation test was too small in view of the six which had previously been mooted for the Transvaal.

[77] *Ibid.*

[78] CO, 551/14, minuting by Lambert, Nov. 14, 1911, on minute 1252 by Botha, Oct. 21, 1911.

[79] This phrase was no doubt added to assuage the Cape fear of being invaded by large numbers of Natal Indians. On the other hand, the Indians could claim that section 7 excluded Natal Indians from the Cape, a province they had always in the past been able to enter with relative ease.

South Africa's English newspapers were critical of many of the facets of the draft act which seemed to run counter to the precepts of British liberalism. For example, the Johannesburg *Star* of January 31 wrote:

The new Bill . . . goes beyond the bounds of either equity or expediency. It defines the illiterate "prohibited immigrant" as any person who is unable to pass a dictation test, that is to say, when an Immigration Officer dictates to him not less than 50 words in the language selected by such an officer, fails to write out these in that language to the satisfaction of that officer. Here we have the most arbitrary power placed into the hands of a government official. There is no mention of a European language plus Yiddish, so that the official can make his choice as to what education test he can impose. It is useless to say that there is a Board of Appeal, because the preliminary inconvenience and loss of money which may result from the action of an arbitrary officer— possibly of anti-Semitic tendencies—will not be compensated for by the reversal of his decision after many days. But, worse still, the officer can select the language in which the dictation test is written. This gives him absolute power to impose one European language on an immigrant who is literate and even a skilled scholar in another. There are no words in the Bill to provide that the language selected shall be one of the commonly spoken in the country from which the immigrant comes or by the race to which he belongs. . . . We do not say that the Act will be administered at once in this sense, but we know sufficiently of the way comparatively harmless Acts are carried out to make it incumbent on our legislators to see that no loophole is left for a "regulation" of the Department to sanction such abuse.

On January 30, [80] and again on February 15, [81] Gandhi telegraphed Smuts. He particularly objected to the almost absolute power of determining an immigrant's status being left in the hands of the immigration officers. The existence of boards was no protection as bitter experience had proved. There must be an appeal to the courts of the land. Section 28, which now specifically named the hated Free State Law

[80] *Works*, XI, 216.   [81] *Ibid.*, 217.

in the body of the bill, was, of course, totally unacceptable to the Indian community.

The relevance of Gandhi's doubts was manifested by the case of an Indian boy, Nathalia, who was several times refused permission to land and join his father. In the course of his misadventures, Nathalia was sent back to India twice, and the last time returned to South Africa with documents proving his relationship. But the immigration officer simply refused to accept their authenticity. When the case was appealed to the supreme court, the judges held themselves empowered to intervene only if there was an indication that the immigration officer had not sufficiently considered the evidence. "It seemed a rather pitiful thing," the judgment concluded, "that this boy should be moved about as he had been. The court was powerless to interfere here, and he could only add that he made this statement with regret, because he thought that ordinary justice, if nothing else, would have dictated permission for the boy to land. Mr. Justice Broome said he regretted that the rule must be discharged in the present state of the law." [82] Harcourt immediately cabled Gladstone in familiar terms: "As your Ministers are aware His Majesty's Government have always regarded it as a matter of great importance that decision of Immigration Officers on question affecting rights of Indians already established in South Africa should be open to judicial review." But, he disingenuously concluded, "the reoccurrence of such a case is precluded by the terms of the Immigration Bill now before Parliament and he . . . [did] not propose to take any action in the matter." [83]

When the draft immigration bill reached the floor of parliament for its second reading, it came under heavy fire. It was discussed extensively in the house of assembly during mid-June, but was unable to muster sufficient support to pass on to the next stage. Most critics felt that the bill was too permissive as far as Indians were concerned, and a possi-

[82] CO, 551/35.   [83] CO, 551/34, tel., sec. of state, March 13, 1912.

ble danger to white immigration. The member from Bechuanaland (Wessels) claimed that "the competition of the
Asiatic was such that no European could stand up against
him, and he would like it to be laid down clearly that in future no Asiatic should be allowed to come into the
country." [84] C. G. Fischerdt also demanded a more restrictive measure. "They would be told," he asserted, "that, if
they passed a prohibitive clause, the law would be vetoed. If
it were, let them pass it again and let them understand in
the United Kingdom that that was what they meant to stand
by." [85] Of course, not all the dissent was from the right.
More liberal members agreed with T. L. Schreiner of Tem-
buland, who felt that Indians should be allowed to move
freely from one province to another. "They had been allowed to come into this country on certain terms, and they
were bound, as they were British subjects, to see that the
rights which they at present possessed were not taken away.
The bill to his mind seems to take away these rights." [86]

Smuts was not particularly concerned about the small liberal opposition to the immigration bill, but he did his best
to assuage the fears of the more conservative opponents.

The difficulty in working the Immigration Law in this country
was considerable, because whilst, on the one hand, they were
most anxious to foster the immigration of white people, they
were equally anxious to keep Asiatics out. (Hear! Hear!) They
had therefore to pass a law applying in the same terms to all sections, but aiming at bringing certain people in and keeping others out. It looked almost like a Chinese puzzle.

The government had decided, on the advice of the British
Government, to adopt the Australian dictation test. But the
great power placed into the hands of the government, Smuts
assured the house, would be used with great care.

There was not the slightest intention of making it more difficult
for white people to come into the country than it was today. The

---

[84] Union *Hansard,* June 14, 1913.   [85] *Ibid.*   [86] *Ibid.*

intention was rather the other way. In the past there had been too great a tendency under their existing legislation to lay stress on purely educational qualifications. (Hear! Hear!) A man who wanted to come into this country, and was physically fit and otherwise might be a good citizen was asked to test his knowledge in some European language. Some of these languages did not concern them in this country in the least. A man who had a very high knowledge of Yiddish did not impress him, and the same applied to Russian and many other languages. What they did want in this country was a certain type of character and physical fitness, and they should not look too much to immigrants' literary attainments or educational attainments or educational qualifications in languages of little use in this country.[87]

Smuts's rhetoric was all in vain, as he rather suspected it would be, and the immigration bill was withdrawn again in order that still another measure might be prepared for introduction during the next session of parliament. As Gladstone explained to Harcourt:

Some members disliked it because it appeared that it might at some period be applied to facilitate the admission of Indians; others disliked it because they feared that it might be used to exclude Europeans; others again were averse on general grounds from entrusting any public department with such arbitrary powers.

The governor-general explained that much of the prime minister's own party was unfriendly to the bill, that the Labor party opposed it, and that a large proportion of the United party's rank and file were frankly hostile.[88]

[87] *Ibid.*, May 30, 1912. Smuts's statement was probably aimed at the Jewish opponents of the immigration bill. A relatively high percentage of the white immigrants into South Africa in the early years of the twentieth century were Jewish. Previous provincial legislation had usually stipulated a knowledge of any European language, including Yiddish, as a qualification for entrance into South Africa. The proposed new law permitted dictation in a language of the immigration officer's choice.

[88] CO, 551/27, gov.-gen. to sec. of state, June 25, 1912.

On the whole, 1912 was a rather quiet year. Other than the immigration legislation, however, two issues constantly reasserted themselves. The difficult question of the status of polygamous marriages was becoming ever more threatening. "Both under the laws of South Africa and under the practice in the past polygamous marriages have not been recognised," Gladstone telegraphed Harcourt, "and Ministers are unable to provide any facilities . . . which would have the effect of altering the present position." [89] Although the legal position of polygamous marriages was not yet a major concern to the Indians, they were beginning to feel a pressure to which they would sooner or later have to respond. First there had been the Bai Rasul case, and now, in February 1912, the court, in Fatima *vs*. Rex, again ruled that a Muslim or Hindu was entitled to bring only one wife into the Union,[90] a decision exacerbated by the stated policy of C. W. Cousins, the Transvaal's acting immigration restriction officer, who would only accept the testimony of a superior European magistrate in India as proof of marriage and not that of an Indian judge.[91]

Of greater urgency for the moment was the recrudescence of the licensing question in an acute form. Under the South Africa Act, jurisdiction over licensing affairs fell to the Union Government. It was one of the few advantages the Indians gained from union, and was resented by the provinces, especially Natal. On April 10, 1911, a resolution from the Natal Provincial Council was presented to parliament. It requested:

That in terms of Section 87 of the South Africa Act of 1909, this Council begs to recommend to the Parliament of the Union of South Africa the passing of legislation having for its purpose the granting to their Provincial Council the power to pass legislation

[89] NAI, April 1912, tel., gov.-gen. to sec. of state, Jan. 7, 1912.
[90] CO, 551/35.
[91] *Ibid.,* So. Af. Brit. Ind. Comm. to Col. Off., Aug. 10, 1912.

for the granting and withholding of all trading licenses in the Province.[92]

Harcourt, in due course, noted that legislation to this effect was being contemplated, and he asked to be informed how this would affect the Indian position in the Union.[93] In a month Gladstone replied. He admitted that the governor-general could not as easily interfere in matters transferred to the provinces as he could in those maintained at the Union level. On the other hand, the provisions of section 147 of the South Africa Act vested in the governor-general in council "the control and administration . . . of matters specially or differentially affecting Asiatics throughout the Union," and Gladstone thought this provision would probably restrain any provincial council from passing an ordinance explicitly discriminatory to Indians. After years of experience, he contended that where the original jurisdiction lay was of little moment as long as local authorities, actuated by racial animus, administered the law. "It is easy to regret," he concluded, "but it is impossible to deny, that public opinion throughout the country is growing increasingly restive in its attitude towards the Asiatic trading competiton. The danger may be imaginary. The anxiety and intolerance are real." [94]

Gladstone, however, did not expect the government to proceed with the measure, and it was with some surprise that he informed the Colonial Office on June 12 that Smuts had given notice the previous week of his intention to introduce an act which, among other things, transferred legislative jurisdiction in licensing matters from the Union to the provinces.[95] In Natal such a change would do little to alter the *status quo*. In the Transvaal, however, an applicant

[92] Union *Hansard,* April 10, 1912.

[93] NAI, Oct. 1912, procs. 14–15, sec. of state to gov.-gen., April 19, 1912.

[94] *Ibid.,* gov.-gen. to sec. of state, May 21, 1912.

[95] *Ibid.,* gov.-gen. to sec. of state, June 12, 1912.

could, as matters stood, get a trading license merely by paying a prescribed fee, and if his application was refused, he could appeal to the courts. This situation the government was determined to change, and as it was doubtful that the Transvaal local government ordinance could effectively do the job without the necessary transfer of authority from the Union to the province, the new law was decided upon. Under the prevailing situation, Gladstone averred, "Indian trading had developed to an alarming extent, and it would not be possible for the Government to place themselves into dire conflict with the strong public feeling which has been aroused." Gladstone would do all he could to protect Indian license-holders and to ensure that they enjoyed right of appeal to the courts, but he was not prepared to go very far to attain these ends. As he wrote Harcourt rather shamefacedly,

I felt that it would be impolitic to stand out for further concessions before signing my recommendations. . . . Continued delay in furnishing the recommendation would probably have involved abandonment of the Bill, and the irritation caused thereby could not have been expected to predispose Ministers favourably towards any future representations which I have to make on the Indian question. I, therefore made the recommendation and it was duly announced in the House of Assembly yesterday. . . .

I regret that it has not been in my power to secure more favourable terms.[96]

Although he could report that he had induced his government at least to guarantee the *status quo* in the Cape and Natal,[97] where only existing licenses received any protection, Gladstone was totally unsuccessful in convincing the ministers that the right of all applicants for new licenses in the Transvaal should be preserved. The governor-general hoped, however, that

[96] *Ibid.*

[97] This had been accomplished by the addition of a fifth subclause to section 10.

my action will commend itself to your judgment. A refusal to accept Ministerial advice, and to make the desired recommendation for the financial clauses before the time appointed for the second reading stage might have been open to criticism from the point of view of constitutional propriety, and in any event, I doubt whether, in the present stage of public opinion, my Government could have gone further than they have actually gone to meet my representations.[98]

Botha and his ministers had won the battle but they were to delay gathering the fruits of victory. Due to the press of time, they dropped the bill from consideration during the current session of parliament, and it was not passed into law until the following year.

For the Indians, the year 1912 reached its apogee with the arrival in the Union of Gopal Krishna Gokhale, the most revered Indian political leader of his day. Gokhale had kept in close touch with Gandhi and the Indian situation in South Africa for fifteen years. He was undoubtedly the most prominent Indian ever to visit the southern part of the African continent, and he came with the blessings of both the British and Indian governments.[99] Well advised by the wily Smuts, the Union Government made Gokhale a state guest and showered him with flattery and adulation. From the time of his arrival in Cape Town on October 22, a private railway carriage was placed at his disposal, and throughout his one-month tour red carpets and illuminations greeted him at every stop. Gandhi, who acted as Gokhale's secretary (and valet), became more and more uneasy as he watched the effect this treatment was having on his great guest—dulling the edge of his resentment. In a sense, the Union Government was stealing the Indians' saviour.

Gokhale saw all the prominent members of the govern-

[98] *Vide* n. 88.

[99] It should be remembered that Gokhale had entered the motion calling for the end of Indian indentured immigration to Natal into the Indian legislative council.

ment, and on the 12 of November had lunch with the governor-general. The one reform Gokhale was determined to achieve while in South Africa was the repeal of the £3 tax in Natal, and upon leaving the Union he was convinced that he carried with him a promise to that effect from the government. As he landed in Bombay on December 13, he was full of optimism: "The actual working of the Immigration Law . . . will," he told the crowd that greeted him at the dock,

I expect, become milder and more considerate. Then that outrageous impost, the three-pound license tax, will, I fully expect, go in the course of this year. In fact, I may mention that Ministers have authorised me to say that they will do their best to remove the grievance as early as possible. In the matter of education also,[100] the position will materially improve and the actual administration of laws such as the Gold Law and Townships Act will tend to become less and less burdensome.

The provisional agreement between Smuts and Gandhi, Gokhale also thought, presaged the passage of an acceptable immigration bill.[101]

Whether Gokhale had actually been promised the removal of the £3 tax was to become a question of major importance. In March 1913 the government contended that ministers had only agreed to "give consideration to the points raised by him [Gokhale] more especially in regard to the £3 im-

---

[100] *Works*, XI, 439; *Indian Opinion*, Jan. 18, 1913, quotes the following notice in the *Natal Provincial Gazette:* "No Native, Indian or Coloured children are to be admitted to schools other than those specially provided for them.

"No pupils under Standard II may be admitted to an Indian School under European teachers.

"No subject included in the Standard Syllabus for Primary Schools may be taught during ordinary school hours in an Indian School in charge of European teachers.

"No pupil who has passed Standard IV will be allowed to remain in an Elementary Indian School."

[101] SANA, prime minister's office, 12/4/1912, proof 672, extract from the *Times of India*, Dec. 21, 1912. Also *Works*, XI, 576–587.

posed on Indians in Natal who had served their indentures." [102] Seven months later Gladstone remarked rather defensively: "It will be remembered that Ministers have never admitted the existence of any definite undertaking." [103] Gokhale's version of the promise was as follows:

I was assured that the Government realised the iniquity of the £3 licence Tax and that from a financial point of view its proceeds were negligible, and that the earliest opportunity would be taken of abolishing it. On my asking for the authority to announce this, I was told that it was necessary for the Ministers to mention the matter to Natal members, and I should, therefore, merely announce in general terms that the Ministers had promised their most favourable consideration to my representations in the matter and that I had every confidence that the tax would be repealed in the new Parliament.[104]

W. K. Hancock, in the first volume of his biography of Smuts, contends that although the ministers aroused expectations they could not fulfill, they stopped short of giving a pledge and that Gokhale himself, as he left his interview with them, merely "supposed" that the tax would be abolished.[105]

Gandhi, for his part, believed that the promise had been given but that the government had no intention of keeping it. He described his conversation with Gokhale immediately after the meeting:

Gokhale's interview with the ministers lasted for about two hours, and when he returned he said, "You must return to India in a year. Everything has been settled. The Black Act will be repealed. The racial bar will be removed from the emigration law. The £3 tax will be abolished." "I doubt it very much," I replied.

[102] Cd. 6040, minute paper 127, ministers (Botha) to gov.-gen., March 11, 1913.

[103] NAI, Feb. 1912, procs. 1–3, gov.-gen. to sec. of state, Oct. 9, 1913.

[104] W. K. Hancock, *Smuts: The Sanguine Years, 1870–1919* (Cambridge, 1967), 342.

[105] *Ibid.*, 342–343.

"You do not know the ministers as I do. Being an optimist myself, I love your optimism, but having suffered frequent disappointments, I am not as hopeful in the matter as you are. But I have no fears either. It is enough for me that you have obtained this undertaking from the ministers. It is my duty to fight it out only where it is necessary and to demonstrate that ours is a righteous struggle. The promise given to you will serve as proof of the justice of our demands and will redouble our fighting spirit if it comes to fighting after all. But I do not think I can return to India in a year before many more Indians have gone to jail."

Gokhale said: "What I have told you is bound to come to pass. General Botha promised me that the Black Act would be repealed and the £3 tax abolished. You must return to India within twelve months, and I will have no more of your excuses." [106]

In Gandhi's mind the issue was clear. Gokhale had been promised the repeal of Act 2 of 1907, and this was already assured. The government had also pledged the abolition of the £3 tax in Natal. If the ministers failed to keep their word, the Indians would have to recommence their struggle. As Gandhi admitted:

If Gokhale had not come over to South Africa, if he had not seen the Union ministers, the abolition of the £3 tax would not have been made a plank in our platform.

If the Satyagraha struggle had closed with the repeal of the Black Act, a fresh fight would have been necessary against the £3 tax, and not only would the Indians have come in for endless trouble, but it is doubtful whether they would have been ready so soon for a new and arduous campaign. [107]

The stage was now set for the final great *satyagraha* campaign that Gandhi was to lead in South Africa. The old familiar issues were again to be the subjects of contention, but the twin foci of the renewed struggle were to be the polygamous-marriage and £3-tax questions. But the time was not yet. The government still had to make its intentions clear.

[106] *Satyagraha,* 268.   [107] *Ibid.,* 269–270.

On March 11, 1913, the Union ministers were able to forward to Gladstone the draft of the immigration bill they intended to introduce into parliament during the current session. The bill, Botha explained, was in the main the same as its predecessors. There were, however, some significant changes.[108] Regular boards of appeal to which prohibited immigrants could appeal their cases were established, but section 3 limited the jurisdiction of the courts to matters concerning domicile, and by later amendment, to questions of law, including domicile. Section 4 was considerably altered. A new subsection, 4(1)(a), was added so that a prohibited immigrant was not only a person who failed the dictation test, but also "any person or class of persons deemed by the Minister on economic grounds or on account of standard or habits of life to be unsuited to the requirements of the Union or any particular province thereof." [109] To satisfy the critics of the dictation test as a threat to European, and particularly Jewish, immigration, section 4(1)(b) now stipulated that a prohibited immigrant was

any person who is unable, by reason of deficient education, to read and write in any European language to the satisfaction of an immigration officer, or, in case of appeal, to the satisfaction of the board; and for the purpose of this paragraph Yiddish shall be regarded as a European language.

Indians, consequently, were faced by two barriers that could be used to prevent their entrance into the Union, while a whole class of opponents to the immigration bill had been effectively disarmed.

Section 4(4) of the law curtailed the ports at which "persons belonging to classes described in paragraph (a) of subsection (1) of this Section" (i.e., Indians) could apply for entry or re-entry into the Union. The reason given for this circum-

[108] Cd. 6940, minute 242, ministers to gov.-gen., March 11, 1913.
[109] This was the method of exclusion prescribed in the Canadian immigration law.

scription was that the Portuguese tended to permit too many prohibited immigrants to enter through Komati Poort.[110] The limitation on absence from the Union to three years established by the previous draft law was removed and section 30 essentially defined domicile as three years' residence in the Union while not under contract of indenture. The new section 4(2) attempted to deal once more with the sensitive issue of Indian freedom of movement. It stated that nothing in Subsection (1)(a) should be construed

(a) as enabling a person to be deemed a prohibited immigrant in the Cape of Good Hope or Natal if, being at the commencement of this Act lawfully entitled to reside in any Province, he shows or has shown that he is able to comply with the requirements described in Section *three* (a) of Act No. 30 of 1906 of the Cape of Good Hope, or of Section *five* (a) of Act No. 30 of 1903 of Natal,[111] or

(b) as abrogating or affecting any right conferred by Act No. 36 of 1908 of the Transvaal upon the lawful holder of a certificate of registration defined in that Act.

Section 5(h) of the old bill was retained, except that the term "European" was substituted for "white."

The ministers had in the hiatus between the demise of the previous immigration act and the introduction of the current one still not been able to shake the resolve of the Free State members, and section 7 of the new bill differed little from section 28 of the old. "Any such person," it read,

as is described in Chapter XXXIII of the Orange Free State Law Book shall notwithstanding that he is lawfully resident in a particular Province or that he has been permitted to enter the Union continue to be subject in all respects to the provisions of Sections *seven* and *eight* of the said Chapter XXXIII, and if he acts in contravention of those provisions, he may be dealt with

[110] *Vide* n. 108.

[111] The restrictive clauses of the respective provincial immigration acts.

under this Act as a prohibited immigrant in respect of the Orange Free State.

Schedule 2 of the act did, as had the previous Union draft immigration acts, duly repeal Transvaal Act 2 of 1907, with the exception of those parts dealing with the registration of minors, and the Transvaal Immigrants' Restriction Acts of 1907 and 1908.

Thus far the Indians had gained little and lost much. A new impediment had been erected to secure the Union against their presence. No appeals were, in essence, to be allowed from the decisions of the immigration boards. The ports through which they could re-enter the Union were to be severely limited and the hated Free State proviso still remained. The most severe crisis, however, was to erupt over the provisions concerning domicile and hence also marriage. Section 5(e) of the second draft immigration bill had exempted from the designation prohibited immigrant, "subject to the provisions of section *seven,* any person born in any part of South Africa included in the Union." Section 5(e) of the 1913 bill referred to

any person born before the commencement of this Act in any part of South Africa included in the Union whose parents were lawfully resident therein and were not at that time restricted to temporary or conditional residence by any law then in force, and any person born in any place after the commencement of this Act whose parents were at the time of his birth domiciled in any part of South Africa included in the Union.

The status of all indentured and formerly indentured Indian laborers was consequently placed in jeopardy, for it was not clear whether "conditional residence" referred to Indians who were paying Natal's £3 tax. Section 5(g) countenanced only the entrance of the wives and minor children of domiciled persons whose marriages had been "monogamous" and "duly celebrated according to the rites of any religious faith outside the Union."

The attack on Indian marriages vis à vis the rights of wives to enter the Union also continued in the courts. In June 1912, in the case of Sukina *vs.* Rex, a Johannesburg judge (Jordan) extended the Fatima *vs.* Rex decision by declaring all polygamous marriages illegal. Botha subsequently issued a minute in which he stipulated that should no marriage certificate be extant (which was almost certain in an Indian marriage), a certificate of a superior magistrate would have to be obtained attesting that the judge *personally* knew that the woman involved was indeed the wife of the applicant in the Union. If the magistrate could not fulfill this requirement, he could alternatively hold an inquiry under oath, establish the facts, and forward the evidence.[112] On Friday, March 14, 1913, in the case of Esop *vs.* the Minister of the Interior, Mr. Justice Malcolm Searle, of the Cape provincial division of the supreme court, handed down a ruling that, more than any other factor, was to usher in a renewal of *satyagraha.* The Bai Rasul and Fatima cases had determined that a Hindu or Muslim might bring into the Union one wife of a polygamous marriage, but not more than one. Judge Jordan declared all polygamous marriages illegal. Searle added to the force of these previous decisions the judgment that only those marriages performed according to Christian rites and recorded by a registrar of marriages were legal. As Gandhi remarked:

This terrible judgment thus nullified in South Africa at a stroke of the pen all marriages celebrated according to the Hindu, Musalman and Zoroastrian rites. The many married Indian women in South Africa in terms of this judgment ceased to rank as wives of their husbands and were degraded to the rank of concubines, while their progeny were deprived of their right to inherit the parents' property. This was an insufferable situation for women no less than men, and the Indians in South Africa were deeply agitated.[113]

[112] NAI, March 1913, procs. 2 and 3, minute 1010 by Botha, Nov. 24, 1912.

[113] *Satyagraha,* 266.

The Colonial Office was far from sympathetic to the Indian dilemma. "This agitation about wives," an office minute read,

is not one which we should give any countenance whatever. The judgment in this case is merely repetition of what we have always understood to be the law of S. Africa. . . . It is preposterous I think that a small community (say 150,000 all told) should expect to force a different—and frankly a lower, alien—view of marriage on S. Africa.[114]

The lines of battle were now clearly drawn, but the Indians still awaited the results of the debate on the draft bill in parliament and of the negotiations that were constantly in progress. The proceedings in the house of assembly could not have provided much cheer. The minister of the interior, now Abraham Fischer,[115] expounded on the draft bill in moving the second reading. "As to the admission of wives," he declared,

a decision was given out a couple of years ago by the Transvaal High Court that when a man sought admission of a woman on the ground that she was his wife, he must prove she was his only wife. (Laughter.) A man was entitled to have only one wife, which some people maintained was quite sufficient. (Laughter.)

Fischer realized that the Union was part of an empire which believed that

no one's rights should be taken away, whatever race or colour . . . but they wanted to be masters in their own house, and they wanted to be in a position to say whom they did not want in the country. . . . It was no use hiding their light under a bushel,

114 CO, 551/43, minute paper 35017, Oct. 8, 1913, minuting by H. L. (probably H. C. M. Lambert, now a principal clerk), Oct. 15, 1913.

115 Smuts had been minister of the interior, mines and defense in the first Botha ministry of May 31, 1910 to Dec. 19, 1912. In Botha's second ministry, which held office from Dec. 20, 1912 to Sept. 1919, he kept the defense and mines portfolios while Abraham Fischer assumed the ministry of the interior.

for they all knew it was the intention of South Africa to exclude the Asiatics. It was undesirable that this country should be encroached upon by Asiatics. They believed that it was not a matter of selfish policy whether a few Asiatics should compete with them in trade or an acre of land, but it was a matter of the self-preservation of the white man in South Africa. In regard to the legislation, therefore, they would avoid as far as they could naming anyone by name or any race by name, and excluding them on that account, but they must make it clear that they deemed the European civilisation the desirable one from which to seek progress and advancement of the country. . . . Let them be honest about it. One race would have to be the master, and they who were masters at present had better remain masters.[116]

It was essentially the same speech that had been given by many different men in many different settings, and as usual the sentiments expressed were cheered to the rafters. Fischer concluded by making it clear that as far as white immigrants were concerned, the dictation test would "be conducted plainly in the language the candidate said he knew." [117]

There was once more opposition to the draft bill from both the left and the right. In the senate, Senator de Villiers of the Orange Free State wished to exclude Indians *eo nomine* from the Union, while Senator W. P. Schreiner of the Cape criticized the harshness of the marriage and domicile clauses. In the house of assembly, the Cape members, notably J. X. Merriman and Morris Alexander, again led the attack of the liberals upon the measure. In fact, the latter, in trying to ameliorate the unhappy position regarding the legality of Indian marriages, sponsored what turned out to be a most unfortunate amendment. In section 5(g) were inserted the words: "including the wife and child of a lawful and monogamous marriage duly celebrated according to the rites of any religious faith outside the Union and duly registered at the place of celebration and having all the legal consequences of a lawful marriage duly celebrated within the

---

[116] Union *Hansard,* April 30, 1913.   [117] *Ibid.*

Union." [118] As no Indian marriages were ever registered in the sense of European marriages, Alexander's amendment only succeeded in clouding further an already confused issue. Be that as it may, the government, by mollifying the opponents of the dictation test, was able to pass, on the third attempt, an immigration act for the Union. Its multiple defects, however, assured a resumption of active Indian resistance. The only possible hope for averting a crisis lay in the repeal of Natal Act 17 of 1895. But the government was only willing to enter legislation that would exempt females from the payment of the £3 tax, and Gladstone remarked to the secretary of state: "I do not think that any further concession will be obtainable this session." [119]

The viceroy, under considerable domestic pressure from organizations such as the Bombay Presidency Association [120] and the United Provinces Congress Committee, led by Motilal Nehru,[121] began to regret his earlier acceptance of the bill. "I am not at all happy," Hardinge minuted on July 21,

over the fact that we accepted the Immigration Bill, nor am I certain in view of the fact that our telegram of March 22nd was communicated to the Colonial Office that it will not become known that we have done so.

From a further study of the papers I gather that we were under the impression that the revised bill was in terms agreed upon with Mr. Gandhi, while the objections to the bill are summarised in Mr. Polak's telegram of April 23rd received after our telegram accepting had been sent.[122]

As a consequence, the viceroy, on July 20, telegraphed the India office: "We had been under the impression that the bill was drafted in general agreement with Mr. Gandhi's

[118] Cd. 6940, gov.-gen. to sec. of state, May 27, 1913.

[119] NAI, Oct. 1913, procs. 1–3, gov.-gen. to sec. of state, June 5, 1913.

[120] *Ibid.*, Sept. 1913, procs. 25–49. tels. to viceroy, July 3 and July 9, 1913.

[121] *Ibid.*, July 7.   [122] *Ibid.*

views, but the very strong opposition to its terms of which evidence is reaching us seems to indicate that this is not the case, and in the circumstances we feel constrained to withdraw acceptance of bill as revised and passed." [123] The opposition of the Government of India was centered on the marriage clause, a position largely based on the opinion that no Muslim or even Hindu marriage could properly be termed "monogamous." [124] With the fate of the bill once again in the balance, Fischer assured Hardinge that despite the wording of the law, it was his government's intention to admit one wife of a domiciled Indian regardless of the rites under which the marriage was performed.[125] The Government of India was still not totally satisfied with the bill, but it removed its opposition to the signification of the royal approval upon receipt of Fischer's undertaking.[126] As for the Colonial Office, it had always been determined to see the bill passed; and its main concern was assuaged when Fischer informed Gladstone: "I can give the assurance that in the proposed annual return of persons prohibited from entering the Union, or removed therefrom, race will never be given as a reason for such prohibition or removal." [127]

On June 21, Gandhi telegraphed Gokhale: "Going Transvaal to present final letter to Minister. If reply satisfactory and fresh settlement made, no passive resistance. The act appears to contain four fatal objections. Not very hopeful. Failing settlement, passive resistance starting . . . July." [128] Gandhi delivered his letter to E. M. Gorges, the secretary for the interior, on June 21. The four areas of concern which he outlined were: (1) The definition of "domicile" in section 30, according to which Indians who arrived in South Africa after the passage of the Natal Indian Immigration Law

[123] *Ibid.*   [124] *Ibid.*, viceroy in council to sec. of state, July 3, 1913.
[125] *Ibid.*, tel., gov.-gen. to sec. of state, April 20, 1913.
[126] *Ibid.*, Ind. Off. to Col. Off., Aug. 9, 1913.
[127] *Ibid.*, min. of int. to gov.-gen., April 4, 1913.
[128] *Works*, XII, 117–118.

Amendment Act of 1895 and their descendants were prohibited immigrants.[129] (2) The fact that if this definition was correct, the descendants of indentured Indians would not be able to enter the Cape. (3) The Free State stipulation contained in section 7 of the act. (4) The marriage question.[130] On August 19, Gorges replied. In regard to Gandhi's first point, the government was willing to admit that an Indian who had resided in Natal and paid the £3 tax for three years had acquired domicile. Concerning the second stipulation, Gorges manifested some surprise as Gandhi had on February 15 contended that "if the present legal position namely the ability of educated Asiatics to enter Natal or the Cape . . . by passing the education tests provided by the respective laws of the Province is retained," the Indians would have no cause to complain.[131] Gorges consequently claimed that the government had not been aware, until a few weeks earlier, that the Indians had any strong feelings on the subject, and that it thus had every right to maintain its stated position. Gorges repeated the government's commitment to admit to the Union one wife of a domiciled Indian, regardless of the nature of the marriage rites,[132] but the secretary was unable to say anything of substance on the Free State issue.[133] In

[129] Gandhi referred to the case of Subrayen, who had served under indentures which had expired in 1906. He then paid the £3 until May 1911, at which time he left for India. Subrayen returned in November 1912, and was refused admission into Natal. Upon appeal, "the Court held that Subrayen's residence in Natal as free Indian on payment of the tax did not come within the meaning of the words 'or the like' following after 'indenture' [in] section 32, and he was entitled to exemption from operation of the Act under Section 4." *Works*, XII, 128; Gandhi to sec. of interior, July 4, 1913.

[130] *Ibid.*

[131] Gandhi admitted that he was not aware of this problem at first. Cd. 7111, Gandhi to Gorges, Aug. 24, 1913.

[132] Despite this assurance, the government, in October 1913, fought and won the case against the admission of a certain Kulsambibi, who they claimed had been married under the rites of a religion that recognized polygamy.

[133] *Works*, XII, 588–589; Gorges to Gandhi, Aug. 19, 1913.

mid-October, the Indians published their formal demands: the removal from the immigration law of three of the four fatal flaws discussed by Gandhi. The amelioration of the first blemish had already been conceded by Gorges.

The immigration act came into operation on August 1, 1913, and at the initial meeting of an appeals board an untoward incident occurred. Percy Binns, the chairman, read out in open court the instructions he had received from General Smuts.[134] In the communication, the minister had stated that "under the powers conferred upon him by sub-section 1 of Section 1 of the Immigration Regulation Act, 1913, he deemed every Asiatic person to be undesirable on economic grounds etc." [135] Gladstone was aroused because the intention to differentiate was publicly proclaimed. He was again driven by an obsession to maintain the fiction of an empire where all subjects, regardless of race, were accorded equal consideration. He emphasized that the secretary of state had assumed "that in any published instruction with regard to the administration of the law, Ministers have no intention of differentiating formally between different races." The secretary of state, Gladstone claimed, had been placed in a "difficult and invidious position." [136] As for India, the governor-general thought Binns's public statement would have a very unfortunate effect there. "Can anything be done to remove it?" he asked.

Is it more difficult for the Immigration Officers to restrict an individual or class on economic grounds, than to reject an edu-

[134] Although Smuts did not hold the interior portfolio in Botha's cabinet after 1912, he did, as the prime minister's closest ally, assume wide responsibilities in sensitive areas. Despite the fact that Abraham Fischer had become minister of the interior in 1912, it was Smuts who retained the fundamental jurisdiction over relations with the Indian population.

[135] NAI, Nov. 1913, procs. 3 and 4, gov.-gen. to prime minister, Aug. 18, 1913. It should be noted that the Indians claimed a £26 deposit was required in order to file an appeal. *Ibid.*, Durban Indians to Lord Ampthill, Sept. 8, 1913.

[136] *Ibid.,* gov.-gen. to prime minister, Sept. 6, 1913.

cated Hindoo because he will fail in a selected language under the dictation test? In each case it would be known that it was the intention of the Government to restrict because the individual was an Asiatic. Why then is it necessary to lay down publicly a general principle of differentiation against a race when any single individual can be excluded on "economic" or other grounds? [137]

Gladstone was dealing with a much more substantive issue when he protested the presence of the chief immigration officer as one of the three members of the appeals board, "thus making him judge of his own department." [138] But in both cases his ministers turned a deaf ear,[139] while the secretary of state seemed little concerned.[140]

The failure of the British Government to disallow the immigration act, and of the Union Government to render satisfaction on the Free State and £3 tax issues, forced Gandhi once more to ask his disciples to withdraw their support from certain of the laws of the Union of South Africa. On September 13, in inaugurating the new campaign, Gandhi wrote in *Indian Opinion:*

A settlement without a settlement spirit is not settlement. . . . It is much better to have an open fight than a patched-up truce. The fight this time must be for altering the spirit of the Government and European population of South Africa. And the result can only be attained by prolonged and bitter suffering that must melt the hearts alike of the Government, and of the predominant partner.[141]

Satyagraha is essentially a majority weapon. What must that old political campaigner Gokhale have thought when Gandhi informed him that his "army of peace" consisted of at least sixteen and at most sixty-five *satyagrahis*.[142] But Gan-

[137] *Ibid.*   [138] *Ibid.*

[139] *Ibid.,* prime minister to gov.-gen., July 28, 1913 and Aug. 21, 1913.

[140] NAI, Feb. 1914, procs. 1–3, Col. Off. to Ind. Off., Oct. 11, 1913.

[141] Nanda, *op. cit.,* 113.   [142] *Ibid.*

dhi's methods often prospered best when the odds against success were the longest.

On September 15, a "pioneer party" of twelve men and four women, including Gandhi's wife, Kasturba, left Durban for Volksrust, there to cross the border into the Transvaal illegally. Kasturba and her companions were duly arrested, deported, and, when they attempted to cross the border again, sentenced to terms of hard labor ranging from one to three months. Others followed the "pioneer party's" lead, and the government's discomfiture began to grow, even though Gandhi informed the *Transvaal Leader* that the struggle was to be limited to about a hundred passive resisters.[143]

The renewal of open hostilities between the Indians and the government did not mean that Gandhi had stopped communicating with his adversaries. A stream of correspondence crossed the desks of relevant ministers, and as a result the gap between the two rival camps grew constantly smaller. Six days after Gandhi's statement in *Indian Opinion,* Gladstone was able to inform Harcourt that the Free State problem had essentially been solved on the lines of a suggestion previously made by Gandhi. Section 19 of the immigration act required every immigrant to make out a declaration when asked to by an immigration officer. If the disabilities under which an immigrant might suffer, including the relevant sections of chapter XXXIII of the Orange Free State Law Book, were printed on the back of the form, "then there need be no repetition of the declaration when a British Indian is recognised as an immigrant for the Free State," and it would follow that the odious section 7 could, by amendment, be removed from the immigration act.[144]

The solution of the Free State issue still left the question of the £3 tax unsolved, and the struggle consequently contin-

---

[143] *Works,* XII, 218; interview to the *Transvaal Leader,* Sept. 24, 1913.

[144] NAI, Feb. 1914, procs. 1–3, gov.-gen. to sec. of state, Sept. 18, 1913.

ued to gather momentum. Harcourt persisted in misunder-
standing Gandhi. He was "disposed to think that Mr. Gandhi's attention has been concentrated on questions which are
of comparably small practical importance." [145] But not
everyone agreed with the secretary of state. All manner of
Indian organizations throughout the world (such as the
Awakened India Society of Cape Town) poured their protests upon London. Lord Ampthill, a former governor of
Madras and at one time acting viceroy of India, spoke
strongly and frequently in the House of Lords, and the Government of India, under heavy pressure from its constituents, felt progressively more uneasy.

On October 17, the struggle entered a new phase when
Gandhi visited the Natal coal fields near Newcastle. He
urged the indentured miners to strike until the government
removed the £3 tax, and seventy-eight workers ceased work
and were arrested and sentenced to two weeks' imprisonment at hard labor. Soon 3,000 Indians from the Newcastle,
Cambrian, and Durban Navigation Collieries were on strike.
On October 22, railway employees at Dannhauser struck,
and 1,500 workers decided to walk from there to the Transvaal border and court arrest.

The Union suddenly found itself faced by a serious threat
and its response became increasingly more desperate and
coercive. The mine operators cut off the water and electric-
ity to the miners' quarters, driving them forth and making
Gandhi suddenly wealthy in poor men. On October 26,
eight hundred more miners went on strike. What was Gandhi to do with his unemployed and hungry followers? The
Indian merchants of the mine area were of little help. If the
government could be induced to arrest and jail them, it
would at least have to feed them. In consultation with Kallenbach, Polak, and his secretary, Sonia Schlesin, Gandhi determined to lead his motley army from Natal into the Transvaal. Hopefully, the authorities would intercept them on the

[145] *Ibid.,* Col. Off. to Ind. Off., Nov. 20, 1913.

way, but if they should fail to do so and if by some miracle the strikers completed the journey successfully, Gandhi intended to incorporate them into the Tolstoy Farm establishment.

They marched forth on October 28—2,037 men and 127 women—on a ration of a pound and a half of bread a day and an ounce of sugar. The thirty-six miles from Newcastle to Charlestown, a town close to the border, were covered in two days. "The pilgrims which Gandhi is guiding," wrote the *Sunday Post,* "are an exceedingly picturesque crew. To the eye they appear most meagre, indeed emaciated; their legs are mere sticks but the way they are marching on starvation rations shows them to be particularly hardy." [146] On November 6, the procession advanced on Volksrust expecting trouble, as some of the local worthies had threatened to shoot the Indians like rabbits. But the border was crossed without incident. At 8:30 P.M., in the Transvaal, Gandhi was arrested, only to be immediately released on bail [147] so that he could rejoin the *satyagrahis.* On November 8, Gandhi was once more taken into custody, this time at Standerton, and again he put up the bail of £50. The following day, when he was apprehended for the third time, Gandhi was not released. The marchers continued in good order to Balfour, where they were stopped and herded onto three special trains bound for Natal. En route they were starved, and upon reaching their destination they were prosecuted, convicted, and imprisoned. The government allowed its more imaginative instincts to come into play. The mine compounds were declared to be outstations of the Dundee and Newcastle jails. The mineowners' European staffs were appointed warders, and work in the mines was made part of the sentence. When the miners refused to go underground, they were whipped, fired upon, and, in general, treated with

[146] Nanda, *op. cit.,* 114.

[147] Gandhi did not usually put up bail, but in this case he did not wish his followers to be left leaderless.

the utmost cruelty. As news of these excesses became generally known, more miners and plantation workers from Tongaat to Umgeni joined their fellows in the field, only to be set upon by the mounted military police.

On November 11, Gandhi was tried at Dundee, Natal, for having induced indentured Indians to leave the province. The court was crowded with Europeans and Indians as J. W. Godfrey, appearing for Gandhi, addressed the bench:

The circumstances which had brought Mr. Gandhi before the Magistrate were well known to all persons, and he was only expressing the desire of the defendant when he stated that the Magistrate had a duty to perform, and that he was expected to perform that duty fearlessly, and should therefore not hesitate to impose the highest sentence upon the prisoner if he felt that the circumstances in the case justified it.[148]

The resident magistrate, J. W. Cross, sentenced the prisoner to a £60 fine or nine months' rigorous imprisonment, and Gandhi, of course, chose the latter. Two days later, Gandhi was moved to Volksrust jail, and on November 14 he was sentenced to a further three months' term by the Volksrust court. Another two days elapsed, then all Indian labor in the Durban area—on the railways, sugar refineries, docks, and corporation facilities—struck work. A clash between the strikers and the police ensued, resulting in the injury of sixteen Indians and the death of one. On November 18, Gandhi was moved to his third place of imprisonment, the Pietermaritzburg jail. All in all, Gandhi was treated worse than he had ever been previously. At first he was made to dig stones and sweep the compound. Later he was confined in a cell just ten feet by eight, which at night was lit only when the guard came on his periodic rounds. Gandhi was not allowed to have even a bench in his place of confinement, nor was he allowed to exercise. He was in general harassed, and every attempt was made to humiliate him. When he was

[148] *Works*, XII, 263–265; *Indian Opinion*, Nov. 19, 1913.

summoned to give evidence in another case, he was marched to court, handcuffed and with legs manacled.[149]

But the passive resistance campaign was having an effect all over the British world. In South Africa, itself, although some newspapers chided the government for indecision and for having become "mere pawns in a game as mad and cruel as has ever been devised by any group of fanatics or of notoriety-loving agitators," [150] others openly sided with the Indians. The *Mercury* urged the government "to purge the immigration act of those features which are incompatible with British notions of justice and are obnoxious to Indians and Europeans alike." Otherwise it could not "be credited with having kept faith with the Indians." [151] The paper felt that the strike of the Indian labor force in Natal would come to an end if the £3 tax were only revoked:

The Government, it is not denied, promised Mr. Gokhale that the tax would be repealed, and they have been urged by the Natal members of Parliament to fulfill that promise. As a matter of equity and of good faith, it behooves the Government to remove the obnoxious tax from the Statute Book. By delaying to do so they only compromised their own dignity and they cannot too soon put themselves right with the Home and local opinion by undertaking that the repeal will be effected at the earliest available opportunity.[152]

Lord Hardinge, the viceroy, in violation of time-honored custom, attacked both London and Pretoria. "It is not easy to find means whereby India can make its indignation felt

---

[149] *Ibid.*, 284–287.

[150] The *Star*, Johannesburg, Nov. 10, 1913. Colonial Office minuting by H. L. (probably Lambert) manifested some measure of exasperation with Gandhi. "Demands such as Mr. Gandhi is making," he wrote on Dec. 23, 1913, "simply make the average S. African desire to kick him and it does not much matter from a purely S. African point of view how soon and how hard he and his friends get kicked."

[151] *Natal Mercury*, Oct. 3, 1913.   [152] *Ibid.*, Oct. 23, 1913.

by those holding the reins of Government in South Africa," he exclaimed in a public speech in Madras.

. . . Your compatriots in South Africa have taken matters into their own hands, organising passive resistance to laws which they consider invidious and unjust, an opinion which we, who are watching their struggles from afar, cannot but share. They violated those laws with a full knowledge of the penalties involved, and are ready with all courage and patience to endure the penalties. In all this they have the deep and burning sympathy of India and also of those who like myself, without being Indian, sympathise with the people of this country.

Hardinge next referred to the measures allegedly being used in South Africa to crush passive resistance, "measures which would not be tolerated for a moment in any country claiming to be civilised." The Government of South Africa, the viceroy agreed, categorically denied the charges leveled against it, but in the process admitted practices which at best were neither wise nor discreet. In the conclusion of his address, Hardinge urged the appointment of an impartial committee to investigate and report on the Indian problem in South Africa in all its ramifications.[153]

The Madras speech almost overnight made Hardinge into perhaps the most popular British figure ever to serve on the subcontinent. An eminent Indian wrote to the *Times* on December 2:

He has transformed an indignant and resenting India into a hopeful and trusting country. People at a distance cannot imagine what danger has been averted and what confidence restored. He has saved India from a rising or a deluge of objectionable statements. He has rescued it from the clutch of scheming extremists. He has brought hesitating India closest to the English throne today, and by a well thought-out and earnest expression of Imperial truth crowned the King-Emperor in every Indian heart. Let critics look for the effects on India's heart and judge.

[153] The *Times*, Nov. 27, 1913.

Even the usually hostile indigenous press had some kind comments to make about the viceroy. *Kaiser-i-Hind,* a Bombay English weekly, claimed that, "Lord Hardinge spoke at that very psychological moment when India's feelings were at the boiling point. His words fell like oil on angry waves." [154] The *Sind Journal,* of Hyderabad, Sind, contended: "Lord Hardinge has, in fact, spoken as would an Indian patriot . . . His speech will ever remain enshrined in the hearts of Indians." [155] Hardinge himself was not blind to the effect his pronouncement had exerted. He noted that the agitation in India before his appearance in Madras was "extremely serious." Many people claimed there had been nothing like it since the Indian Mutiny. "I am fully aware," the viceroy admitted, "that my speech was very unusual in character." But he contended that "it had an almost magic effect."

The agitation calmed down instantly, because people had a feeling of confidence in, and solidarity with, me and my Government, and I think that this has been almost a unique occasion, since the Government of India have had the whole of India behind them. It now remains for the Imperial Government to do their share if they can, for I fully realise the difficulty of the situation with an obstinate Colonial Government, such as that of the Union, where the whole question is regarded from the standpoint of internal politics. It is a great mistake to imagine that Indians want a great deal. They do not clamour at all for free immigration, but what they demand is the fair and proper treatment of domiciled Indians in South Africa who have been allowed to immigrate into that part of the Empire much to the advantage and profit of the planters etc.[156]

In South Africa, Gladstone,[157] Botha, and Smuts were not only irate but pressed for Hardinge's recall. And the British

[154] Report of native newspapers, Bombay, *Kaiser-i-Hind,* Dec. 9, 1913.

[155] *Ibid.,* the *Sind Journal* (English language), Dec. 4, 1913.

[156] Hardinge papers, v. 87, Hardinge to Sanderson, Dec. 11, 1913.

[157] CO, 551/46, min. pap. 267313/14, pvt., gov.-gen. to sec. of state, Dec. 11, 1913.

cabinet, for its part, seriously considered depriving Hardinge of his office, but abandoned the idea in consequence of the high esteem which the viceroy was now enjoying in India.[158]

The situation grew ever more desperate,[159] as Gladstone telegraphed the Colonial Office on behalf of the Natal Indian Congress:

Indian mass meeting, over 5,000 present, strongly condemn Government of Union of South Africa attitude, arrest and imprisonment of Gandhi, Kallenbach, Polak, and others for striking demonstration of feeling against £3 tax, Strikers imprisoned, Mines proclaimed temporary gaols. Brutally assaulted, flogged, some shot at, wounded. One died to-day result flogging. Strikers confined estates under police guard. Thousands continue to come out. Situation getting more serious every hour. Increasing difficulty feeding people and keeping order. Active, prompt, intervention by Imperial, Indian Governments necessary lest greater hardships ensue, even many lives may be lost.[160]

At this darkest hour, however, a new development suddenly shattered the gloom. The Union Government, perhaps as a

[158] Nanda, op. cit., 117, quoting Hardinge of Penshurst, My Indian Years (London, 1948), 91. See also W. K. Hancock and J. Van der Poel, Selections from the Smuts Papers (Cambridge, 1966), III, 138–139, 148–152.

[159] NAI, Feb. 1914, proc. 4, tel., gov.-gen. to sec. of state, Dec. 2, 1913, forwarding figures from Gen. Lukin: north coast Natal—approx. 11,655 coolies in area, 8,564 working, 2,434 on strike, 657 in jail; south coast Natal—5,523 coolies in area, 4,914 working, 189 on strike, 420 in jail; Zululand—1,400 coolies in area, 1,140 working, 65 on strike, 195 in jail. Natal coal area—2,957 employed in the collieries, 2,729 working, 115 on strike, 113 in jail. Ibid., gov.-gen. to sec. of state, Dec. 11, 1913, further figures from Gen. Lukin: coal area—3,680 working, 165 on strike, 167 in jail; north coast Natal—11,000 working, 302 on strike, 810 in jail; south coast Natal—7,864 working, 154 on strike, 92 in jail; Zululand—4,100 working; totals—26,644 working, 621 on strike, 1,069 in jail. Ibid., proc. 16, gov.-gen. to sec. of state, Dec. 18, 1913, forwarding figures as of Dec. 12. In all of Natal, 24,334 coolies were working, 625 were on strike, and 730 were in jail.

[160] Cd. 7111, gov.-gen. to sec. of state, Nov. 18, 1913.

result of Hardinge's speech, on December 11 announced its intention to establish an "Indian Enquiry Commission" to investigate the causes of the strike and the disturbances that occurred in connection with it. With little delay the government appointed the three members of the body. Sir William Solomon, the noted South African jurist, was to be the chairman. Edward Esselen and Lieutenant-Colonel James S. Wylie were to work in conjunction with him.

One of the commission's first actions was to recommend the release of Gandhi, Polak, and Kallenbach, and on December 18 the three prisoners were brought to Pretoria and unconditionally set free. Despite the government's obvious gestures of conciliation, Gandhi was most dissatisfied with the commission's membership. "It is considered that the Commission have been appointed to give fair play," he informed Gokhale, "but it is a packed body intended to hoodwink the public in England and India." [161] Gandhi did not object to Solomon, but Esselen had long been strongly anti-Indian and Wylie's record was no better. In fact, he had been one of the leaders of the anti-Indian demonstration at Durban harbor in January 1897 (see Chapter III). Gandhi wanted the appointment of at least one other commissioner to represent the Indians, perhaps W. P. Schreiner or James Rose-Innes, both of the Cape.[162] But the government stood firm, although a high official in the Government of India, Sir Benjamin Robertson, did sit with the commission.

With no reconstruction of the commission in sight, Gandhi, despite the opposition of both Hardinge and Gokhale, determined to boycott its proceedings and to urge his followers not to give evidence. Gokhale was particularly peeved. He was tired and his diabetes was constantly growing worse. "Gandhi had no business to take a vow and tie himself up,"

[161] NAI, March 1914, proc. 16, sec. of state to gov.-gen., Jan. 6, 1914. summary of communications to Gokhale.

[162] *Works*, XII, 277–281; Gandhi, Kallenbach, and Polak to min. of interior, Dec. 21, 1913.

he growled. "This is politics and compromise is the essence." [163] In January 1914, when the Reverend C. F. Andrews arrived in South Africa to aid the Indian cause, he asked Gandhi whether his opposition to the commission was not just a question of the Indians' honor. "Yes," Gandhi responded vehemently, "that is it, that is it. There is the real point at issue." "Then," said Andrews, "I am sure that you are right to stand out. There must be no sacrifice of honour." Andrews and Gandhi were friends from that moment forth; within two or three days they were "Mohan" and "Charlie" to one another.[164]

The *satyagraha* struggle was still not officially over when Gandhi, accompanied by Andrews, traveled to Pretoria to see Smuts. It was January 9, 1914, and a railway strike was looming on the horizon. As was his custom, Gandhi was not at all anxious to take advantage of the government's embarrassment, and he promised that *satyagraha* would be suspended, at least until the strike was settled. This decision has a profound effect. One of Smuts's secretaries with somewhat strained jocularity told Gandhi:

I do not like your people, and do not care to assist them at all. But what can I do? You help us in our days of need. How can we lay hands upon you? I often wish you took to violence like the English strikers, and then we would know at once how to dispose of you. But you will not injure even the enemy. You desire victory by self-suffering alone and never transgress your self-imposed limit of courtesy and chivalry. And that is what reduces us to sheer helplessness.[165]

On January 16, Gandhi had an interview with Smuts, and throughout the succeeding days numerous conversations took place between Gandhi, Andrews, Robertson, and Smuts. When the discussion began, it became clear that there was already a broad area of agreement. Smuts asked

[163] Nanda, *op. cit.*, 118.   [164] *Works*, XII, 315.
[165] *Satyagraha*, 325–326.

whether Gandhi would be satisfied if the £3 tax were abolished but the license retained. Gandhi at first thought this compromise might be acceptable but later felt that the license should no longer be required after three years' residence in Natal. On the marriage question, Gandhi would be satisfied if statutory recognition were accorded to *"de facto monogamous wives."* Gandhi did not press for new legislation to govern the entrance of Indians from another province into the Cape. He merely asked for an assurance that the law would be so administered that the education test would not apply to such persons. The understanding reached was that this situation would apply as long as there were only a few Indians entering the Cape. Should the number ever increase, the education test would be administered. The Free State issue had, of course, already been settled by Gandhi in correspondence with Gorges, and Smuts was pleased to ratify the agreement of a question which had caused so many previous attempts at an accommodation between the Indians and the government to founder. As a final point, Gandhi asked that the laws of the Union which particularly applied to Indians be administered justly and with due regard for vested interests.[166]

What some of the major actors in the drama thought of Gandhi is of more than casual interest. "General Smuts," Gladstone wrote,

has shown a most patient and conciliatory temper. In spite of a series of conflicts extending over many years, he retains a sympathetic interest in Mr. Gandhi as an unusual type of humanity, whose peculiarities, however inconvenient they may be to the Minister, are not devoid of attraction for the student. . . . It is no easy task for a European to conduct negotiations with Mr. Gandhi. The workings of his conscience are inscrutable to the Occidental mind and produce complications in wholly unexpected places. His ethical and intellectual attitude, based it ap-

[166] NAI, May 1914, proc. 1, gov.-gen. to sec. of state, Jan. 22, 1914.

pears on a curious compound of mysticism and astuteness baffles the ordinary procession of thought.[167]

It was, all in all, a description which many of Gandhi's later adversaries in India might have echoed. Robertson thought Gandhi was

altogether a most extraordinary person, very subtle minded, and always ready to change his ground at a moment's notice. I must say, after having been in contact with him for a fortnight, that I have some sympathy for Smuts—who, by the way, is a personal friend of Gandhi's—when he complains that he never knows what Gandhi is asking for. . . .

Despite what I have written about Gandhi above, he and I get on very well together and are quite friends. I paid him a visit this afternoon at his settlement, ten miles north of Durban, which pleased him greatly. But he has a terrible amount of conscience and is very hard to manage.[168]

Crewe, whose encounters with Gandhi in London must have caused him more than usual frustration, felt that "he is a quite astonishingly hopeless and impracticable person for any kind of deal, but with a sort of ardent, though restrained honesty which becomes the most pigheaded obstinacy at the critical moment." [169]

The report of the Indian Enquiry Commission appeared in April 1914. Much of it was concerned with the events leading up to the passive resistance campaign and an analysis of the various incidents which occurred during the strike. Its most significant sections, however, left to a few paragraphs at the end of some forty pages, contained the recommended changes in both the law and in administrative practice. They are worth repeating in full: [170]

(1) Section 5(g) of the Immigration Regulation Act of

[167] *Ibid.*

[168] Hardinge papers, v. 87, Robertson to Hardinge, Feb. 4, 1914.

[169] *Ibid.*, sec. of state to viceroy, March 20, 1914.　　[170] Cd. 7265.

1913 should be altered to bring it into conformity with the practice of the immigration department, which was "to admit one wife and the minor children by her of an Indian now entitled to reside in any province or who may in future be permitted to enter the Union, irrespective of the fact that his marriage to such wife may have been solemnised according to tenets that recognise polygamy, or that she is one of several wives married abroad, so long as she is the only wife in South Africa."

(2) Instructions should be given to the immigration officers to open registers in each province for the registration by Indians of, say, three or more years' residence in South Africa, who have at present or have had in the past more than one wife living in South Africa, of such wives, who are to be free to travel to and from India with their minor children as long as the husband continues to reside in this country.

(3) There should be legislation on the lines of Act 16 of 1860 of the Cape Colony making provision for the appointment of marriage officers from amongst Indian priests of different denominations for the purpose of solemnising marriages in accordance with the rites of the respective religions of the parties.

(4) There should be legislation for the validation by means of registration of existing *de facto* monogamous marriages, by which were understood marriages of one man with one woman under a system which recognized the right of the husband to marry one or more other wives.

(5) Section 6 of Natal Act 17 of 1895—the £3 tax—should be repealed.

(6) Certificates issued under the Immigration Act of 1913 should remain in effect for three years.

(7) A full-time interpreter should be attached to the immigration department in Cape Town.

(8) A clerk should fill in the application forms for immigrants who desire him to do so.

(9) The practice in Cape Town of taking, in certain cases,

all ten fingerprints instead of just thumbprints should be discontinued.

(10) The resident magistrate in districts having no immigration officer should have the power to issue temporary permits to Indians residing in his district who desire to travel from their home province to another province within the Union.

(11) The £1 fee for a temporary permit or identification certificate should be materially reduced and there should be no charge for its extension.

(12) The present practice of the immigration officer of one province communicating with his counterpart in another province whenever an Indian made an application for a permit to travel should be discontinued.

(13) Domicile certificates issued by the immigration officers in Natal which bear the thumb impression of the holder should be recognized as conclusive evidence of the right of the holder to enter the Union as soon as his identity has been established.

(14) An agreement should be concluded with the Government of India whereby an official inquiry to determine the status of alleged wives and children of Indians domiciled in South Africa would be conducted by a magistrate or other government official. If the appropriate certificate were issued as a consequence of the investigation, it should be accepted as conclusive evidence by immigration officers.[171]

Those of the commission's recommendations which had to be reflected in legislation resulted in the introduction into parliament of Act 22 of 1914—"To make provision for the redress of certain grievances and the removal of certain disabilities of His Majesty's Indian Subjects in the Union and other matters incidental thereto"—commonly referred to as the Indian Relief Bill. Sections 1, 2, and 3 of the measure implemented the commission's recommendations concerning

[171] An agreement on these lines was in short order negotiated. NAI, July 1914, procs. 10–12, viceroy to sec. of state, May 28, 1914.

Indian marriages. To encourage the return of Indians to the subcontinent, section 6 offered a free passage to those Indians and their dependents who were willing to surrender their rights of domicile in South Africa. Section 7 provided for the acceptance of Natal certificates of residence of domicile as conclusive proof of former residence for Indians returning to South Africa from abroad. The £3 tax question was at last settled by the inclusion of section 6 of Natal Act 17 of 1895 in the schedule of measures repealed.

Those outstanding difficulties not covered by the bill were to be settled by administrative action on the basis of the agreements concluded between Smuts and Gandhi in their extensive correspondence. The government would create no impediment to the entrance into the Union of existing plural wives of domiciled Indians. A discharge certificate would be issued to all indentured or reindentured Indians upon the completion of their period of service. The entry of South African-born Indians into the Cape would continue on the same basis as before the passage of the immigration act of 1913, but the government reserved the right to activate the provisions of the act if the number of such entrants "sensibly increases." Gandhi's proposals to Gorges on the Free State question would be implemented, and bona fide passive resisters would not in the future have their convictions used against them by the government.[172]

Gandhi now felt that he could at last obey Gokhale's injunction to return to India. One wonders what Gandhi would have been like without the South African experience. He had landed in Natal as the junior counsel for a commercial firm, earning a salary of £105 per annum. Within a few short years he was receiving £5000 a year in legal fees, all of which he was to contribute to a cause in which he deeply believed. Operating in a sphere where he really had no rivals, Gandhi was able to rid himself of the uncertainty which had

[172] *Ibid.*, Sept. 1914, procs. 5–12, paraphrase of tel., gov.-gen. to sec. of state, July 1, 1914.

caused him to collapse while cross-examining a witness in Bombay, and to emerge not only as a skilled lawyer, respected throughout Natal, the Transvaal, and later the Union, but as a political leader of great maturity, flexibility, and imagination. As Gandhi left South Africa for the final time in July 1914, his constituents flooded him with testimonials and farewell banquets. Even his former rivals were not ungenerous in praise. The *Star,* on July 15, wrote:

As we remarked the other day, he has proved himself a singularly purposeful patriot and a strategist of considerable ability. But with this intense pride in his people has "marched" a feeling for Imperial considerations without which a solution might never have been found, and without which future guiders of Indian opinion in this country will find future policy almost impossible to direct.

Smuts, for his part, exclaimed with obvious relief: "The saint has left our shores, I sincerely hope for ever." [173] Yet, thirty-five years later, in an essay he contributed to a collection titled *Gandhi's Political Method,* Smuts wrote:

It was my fate to be the antagonist of a man for whom even then I had the highest respect. . . . I must frankly admit that his activities at that time were very trying to me. Together with other South African leaders I was busily engaged in the task of welding the old Colonies into a unified State. . . . It was a colossal work which took up every moment of my time. Suddenly in the midst of all those engrossing preoccupations, Gandhi raised a troublesome issue. We had a skeleton in our cupboard.[174]

"[I] would like to make a final appeal to our European friends who take an interest in the British Indian question in South Africa," Gandhi proclaimed in his valedictory.

Let me appeal to them to take a humanitarian view of the question, the imperial view of the question. Rightly or wrongly, for good or evil, Englishmen and Indians have been knit together and it behooves both races so to mould themselves as to leave a

[173] Hancock, *Smuts,* 345.   [174] *Ibid.,* 346–347.

splendid legacy to generations yet to be born, and to show that though Empires have gone and fallen, this Empire perhaps may be an exception and this is an Empire not founded on material but spiritual foundations.

That has been a source of solace all through. I have always believed there is something subtle, something fine in the ideals of the British Constitution. Tear away those ideals and you tear away my loyalty to that Constitution; keep those ideals and I am ever a bondsman. (Cheers.) Both races should see that those ideals of the British Constitution always remain a sacred treasure.[175]

As he sailed away, Gandhi knew not what great task still lay ahead of him in India. Wistfully he wrote from shipboard: "I have been so often prevented from reaching India that it seems hardly real that I am sitting in a ship bound for India. And having reached that what shall I do with myself? However, 'Lead Kindly Light, amid the encircling gloom. Lead Thou me on . . . .' That thought is my solace. . . ." [176]

It is much too easy to confuse what Gandhi accomplished as a human being, his stature as the prophet of a devastating new philosophy of dissent, with the significance of his presence in South Africa to the reformulation of imperial policy and attitudes and to the actual fabric of Indian life. He had returned to the Indians their honor, but Law 3 of 1885 and the Transvaal Gold Law and Townships Act were still on the statute books. Indians lacked the franchise, license abuses were as common as ever, the municipal councils still held sway, and the situation was destined to get worse not better. Gandhi had left South Africa optimistic about the future of his countrymen there, but his optimism was ill-founded. Official pronouncements by statesmen and savants may have espoused an imperial philosophy dedicated to the equality of all British subjects. But Sir West Ridgeway, a former Indian provincial governor and erstwhile chairman of a committee sent to the Transvaal in 1906 to deal with the franchise and

---

[175] *Works*, XII, 505; *Cape Times*, July 20, 1914.
[176] *Ibid.*, 566; Gandhi to A. H. West, Dec. 23, 1914.

electoral system questions, probably represented prevailing British opinion more accurately. In a long letter to the *Times,* he disparaged

academic imperialists at home who dream of a Utopian Empire where all citizens enjoy equal rights. This dream can never be realised; at least not for generations to come. If the Government were to make any attempt to enforce this policy, or even to support it by argument, the break-up of our Empire would follow. Our self-governing colonies—at least at this stage of their development—will not tolerate the entry of coloured races into their midst in any number. It is a question of life and death with them. Theirs must be a white man's country.[177]

[177] The *Times,* Dec. 6, 1913.

Epilogue

THE HISTORY of the Indian community in South Africa is at least in part a case study in moral bankruptcy and imperial futility. The South African governments were only interested in Indian labor and were determined not to countenance Indians as citizens of a "white man's country." The Government of India tended to assume no more compelling a role than that of a great power concerned with some not totally desirable subjects overseas. On the other hand, it was not above currying favor with the millions it ruled on the subcontinent by advocating the rights of their brethren in South Africa. The British Government, the guardian and enunciator of the imperial philosophy of equality, had, for many reasons, not been able decisively to influence racial policy in South Africa since about 1870, and it was vain to expect it to do so after Union. Laws that were controversial at the colonial level could often be effected by the municipalities. No doubt an awareness of the futility of disallowance must have made it very easy for Whitehall to hide behind the façade of responsible government, with its implication of colonial autonomy, and to insist on form rather than substance in colonial legislation. Unable totally to abandon the standards of their age, many of the officials in London and Calcutta must have felt more sympathy for their white cousins in South Africa than for their Indian fellow subjects.

Gandhi had made the world aware of the Indians' dilemma in South Africa. He had fought a battle based on principle, and he had largely prevailed on most of the questions specifically at issue. But it was a much more limited victory than either he or his followers had anticipated. The Government of the Union of South Africa had no intention of abating the pressure on the Indian population. Increased anti-Indian agitation in the Transvaal forced the parliament in Pretoria to pass Act 37 of 1919, "the Transvaal Asiatic Land and Trading Amendment Act," which severely limited the rights of Indians, either as companies or individuals, to own fixed property. The Asiatic Inquiry Commission, appointed the following year under the chairmanship of Sir John Lange, recommended a program of voluntary repatriation to India, and although it condemned existing locations as inadequate, the commission urged the establishment of segregated areas in towns to which Indians would be limited both for purposes of habitation and of business. Natal Indians were finally denied the franchise in municipal elections when General Hertzog became prime minister in 1924, and "The Areas Reservation and Immigration and Registration (Further Provisions) Bill," introduced in 1925, was designed to strengthen the law in regard to Indian immigration and the establishment of locations and to provide for still another registration of all Indians in South Africa. As Dr. D. F. Malan, the minister of the interior, said in moving the measure:

I must say that the bill frankly starts from the general supposition that the Indian, as a race in this country, is an alien element in the population, and no solution of this question will be acceptable to the country unless it results in a very considerable reduction of the Indian population in this country. But, on the other hand, the method of dealing with this question will not be the employment of any forcible means. The method which this bill will propose will be the application of pressure to supplement, on the other hand, the inducement which is held out to the Indians to leave the country.[1]

Due to strong opposition by the Government of India, the Areas Reservation Bill was withdrawn and a round table conference between officials of the governments of India and South Africa instead convened. What emerged was the so-called Cape Town Agreement, under the terms of which the Government of India agreed to cooperate in a program of voluntary repatriation while the Union undertook not to reintroduce the areas reservation bill and to "uplift" those Indians who determined to remain in South Africa.

The voluntary repatriation scheme was from the first a dead letter in the Cape Town Agreement, and the South African Government, cheated of the one success it most desired, returned to the attack. The Mines and Works (Amendment) Act of 1926, commonly known as the Colour Bar Act, reserved certain areas of the mining industry for Europeans and closed them to Indians. During the 1930's and 1940's, a series of enactments to curtail Indian occupation of land was passed. These culminated in the Trading and Occupation of Land (Transvaal and Natal) Restriction Bill of 1943. The Pegging Act, as it was called, essentially froze Indian landholdings in Durban as they then were, for the next three years, and its provisions could be applied to other areas by proclamation, as circumstances warranted. The stipulations of the Pegging Act were made permanent by the Asiatic Land Tenure and Indian Representation Bill. Its passage in 1946 prompted the withdrawal of the Indian agent-general in South Africa, a post established by the Cape Town Agreement, as one of the initial acts of a newly independent India. In South Africa itself, the Indians inaugu-

[1] M. Palmer, *The History of Indians in Natal* (Cape Town, 1957), 94.

rated the first passive resistance campaign since 1913. But without Gandhi's leadership, it was a dismal failure.

Indians, along with other nonwhite peoples of South Africa, became victims of the group areas legislation passed by succeeding post World War II Nationalist governments. Today they are under the jurisdiction of a separate department of Indian affairs. They may only attend a special Indian university in Durban harbor, and their job opportunities are by law severely circumscribed. The government is committed to moving all of South Africa's Indians into separate locations, and they are progressively seeing to the task. The hated Law 3 of 1885, with its stipulation that special areas be reserved for Indians *within* the Transvaal municipalities, must now seem part of an almost golden past. Johannesburg Indians have virtually all been moved to a new township of Lenasia, over twenty miles from the city. Most of them can find employment only in Johannesburg, and the return fare is almost prohibitive for members of a community whose per capita mean income was, in 1958, given as only £40.02.[2]

What the future holds is always hard to predict, but for South Africa's Indians, cut off from an ancestral homeland they no longer know, caught between a disdainful white minority and a hostile black majority, the prospects can be no more than bleak.

[2] L. Kuper *et al., Durban—A Racial Ecology* (London, 1958), 86.

Appendix / The Indian Question in British Central Africa

THE ATTITUDE of the white settlers in Rhodesia toward the Indians who began to filter into the territory in the years preceding the Anglo-Boer War was not dissimilar to that of their cousins further south. Although Southern Rhodesia was under the jurisdiction of the British South Africa Company, and hence closely scrutinized by the Colonial Office, and despite the fact that the number of Indians was always small,[1] the colonists' fervor was in no way abated. The *Rhodesia Herald* of June 4, 1898, played a familiar strain. Coolies, it asserted,

were filthy dirty, and with their uncleanly habits may at any time sow the seeds of deadly epidemic. They live upon what may be termed the smell of an oiled rag, and the result is that in certain branches of business they dislocated trade by cutting-down prices, to the detriment of the legitimate trader, and without a corresponding spending capacity to level matters up. . . .

It would be unwise to counsel violent measures, yet the action which the Salisbury storekeepers took when threatened to check the irrepressible Indian trader, who made his appearance there, unless he promptly quitted, was apparently successful, for since then not one of them has attempted to obtain a footing in the place.

[1] There were only 900 Indians in Southern Rhodesia in 1908 and 2,911 by 1946.

The depth of anti-Indian feeling was manifested in Umtali, when on the night of January 4, 1899, at about nine o'clock, a mob of 1,500, including many of the town's most prominent businessmen and officers of the volunteers, gathered to drive the Indian traders out of the municipality. Furthermore, the acting civil commissioner of Umtali reported, all the principal white storekeepers and two justices of the peace were involved.[2] In the growing riot, Indian merchants were manhandled, their goods scattered abroad, and order not restored until the mounted police intervened. What was alarming about the whole episode was the character of the participants. This was no mob of hooligans but the town's most respected and responsible citizens. To drive the demonstrators' point home, the chamber of commerce wrote:

The majority of the inhabitants are determined to oppose by every means in their power the introduction of Banyan traders into Umtali, as they consider that the displacement of white traders by Asiatics will be very prejudicial to the prosperity of Umtali and Rhodesia generally and take the bread out of a large number of the mouths of Europeans. We would suggest as a peaceful way out of the difficulty that power be given to the Sanitary Board or other representative body here to grant or refuse trading licenses to any whom they may consider to be undesirable inhabitants. This principle is now accepted by the Home Government. In the meantime we trust that the Government will refuse to issue further licenses to Asiatics pending definite decision by the High Commissioner.[3]

The Rhodesian administration in Salisbury took a very dim view of the affair. A public prosecutor was sent to Umtali to bring charges against the perpetrators of the disorder. He reported to his superiors that the trial of the guilty might "possibly have the effect of causing further trouble for a very bitter feeling undoubtedly exists against the influx of

[2] RA, act. civil comm., Umtali to the act. admin., Salisbury, Jan. 5, 1899.

[3] *Ibid.*, encl.

Banyans into the country." [4] The government, however, stood firm. The justices of the peace and the officers of the volunteers were forced to resign,[5] and several of the offenders were duly convicted. The chamber of commerce was informed in no uncertain terms that licenses would continue to be issued to Indians in the usual manner.[6]

In contrast to the Southern Rhodesia settlers, Sir Harry Johnston, in Nyasaland, held a quite different view of the role of the Indian in Central Africa; but he was a man of broad, almost romantic, imperial vision. "I am convinced," he wrote,

that the greater part of the territories we have acquired or are about to acquire in Tropical Africa will never be habitable to any extent by white men unless the climatic conditions can be altered: on the other hand, these territories are to a great extent uninhabited, and offer most attractive conditions of fertile soil and good water-supply. Here natives of India might settle to advantage and in time create wealthy establishments.[7]

Johnston offered Indians thirty-acre estates on the lower Shire, an area not suitable for European habitation,[8] and after the first settlers arrived he was soon able to report that they were thriving in a manner impossible for Europeans.[9]

But Indians farming lands inhospitable to Europeans and Indians competing with white merchants were two totally different matters, and Southern Rhodesia was unable to emulate Nyasaland's apparently happy attitude on the Asian question. The Colonial Office, ever more frequently, came into possession of reports that Indians were treated prejudi-

---

[4] RA, act. pub. pros., Herbert J. Castens, to act. admin., Jan. 19, 1899.

[5] RA, act. admin. to act. civil comm., Umtali, Jan. 6, 1899.

[6] RA, Percy Inskipp, undersec. to sec., chamb. of comm., Umtali, Jan. 16, 1899.

[7] NAI, Jan. 1895, proc. 8, Johnston to for. sec., Nov. 17, 1894.

[8] NAI, Feb. 1895, proc. 8, Johnston to for. sec., Nov. 11, 1894.

[9] NAI, Nov. 1895, proc. 8, Johnston to for. sec., June 1, 1895.

cially when applying for hawkers' or traders' licenses. The company, however, resolutely denied these charges.[10] Regardless, Indians were, without doubt, discriminated against in other ways. Ordinance 134 of 1896, for example, prohibited Indians from drinking alcoholic beverages except on licensed premises. They could only acquire liquor in a bottle on behalf of a European and then only upon presentation of a bona fide note from the white purchaser.

Despite the strong feeling against the immigration of "free" Indians, Southern Rhodesia, plagued with a labor shortage only slightly less severe than that in the Transvaal, was anxious, after the war, to import indentured Indian laborers.[11] The company was willing to pass appropriate legislation,[12] and the Colonial Office, in reply, delineated what it felt to be the Government of India's basic requirements. The company would have to closely supervise the recruitment process, the journey of the laborers to Africa, and their assignments to employers. There would have to be a protector and staff armed with the power to inspect and investigate, and the territorial administration would have to be responsible for the return to India of laborers who had concluded their contractual term or who were unfit to work.[13] Ordinance 18 of 1901 implemented the Colonial Office's advice, adding an enforced savings scheme as an extra inducement to the Government of India. Before negotiations could achieve fruition, however, the envisaged nightmare of hordes of Chinese laborers descending upon the Transvaal and then slowly insinuating themselves into Southern Rhodesia, considerably cooled the territory's ardor. Only the mine owners and the chambers of commerce continued to support the

[10] NAI, Aug. 1898, proc. 2.

[11] A scheme to import Arabs from Aden, although partially implemented, was unsuccessful.

[12] CO, 417/329, Brit. So. Af. Co. to Col. Off., June 5, 1901.

[13] *Ibid.*, Brit. So. Af. Co. to So. Rhod., June 27, 1901.

scheme. The Government of India, sensing the new mood, decided not to continue the conversations.[14]

The closing of the Indian labor issue still left the question of free immigration unresolved, and Southern Rhodesia proceeded to draw its inspiration for a solution from its South African neighbors. Ordinance 10 of 1903 was based on the Cape immigration restriction act. The measure excluded persons from Southern Rhodesia who could not, to the satisfaction of the administrator, write out and sign in the characters of any European language an application to enter the territory. Reminiscent of the Cape act, European agricultural laborers, domestic servants, skilled artisans, mechanics, miners, and workmen could be exempted from the language test through action by the administrator [15] and the executive council. Even the debates on the bill sounded familiar. One member (Frances) announced in the legislature that "he did not think that any man who was born in South Africa and who intended to live in South Africa, wished to see the country flooded by undesirable Asiatics or Indians, or any coloured persons." [16]

Westminster's position vis-à-vis Southern Rhodesia was, however, infinitely more powerful than it was in the case of a colony enjoying the rights of responsible government. As it had in the Cape, the Colonial Office demanded the deletion of the word "European" from the exemption clause and the liberal interpretation of the term "domicile." [17] The territorial government agreed to both these conditions, but found a devious way to indirectly effect its purpose. The

[14] CO, 417/381, viceroy to high comm., March 21, 1903.

[15] The administrator was the ranking British South Africa Company official in the territory. The resident commissioner represented the interests of the Colonial Office.

[16] So. Rhod. leg. counc. debates, Nov. 7, 1902.

[17] CO, 417/372, Col. Off. to For. Off., Sept. 7, 1903; Col. Off. to Ind. Off., Sept. 9, 1903.

amending legislation (Ordinance 13 of 1904), while it removed the offending terminology, empowered the administrator to admit, under exemption from the normal workings of the law, any member of the enumerated classes of persons (domestic servants, skilled artisans, mechanics, miners, and workmen—but significantly not traders) with an engagement to work in Southern Rhodesia. The Government of India, already bloodied by its Transvaal ordeal, was far from satisfied. "We are wholly unable to accept the suggestion," the viceroy's council wrote to the India Office, "that the limitation to European languages of the literary [sic] test is not very material, owing to the discretion allowed to the Administrator. . . . The discretion in question is confined to a very limited class, and is calculated no doubt to meet the needs of the Colony, but not our requirements." [18] The Colonial Office understood the India Office's objections and saw through the casuistry of the Rhodesian legislation, but was not about to interfere now that the veil of decency had been drawn before its eyes.[19]

The Southern Rhodesian settlers were not willing to accept the ordinances of 1903 and 1904 as the final solution of the Indian immigration problem. In 1907, inspired by the Transvaal Asiatic Law Amendment Act, they proposed to follow in that colony's footsteps, "so as to protect the territory from an influx of undesirable immigrants of this class [Asians]." [20] What emerged was Ordinance 4 of 1908—"An Ordinance to restrict the Immigration of Asiatics into this Territory and to provide for the Registration of such Asiatics as are already resident therein." In almost every detail, the law bore the mark of its Transvaal model, and the attorney general in moving the second reading made his purpose clear: "They were now joining," he claimed,

[18] CO, 417/405, viceroy in council to sec. of state, Aug. 11, 1904.

[19] CO, 417/392, minuting by R. H. G. (Graham) on minute paper 30201, Aug. 8, 1904.

[20] So. Rhod. leg. counc. debates, Gordon Forbes, May 9, 1907.

the last link in that chain which must form the cordon around the white people of South Africa. The strength of that chain was its weakest link and if they failed in their duty they were leaving a breaking point in that chain; leaving the door open to any influx of undesirable persons. He did not propose to go into or discuss the principles affecting the rights or wrongs of the Asiatics in this matter. In many cases the Asiatics had been extremely useful, but there was nothing which the Indian had done in this country which could not have been done by white men. If the Indians—he said it advisedly—had kept themselves to that calling that seemed best suited to the Indian at home, the cultivator, there would have been little outcry against them. But they have trespassed enormously on trade and he thought he might fairly state that their competition in trade in this country had been unfair. He did not say it had been underhanded, but they were able to adopt manners and use methods which were quite unacceptable to the scale of civilisation of the European.[21]

Although there were only nine hundred Indians in Southern Rhodesia, the attorney general pointed out that they constituted 6.5 per cent of the population compared with 5 per cent in the Transvaal.[22]

For once, all the great mandarins of empire united in opposition. The high commissioner felt that the measure was too blatantly anti-Indian. "The Ordinance," he wrote Salisbury, "is a measure specially directed against Asiatics as such. . . . No attempt is made in the Rhodesian Ordinance to disguise the compulsory character of its provisions, and no provision is made for any 'voluntary' method of registration." [23] The administrator's reply was weak. He contended that Rhodesia, as a member of the South African Customs Union, was honor-bound to accept the resolution of a conference, held at Pretoria a few months earlier, calling for the passage in all colonies and territories of legislation designed to inhibit Indian immigration into all of Southern

[21] *Ibid.,* June 16, 1908.   [22] *Ibid.*

[23] SANA, high comm. records, high comm. to sec. of state, encl., high comm. to admin., So. Rhod., Sept. 23, 1908.

Africa.[24] The India Office, for its part, gave voice to "grave objections that exist in the case of a territory which is not a self-governing Colony to such legislation as is proposed. Lord Morley is not aware of any circumstances which would justify the permanent exclusion from Southern Rhodesia (except on temporary permits of admission) of all Asiatic subjects of His Majesty who have not already acquired domicile." [25]

The Colonial Office faced with a company territory containing only 14,000 whites was for once resolute in its purpose. "I am not unmindful of the fact," the secretary of state wrote the high commissioner,

that the ordinance has unanimous support of the elected members of the Legislative Council and that it was introduced as a result of repeated requests to the administration. Southern Rhodesia is, however, not in possession of Responsible Government. The Secretary of State and High Commissioner retain considerable powers of control over its administration and their responsibility in assenting to legislation is correspondingly increased.

In view of this responsibility I am not prepared to authorise you to assent to an ordinance which is open to grave objection in principle, which is likely to lead to serious complications, and which, so far as I can judge, is not imperatively required by the position in Southern Rhodesia.[26]

The reaction in Southern Rhodesia was immediate and intense. Petitions, memorials, letters of outrage, and denunciations streamed in from all parts of the territory. At the end of May 1909, the Colonial Office's decision was debated in the legislative council. The treasurer "did not think the Government would have brought forward the Ordinance or Honourable Members opposite supported it, if it had not been imperatively required [hear, hear]. . . . He was bound to say that . . . there had been nothing furtive or hasty in

24 *Ibid.*, admin. to high comm., Oct. 6, 1908.
25 CO, 417/462, Ind. Off. to Col. Off., Sept. 24, 1908.
26 CO, 417/465, sec. of state to high comm., Dec. 12, 1908.

their action. They had always said they intended to do as the Transvaal did." [27] At the end of the proceedings the council asked His Majesty's Government to reconsider its action, "as this Council considers the present conditions are detrimental to the interests of the white race and a cause of serious danger to the progress and welfare of the country." [28] The whole situation was probably best summed up by one of the members of the legislature, a certain representative Longden. If the British Government had disallowed the Transvaal's Asiatic legislation, he contended,

it would have been followed by such a howl of indignation as would have given the Imperial Government a great deal of trouble. There was no such danger in Rhodesia because the population was small.

It seemed to him an extraordinary admission on the part of the Imperial Government to say that it was only when dealing with the weaker countries that they had the courage of their convictions.[29]

Even triumphs over weak adversaries were all too often ephemeral. Ordinance 7 of 1914—"An Ordinance to regulate the entry of immigrants and to prohibit the entry of undesirable persons into Southern Rhodesia"—quietly reimplemented the clause of the immigration restriction ordinance of 1903 which limited the exemption from the language test to "persons of European descent." [30]

While the settlers wished to prevent further Indian immigration into Southern Rhodesia, they were no less determined to limit the horizons for those already in the territory. In May 1903, the administrator, Sir W. H. Milton, informed the company that

[27] So. Rhod., leg. counc. debates of May 27–28, 1909.
[28] RA, admin. to res. comm. for transmission to high comm., June 4, 1909.
[29] *Ibid.*   [30] Ord. no. 7, 1914, sect. 7(5).

the commercial community propose during the coming session to urge, through their local members, that immediate steps should be taken by legislation to regulate the issue of licenses with a view to excluding what are termed "undesirables" from the right to obtain Trading Licenses. This, of course, is aimed at the Banyan trader. In their action the merchants will, I believe, obtain practically unanimous support from the whole community. There is no doubt that the Indian trader is, year by year, obtaining a firmer foothold in the country, and, by cutting prices to a level below that allowing a margin of profit to the European, his presence tends to the possibility of the eventual exclusion of the latter.

The proposal which the mercantile community propose to bring forward is based on the precedent of the Natal law, under which a local board for the consideration of applications and licenses was established, very much upon the principle which governs the issue of liquor licenses.[31]

The Colonial Office was most reluctant to approve any scheme inspired by the Natal model, but the settlers kept up the pressure and acted to deprive Indians of licenses without the necessary legal sanction.[32] In their attitude they had at least the sympathy of governmental officials at all levels. The civil commissioner of Victoria, for instance, was

strongly of opinion that the holding of licenses by an Indian or any Asiatic does, to a certain extent, seriously affect the welfare of European residents in this District, and that on no grounds can the holding of trading licenses by Asiatics or other coloured foreigners be considered to be accounted beneficial to the community.

. . . It is well known that the wants of the ordinary Indian are probably nil as compared with those of the European; for instance, he is no customer of the local European storekeeper: he spends little on his diet, which consists, for the most part, of

[31] NAI, March 1904, procs. 21–23, admin. to Brit. So. Af. Co., May 21, 1903.

[32] RA, minuting by treasurer on no. 15, Gordon Huntley, civil comm., Victoria, to asst. treasurer, Salisbury, Jan. 14, 1905.

fowl, rice and oil or fat; he likewise spends little on dress and nothing on anything else, but he hoards up his money, which he eventually takes out of the country. If he can find a business man foolish enough to give him credit and to trust him with goods, he not infrequently decamps and is lost to sight for all time. . . . The Asiatic is in a position to supplant and drive out the white trader, who is, from every point of view, of so much greater value to the country.[33]

Southern Rhodesia's wishes were reflected in Ordinance 2 of 1908—"An Ordinance to regulate the trade of General Dealers and Hawkers, and to amend the law relating to Stamp Duties and Licenses." As originally conceived, the bill closely followed the Natal Licensing Act. Applicants for new licenses were left to the mercy of local authorities; although vested interests were theoretically protected.[34] The Colonial Office, however, objected and was prepared to disallow the measure as it stood.[35] In its final form, consequently, the Southern Rhodesian licensing ordinance required "every decision of any Council or Board . . . [to] be submitted to the Administrator, who, with the advice of the Executive Council may after due enquiry, order the issue of any license for which a certificate has been refused." [36] Furthermore, section 6 of the law required two-thirds of the members of a local board voting and forming an absolute majority of the body to acquiesce in the refusal to issue a license to trade.[37]

Agreements between London and Salisbury as to the specific wording of Southern Rhodesian legislation notwithstanding, the settlers could often achieve their purpose by means of municipal by-laws, not subject to immediate Colo-

[33] *Ibid.*, Huntley to asst. treasurer, Jan. 15, 1905.   [34] CO, 417/463.
[35] *Ibid.*   [36] Ord. 2 of 1908, sect. 12.
[37] Section 18 of Ordinance 6 of 1910 strengthened some of the provisions of the licensing ordinance of 1908. Section 11 of the new law forbade Sunday selling—a provision directed against the Indian merchants.

nial Office scrutiny, or through the administration of an ordinance by the territorial authorities in a manner directly contrary to its provisions. Of the latter circumstance, the laws relating to prospecting and the filing of mining claims were a case in point. Despite the legal right of Indians and other colored persons to prospect and to operate mines, they were in fact never issued permits to do so. When an Indian named Pathan Sekam applied for a prospecting license, he was refused, and his solicitors, as a consequence, addressed the secretary of mines in Salisbury:

We applied on his behalf yesterday and were informed that the License could not be granted (under Section 8 of the Ordinance) without the authority of the Administrator. As we have known of very many Licenses issued without any such authority, indeed we cannot recollect a case where such authority was demanded prior to the issue of a Prospecting License, this refusal of a License would seem to point to special restrictions directed against those British subjects who come from the Indian Empire. We shall be glad if you will inform us whether the License was refused because our client is a British Indian and, if so, whether any other Nation or class or race of people are under similar disability.

It would certainly be anomalous if a British Indian who is allowed to own land and houses and, so far as we know, to own gold mines, were not allowed to carry on the calling of a prospector.[38]

Despite the fact that the secretary of mines was on record as saying, "Our custom is not to issue prospecting licenses to coloured persons," [39] the official line was that each application was decided on its own merits. After the rejection of Sekam's claim, however, the administrator saw fit to warn his subordinates to be sure that "in such cases care . . . be taken that the reply refers only to the individual application and

[38] RA, mines and works dept., Roberts, Letts, and Gill to the sec. of mines, Salisbury, Aug. 2, 1917.

[39] *Ibid.*, sec. of mines to mining comm., Umtali, Sept. 10, 1904.

not to any race or class." [40] The territorial authorities clearly understood that they were perverting the law by not granting prospecting licenses to Indians and colored persons, but they continued the practice, cloaking their purpose in various guises.[41]

There was considerably less anti-Indian feeling in Northeast and Northwest Rhodesia. The former was administered from Blantyre, Nyasaland, and attitudes toward Indians there reflected Nyasaland's considerable tolerance for the presence of Asians. Northwest Rhodesia was peopled largely by settlers more imbued with South African attitudes toward Indians, and Northwest Rhodesia Ordinance 38 of 1908 legislated against the immigration of "undesirables"—although there was no provision for a language test. Northern Rhodesia [42] Proclamation 15 of 1915 did, however, require immigrants to read and write a European language to the satisfaction of an immigration officer.

Nyasaland, on the whole, adhered to the generally liberal philosophy of Sir Harry Johnston. Neither Nyasaland Ordinance 6 of 1905 nor Ordinance 4 of 1913, both concerned with immigration, prescribed a language test. Although white merchants in Nyasaland agitated for restrictions on Indian traders, the matter was not treated with accustomed sympathy in the legislative council.[43]

[40] *Ibid.*, mines and works dept., minute no. 8555/774, by administrator, Aug. 13, 1917.

[41] *Ibid.*, act. sec. for mines and works to the sec., dept. of the administrator, Aug. 28, 1923.

[42] Northeastern and Northwestern Rhodesia were combined into Northern Rhodesia in 1911.

[43] Summary of the proceedings of the Nyasaland leg. counc., May 6, 1909. The Asian population of the Rhodesias and Nyasaland in 1961 was: Southern Rhodesia—6,990; Northern Rhodesia—7,740; Nyasaland—10,580. The figures for 1911 had been 870, 39, and 115, respectively.

Selected Bibliography

BOOKS

Ashe, G. *Gandhi*. New York: Stein and Day, 1968.

Burrows, H. R. *Indian Life and Labour in Natal*. Durban: South African Institute of Race Relations, 1953.

Calpin, G. H. *Indians in South Africa*. Pietermaritzburg: Shuter and Shooter, 1949.

Desai, D. M. *The Indian Community in Southern Rhodesia*. Salisbury: Herold, 1949.

Dotson, F., and L. O. Dotson. *The Indian Minority of Zambia, Natal, Rhodesia and Malawi*. New Haven: Yale University Press, 1968.

Ferguson-Davie, C. J. *The Early History of Indians in Natal*. Johannesburg: South African Institute of Race Relations, 1952.

Fisher, L. *The Life of Mahatma Gandhi*. New York: Collier, 1966.

Gandhi, M. K. *Collected Works*. Delhi: Government of India, 1958–.

———. *Satyagraha in South Africa*. Ahmedabab: Navajivan, 1928.

———. *The Story of My Experiments with Truth*. Boston: Beacon, 1957.

Hancock, W. K. *Smuts: The Sanguine Years, 1870–1919*. Cambridge: At the University Press, 1967.

———. *Survey of British Commonwealth Affairs*. Vol. I, *Problems of Nationality, 1918–1936*. Oxford: Oxford University Press, 1957.

Hancock, W. K., and J. Van Der Poel. *Selections from the Smuts Papers*. 4 vols. Cambridge: At the University Press, 1960.

Headlam, C. (ed.). *The Milner Papers, 1897–1904*. 2 vols. London: Cassell, 1931–1933.

Hellman, Ellen (ed.). *Handbook of Race Relations in South Africa*. Cape Town: Oxford University Press, 1949.

Joshi, P. S. *The Tyranny of Colour: A Study of the Indian Problem in South Africa*. Durban: Commercial Printing Co., 1942.

Kondapi, C. *Indians Overseas, 1838–1949*. Bombay: Oxford University Press, 1951.

Kuper, H. *Indian People in Natal*. Pietermaritzburg: Natal University Press, 1960.

Kuper, L., H. Watts, and R. Davies. *Durban: A Racial Ecology*. London: Jonathan Cape, 1958.

Nanda, B. R. *Mahatma Gandhi*. London: George Allen and Unwin. 1958.

Narain, Iqbal. *The Politics of Racialism*. Admedabab: Navajivan. 1957.

Palmer, Mabel. *The History of the Indians in Natal*. (Natal Regional Survey No. 10.) Cape Town: Oxford University Press, 1957.

Pyarelal. *Mahatma Gandhi: The Early Phase*. Admedabab: Navajivan. 1965.

Pyrah, G. B. *Imperial Policy and South Africa, 1902–1910*. Oxford: Oxford University Press, 1955.

Sacks, Benjamin. *South Africa: An Imperial Dilemma*. Albuquerque: University of New Mexico Press, 1967.

Smith, William R. *Nationalism and Reform in India*. New Haven: Yale University Press, 1938.

Thompson, L. M. *Indian Immigration into Natal (1860–1872)*. Cape Town: Archives Year Book of South African History, 1952.

———. *The Unification of South Africa, 1902–1910*. Oxford: Oxford University Press, 1960.

Thornton, A. P. *The Habit of Authority*. Toronto: University of Toronto Press, 1966.

Woods, C. A. *The Indian Community of Natal: Their Economic Problem*. (Natal Regional Survey No. 9.) Cape Town: Oxford University Press, 1954.

GOVERNMENT DOCUMENTS
AND MANUSCRIPT MATERIALS

India

National Archives of India

A and B Proceedings from the following departments:
Home, Public, 1859–1870.
Revenue, Agriculture and Commerce—Emigration, 1873–1879.
Home, Revenue and Agriculture—Emigration, 1879–1881.
Revenue and Agriculture—Emigration, 1881–1906.
Commerce and Industry—Emigration, 1906–1914.
Legislative Proceedings, 1863–1914.
Papers with Acts, 1864–1910.

Great Britain

Public Record Office

C[olonial] O[ffice] 3, British South Africa Company Ordinances.
CO 48, Cape Colony, 1880–1910.
CO 179, Natal, 1859–1910.
CO 224, Orange River Colony, 1901–1910.
CO 291, Transvaal, 1877–1881, 1901–1919.
CO 292/6, 7, Transvaal Acts.
CO 417, High Commissioner, South Africa, 1880–1914.
CO 427, Zululand, 1891–1896.
CO 525, Nyasaland, 1904–1914.
CO 551, Union of South Africa, 1910–1914.
CO 549, Transvaal and Orange River Colony, 1903–1908.
CO 632/1, Union Acts.

Colonial Office

Statute Law of the Transvaal.

Parliamentary Papers

C. 7911(1895)—Papers relating to the grievances of Her Majesty's Indian subjects in the South African Republic.

C. 7946(1896)—Continuation of C. 7911, further papers.

C. 8596(1897)—Proceedings of a conference between the secretary of state for the colonies and the premiers of the self-governing colonies.

Cd. 1640(1903)—Minutes of the proceedings of the South African Customs Union Conference, Bloemfontein.

C. 1683(1903)—Correspondence relating to a proposal to employ Indian coolies under indenture on railways in the Transvaal and Orange River Colony.

Cd. 1684(1903)—Despatch from the Governor of the Transvaal respecting the position of British Indians in that colony.

Cd. 2239(1904)—Correspondence relating to the position of British Indians in that colony.

Cd. 3251(1906)—Transvaal Asiatic Law Amendment Ordinance of 1906.

Cd. 3308(1907)—Correspondence relating to legislation affecting Asiatics in the Transvaal.

Cd. 3404(1907)—Published proceedings and precis of the Colonial Conference, 15–30 April, 1907.

Cd. 3406(1907)—Published proceedings and precis of the Colonial Conference, 30 April–14 May, 1907 [cont. of Cd. 3404(1907)].

Cd. 3887(1908)—Further correspondence relating to legislation affecting Asiatics in the Transvaal.

Cd. 3892(1908)—Further correspondence relating to legislation affecting Asiatics in the Transvaal.

Cd. 3994(1908)—Correspondence relating to the Transvaal Indentured Labour Laws Temporary Continuance Act, 1907.

Cd. 4327(1908)—Further correspondence relating to legislation affecting Asiatics in the Transvaal.

Cd. 4584(1909)—Further correspondence relating to legislation affecting Asiatics in the Transvaal.

Cd. 5194(1910)—Report of a committee on emigration from India to the crown colonies and protectorates.

Cd. 5363(1910)—Further correspondence relating to legislation affecting Asiatics in the Transvaal.

Cd. 5579(1911)—Correspondence respecting a bill to regulate further immigration into the Union of South Africa, with special reference to Asiatics; together with the draft bill, and the acts, regulations and statistics relating to immigration into the Commonwealth of Australia.

Cd. 6087(1912)—Correspondence relating to the position of British Indians under the Gold Law and Township Amendment Acts, 1905, of the Transvaal.

Cd. 6283(1912)—Continuation of Cd. 5579. Further correspondence respecting a bill to regulate further immigration into the Union of South Africa, with special reference to Asiatics.

Cd. 6940(1913)—Continuation of Cd. 6283. Further correspondence respecting a bill to regulate further immigration into the Union of South Africa, with special reference to Asiatics.

Cd. 7111(1913)—Correspondence relating to the Immigrants Regulation Act and other matters affecting Asiatics in South Africa.

Cd. 7265(1914)—Report of the Indian Enquiry Commission.

65 (Lords)—Transvaal Registration Bill. Further papers as regard the Transvaal Registration Bill (The Lord Ampthill).

Parliamentary Debates—1884–1913.

Private Papers

Birmingham University
  Chamberlain mss.
Bodleian Library (Oxford)
  Nathan mss.
British Museum
  Gladstone mss.
  Kimberley mss.
  Ripon mss.
Cambridge University Library
  Hardinge mss.
India Office Library
  Argyll mss.
  Cross mss.
  Curzon mss.
  Elgin (9th Earl) mss.
  Hamilton mss.
  Kilbracken (Godley) mss.
  Lansdowne mss.

Lytton mss.
Northbrook mss.
Rhodes House (Oxford)
Nathan mss.
Public Record Office
Carnarvon mss.

Republic of South Africa

Cape Archives (Cape Town)

Letter Books, Administrative and Convict Service, 1899–1904.
Votes and Proceedings of the House of Assembly, 1870–1910.
Acts of the Cape Parliament, 1870–1910.
Cape Parliamentary Debates, 1870–1910.
Cape Government Gazettes, 1870–1910.

Natal Archives (Pietermaritzburg)

Government House Series, 1859–1910.
  General and South African Correspondence.
  Correspondence with the High Commissioner.
  General Despatches.
  Confidential Despatches.
  Secret Despatches.
  Minutes to Ministers.
  Telegrams and Despatches to and from the Secretary of State
    for the Colonies.
Prime Minister's Office.
  Prime Minister's Meetings, 1904–1910.
  Minutes of Meetings, 1903–1909.
  Prime Minister's Private Papers, 1899–1910.
  Minute Papers and Confidential Minutes, 1900–1910.
  Letters dispatched and received, 1900–1910.
Archives of the Executive Council.
  Minutes of Meetings, 1871–1910.
  Original Certified Bills, 1898–1910.
  Register of Papers Laid before the Executive Committee,
    1879–1889.
Colonial Secretary's Office, 1880–1910.
Natal Parliamentary Papers, 1857–1910.

Votes and Proceedings.
Documents Presented.
Clerk of the Legislative Council—Letter Books.
Select Committees.
  Bills.
  Messages.
  Petitions.
  Rough Minutes.
  Miscellaneous (Legislative Assembly and Council).
Legislative Council (Responsible Government).
  Documents Presented.
  Bills Passed.
  Sessional Papers.
  Government Notices.
Natal Parliamentary Debates, 1857–1910.
Natal Government Gazettes, 1859–1910.
Natal Provincial Gazettes, 1910–1914.
Natal Government Notices and Proceedings, 1859–1910.
Minutes of the Provincial Council, 1910–1914.
Ordinances of the Provincial Council, 1910–1914.
Natal Blue Books, 1859–1914 (containing annual reports of the Protector of Indian Immigrants, the Indian Immigration Trust Board and the report on Indian schools).
Statutes of Natal, 1845–1910.

South African Republic (in South African National Archives, Pretoria)

Correspondence of the British Resident in the Transvaal, 1881–1884.
Correspondence of the British Agent in the Transvaal, 1890–1899.
Executive Council Resolutions, 1886–1899.
Volksraad Debates, 1856–1899.
Gazettes and Minutes of the Volksraad, 1856–1899.
Wetboek, 1854–1899.
Notule Volksraad, 1856–1899.
ZAR Green Books.
  Officiele Bescheiden Gewisseld met de Engelse. Refeering in zake de Conventie van London. Geslotten den 27 sten Februarie, 1884, ZAR–9 Juni 1884.

Correspondentie van de Zuid-Afrikaashe Republik met betrekking tod de Kwest van Asiatische Gekleurde Personnen.

ZAR—No. 1 van 1894.
ZAR—No. 2 van 1894.
ZAR—No. 1, 1899.

Transvaal, 1902–1910 (in South African National Archives, Pretoria)

Ordinances and Laws, 1900–1910.

Records of the Colonial Secretary's Office, 1901–1907.

Executive Council Minutes, 1902–1910.

Governor's Papers, 1902–1910.

Minutes, Votes and Proceedings of the Legislative Council, 1902–1910.

Legislative Council Debates, 1903–1910.

Minutes and Correspondence of the Executive Council, 1903–1906.

Records of the Lieutenant Governor of the Transvaal, 1903–1906.

Legislative Assembly Debates, 1907–1910.

Minutes, Votes and Proceedings of the Legislative Assembly, 1907–1910.

Records of the Prime Minister of the Transvaal, 1907–1910.

Gazettes, 1900–1910.

Union of South Africa, 1910–1914 (in South African National Archives, Pretoria)

Minutes by the Governor General.

Archives of the secretary to the department of the prime minister.

Minutes, Votes and Proceedings of the Union Parliament.

Union Debates.

Select Committee Reports.

Government Gazettes.

Union Government Blue Books.

U.G. 55(1913) Witwatersrand Disturbances.

U.G. 56(1913) Witwatersrand Disturbances.

U.G. 6(1914) Industrial Disturbances.

U.G. 14(1914) Report of the Indian Enquiry Commission.

Rhodesia–Central Africa Archives (Salisbury)

Southern Rhodesia Council Debates, 1899–1916.
Southern Rhodesia Legislative Council Proceedings and Ordinances, 1899–1920.
Statute Law of Southern Rhodesia.
Correspondence with the High Commissioner, 1898–1899.
Land Settlement Department.
Indians: Issue of leases, 1905–1914.
Administrator's Office.
Immigration: Petition by British Indians, 1916.
Treasurer Correspondence.
Trading licences for Indians, 1904–1905.
Report of the Immigration Department, 1902.
Board of Enquiry Report into question of trading by undesirable persons, 1904.
Statute Law of North Eastern Rhodesia, 1908–1911.
Satute Law of North Western Rhodesia, 1899–1911.
Statute Law of Northern Rhodesia, 1911–1916.
Summary of the Proceedings of the Nyasaland Legislative Council, 1899–1909.

Nyasaland (Malawi) Archives (Zomba)

Nyasaland Orders in Council in Force, December 31, 1913.
Supplement 1914.
Nyasaland Orders in Council in Force, December 13, 1919.
Nyasaland Orders in Council.
Proceedings, Rules, etc., 1914–1918.

NEWSPAPERS

Natal

Natal Mercury, 1859–1916.
Natal Witness, 1859–1916.
Indian Opinion, 1903–1916.

Transvaal

The *Star* (Johannesburg), 1899–1916.
Rand Daily Mail (Johannesburg), 1899–1916.
Standard and Diggers News, 1892–1900.
De Volkstem, 1882–1888.

Cape

Cape Times, 1885–1916.

Rhodesia

Rhodesia Herald, 1898–1916.

Britain

The *Times* (London), 1859–1916.

India

Reports of the Native Press (Bengal, Bombay, Madras), 1880–1916.

Index

Gandhi in South Africa

Designed by R. E. Rosenbaum
Composed by Vail-Ballou Press, Inc.
in 11 point linofilm Baskerville, 2 points leaded,
with display lines in Palatino.
Printed by offset by Vail-Ballou Press
on Warren's 1854 Text, 60 pound basis,
with the Cornell University Press watermark.
Bound by Vail-Ballou Press
in Columbia Bayside Linen
and stamped in All Purpose black foil.